'Psychoanalysis, from the first, preferred reason over religion, even as it acknowledged religion's extraordinary powers. Religious commitments, beliefs and practices invest all sorts of human activities; such phenomena do not always admit to their own religious character. In this ambitious, rigorous and polemical book, which draws on an impressive range of scholarship, Tamas Pataki takes up the challenge of analysing and combating the pathological aspects of religions, from the ancient entrance of spirits into human affairs, through the development of the monotheisms, to the unconscious psychic investments that continue to sustain them.'

Justin Clemens, *Associate Professor at The University of Melbourne is author of* Psychoanalysis is an Antiphilosophy *and co-author of* Barron Field in New South Wales.

'Pataki is a philosopher who explores the evolution of religion through a critical atheistic perspective pivoting on psychoanalytic object-relations theory. It is this aspect of his thought that provides a much-needed depth of understanding of religious fundamentalism and extremism, the dominant themes of this timely book. Well informed by prehistoric and anthropological scholarship and argued with exceptional clarity, this revised version of his *Religion, Narcissism and Fanaticism* offers a sobering critique in the current historical context when much of humankind is becoming overinflated by its divine images and their correlative this-worldly identities.'

Dr Jadran Mimica, *Senior Lecturer, Department of Anthropology, The University of Sydney and author of* Humans, Pigs and Souls.

Religion, Narcissism and Fanaticism

Religion, Narcissism and Fanaticism traces the historical and psychosocial development of religiosity and applies anthropological and psychoanalytic perspectives to the understanding of religions, particularly their fanatical and fundamentalist expressions.

Religious ideology, practices and institutions satisfy many human needs, including those arising from our hysterical, obsessional and narcissistic dispositions: the need to segregate the good and bad aspects of our personalities; to belong to an idealized group; and to feel secure and special by identifying with, or living in the orbit of, a supposedly omnipotent figure. But these needs and their modes of satisfaction are distorted by religions which may then nurture and accommodate malign characteristics (especially in the case of the monotheisms), narcissistic inflation or grandiosity. The book shows how interactions between religious ideology and personal development become intricated in the narcissistic pathology which underlies much of the violence and religious aggression in the world today. It presents both a new account of the historical and psychosocial development of religiosity and a powerful polemic against the religions which delusorily satisfy some of the very needs they create.

The book will appeal to psychoanalysts, anthropologists, philosophers, sociologists and all those interested in the place of religion in the modern world.

Tamas Pataki is Honorary Senior Fellow at the University of Melbourne. Author of *Against Religion*, *Wish-fulfilment in Philosophy and Psychoanalysis*, and co-editor of *Racism in Mind*. He has also published journal articles and book chapters on the philosophy of mind and religion, most recently in *The Routledge International Handbook of Psychoanalysis and Philosophy*.

Religion, Narcissism and Fanaticism

The Arrogance of Gods

Tamas Pataki

Routledge
Taylor & Francis Group

LONDON AND NEW YORK

Designed cover image: © Getty Images

First published 2024
by Routledge
4 Park Square, Milton Park, Abingdon, Oxon OX14 4RN

and by Routledge
605 Third Avenue, New York, NY 10158

Routledge is an imprint of the Taylor & Francis Group, an informa business

© 2024 Tamas Pataki

The right of Tamas Pataki to be identified as author of this work
has been asserted in accordance with sections 77 and 78 of the
Copyright, Designs and Patents Act 1988.

All rights reserved. No part of this book may be reprinted
or reproduced or utilised in any form or by any electronic,
mechanical, or other means, now known or hereafter invented,
including photocopying and recording, or in any information
storage or retrieval system, without permission in writing from
the publishers.

Trademark notice: Product or corporate names may be
trademarks or registered trademarks, and are used only for
identification and explanation without intent to infringe.

British Library Cataloguing-in-Publication Data
A catalogue record for this book is available from the British Library

ISBN: 978-1-138-69812-3 (hbk)
ISBN: 978-1-032-72494-2 (pbk)
ISBN: 978-1-315-51981-4 (ebk)

DOI: 10.4324/9781315519814

Typeset in Sabon
by Apex CoVantage, LLC

Contents

Acknowledgements and permissions   *x*

Introduction   1

PART I
Theory   **5**

1   The advent of spirits and the birth of religion   7

     Spirits and religion   7
     Religion in the Palaeolithic   10
     Language and spirits   16
     Enter spirits   18
     Spirits and shamanism   21

2   Mysticism, intellectualism and the poverty of cognitivism   28

     Sorting out   28
     The mystical path to spirits   29
     Cognitivism   31
     Tylor revived   39
     And Freud   42

3   For the love of gods   48

     Explanation and communion   48
     Anthropomorphism   50

viii Contents

*Monotheism as progress towards personal
communion 53*
Communion and attachment 59

4 Narcissism in religion   68

Shamanism and narcissism 68
Narcissism and identification 71
Narcissistic relations 73
The inculcation of religion 75
Freud on narcissism and magic 78

PART II
Polemic   **85**

5 The new atheism and the new fanaticism   87

What is the new atheism? 87
Fundamentalism and fanaticism 92
Features of fanaticism 96

6 Sexual morality and law   104

Religion and morality 104
Sexual morality 105
Origins: the fear of women 107
Hatred of the homosexual 110
Family and envy 113
Law 115

7 Aggression in religion   123

Forms of religious aggression today 123
Errors of the apologists 124
An intrinsic connection 131

8 Reason and religion   142

Reprise 142
The subordination of reason 143

Narcissistic wounds 148
The evasion of reality 150
Unfinished conclusion 151

Appendix: on wish-fulfilment	156
Bibliography	163
Index	173

Acknowledgements and permissions

I am grateful to Michael Levine, Alan Lux, Glenn Newbery and Andy Sims, each of whom read portions of the book and provided helpful comments. My greatest intellectual debt and gratitude are to Agnes Petocz. Her erudite and searching commentaries on every chapter, and the correspondence that followed them, made this a far better and, hopefully, truer book than it otherwise would have been. The errors that remain are of course all mine. The book was long in writing. I wish to thank the editorial staff at Routledge whose patience, assistance and courtesy over the many years of my procrastinations has been unfailing. Especially, I would like to thank AnnaMary Goodall, Kate Hawes, Georgina Clutterbuck and Aakriti Aggarwal. And my thanks go, also, to Michael Benge's superb editing. To Jintao, as always, flows my deepest gratitude: without whom, nothing.

I sincerely thank Oxford Publishing Limited for kind permission to use some passages in an amended form that first appeared in my article 'Wish-fulfilment' in R. Gipps and M. Lacewing (eds) *The Oxford Handbook of Philosophy and Psychoanalysis* (Oxford: Oxford University Press: 2019), and Taylor and Francis Group for kind permission to use in an amended form some passages from my article 'Narcissism in religion' in Aner Govrin and Tair Caspi (eds) *The Routledge International Handbook of Psychoanalysis and Philosophy* (Oxford and New York: Routledge: 2023).

Introduction

The main ideas weaving through this book are as follows. Some time in the Upper Palaeolithic era, modern humans invented the ideas of soul and spirit. The disposition of souls explained such enigmas as death, illness and dream life. Spirits, soul-like supernatural beings with extra-human powers, populated a supernatural world inhering in deep caves, rivers and lakes, and their activity explained a good deal about processes in the natural world. Humans supplicated and propitiated these spirits and eventually exalted them into gods. By means of magic, ritual and sacrifice, by living in their orbit or by identifying unconsciously with the spirits and gods, people found instrumental means to allay their feelings of insecurity in exacting environments, and to regulate their self-regard and self-esteem – their narcissistic economy. The gods and spirits dwelling in inaccessible places entered the human psyche. To have powerful, immortal gods and spirits on your side, or, even better, to believe that they are inside, certainly enhances security and self-esteem. The artifices of the emerging religions enabled the devout to live in the pale radiance of the protective divine. The evolution of monotheism complicated religious sensibility and opened avenues for unprecedented narcissistic inflation or grandiosity; now only one religion possesses the Truth and there is only one path to the divine. This precarious conception leads inevitably to fear and hatred of those who challenge the narcissistic investments in religious supremacy. Compared to primitive and pagan religions, monotheism, with its increased emphasis on maintaining self-esteem through communion with an abstruse, omnipotent, incorporeal deity (as opposed to earlier manipulations of human-like spirits and gods) regresses towards increased delusionality. The malign consequences of that development are explored in the last four chapters of the book. The theoretical framework is set out in the first four. It is possible to begin reading the book at Chapter 5 and to turn back as required.

When an earlier, much slimmer, essay of mine came out some years ago, in the shadow of the 9/11 terrorist attacks on New York, some critics remarked that I had written only about religion at its worst, that

DOI: 10.4324/9781315519814-1

2 Introduction

nothing I had written about was worthy of the name of religion.[1] I suppose they had in mind some True Religion or Ideal Religion, possibly *their* religion operating in its highest gear. I am sure they did not have in mind the religion of the Aztecs or ancient Romans. In any case, what I had written about fell short of their Ideal. I had discussed religion in that book, as I do in this, from what is sometimes called the anthropological point of view. That view takes in religion in its large expressions, the beliefs, practices and institutions to which majorities in various cultures are committed, not the refinements of the philosophers and the exceptions of the saints. Religions are many and diverse, and the metric of commitment varies wildly. Since I am predominantly interested in the psychology and anthropology of religion, it makes sense to consider as closely as possible the longest arc of religious expression, from its emergence to the present. It goes without saying that such a consideration will be selective. A consideration of religion in the large is unlikely to perch on religion at its finest or on all that is most worthy, as its defenders may believe, of the name of religion.[2] But it will give a less distorted and misleading account of the psychology of this pan-human phenomenon than the current preoccupation in philosophy and psychology with Christianity and, more recently, Buddhism.

Despite the overall asperity of the critical aspect of the book, I do not of course wish to deny that religion can be charitable, hospitable, tolerant, benign, not seeking to impose itself on non-conformists or secular administration. Nor do I believe, speaking quite generally, that religions are lacking in positive virtues (as opposed to restraint of vice). But in fact these things are pale in the historical record and in current religious dispensations. Lucretius was not far off in saying that religion has brought untold misery to the human race. Whatever it is at its best, the peril – the immediate peril – lies with religion at its worst, when it has become fundamentalist and fanatical and close to the levers of power, as it has particularly in the United States, Russia and parts of the Islamic world. The important thing then is to analyse its intellectual and moral vices, not its occasional virtues. It would be perverse to do otherwise.

The reader will not find here arguments about the existence of gods, although the naturalistic underpinnings and trend of the work have obvious sceptical implications. Apart from honing the skills of metaphysicians, I do not believe that these arguments have much value. But even in the unlikely circumstance that one or another can be salvaged in some diminished form it would have little consequence for the arguments against religion presented in this work. Rarely do the motivations to religious belief and practice, which are among the main concerns of this book, have much relation to evidential or rational considerations. The intellectual and social climate today is not favourable to psychological exploration of motive and self-understanding that turns on subjective

Introduction 3

examination, or the reconstructions of childhood experience such as we find in attachment theory, psychoanalysis and other psychodynamic theories. A kind of hatred of insight and self-examination have emerged in alliance with a global lurch towards reactionary authoritarianism and puritanical religion. This is a dire situation, for the disease resists the very thing that might contribute to curing it. Yet it seems to me evident that the exploration of religiosity *must* turn to the disciplines that make a study of religious motivation and emotion, as well as those that have made a study of cultural and historical context and doctrinal content. Religion does not exist in isolation, it does not have a language of its own, it does not have a field of thought and emotion specific to it. Whatever religion's links are to the supernatural, religiosity is an exclusively human thing. Because the human-to-human relation is fundamental the relation between the individual and the divine takes on human contours. That is the field of our interest here. It goes without saying that psychological and anthropological analyses do not have decisive implications for the metaphysics of religion. They can, however, cast familiar things in a new light and insert scepticism where before there was certainty.

Notes

1 Pataki 2007.
2 The notion of True Religion, a common resort of the apologists whenever some religiously inspired atrocity enters the scene, can be taken to absurd lengths, as it is dramatically in Mark Johnston's *Saving God* (2009). Johnston says that the essence of true, genuine or real religion is a salvific core: 'the demanding core of true religion' is 'radical self-abandonment to the Divine as manifested in the turn toward others and toward objective reality' (24). But the Divine, God, or in his favored terminology, 'the Highest One' is by no means supernatural. On the contrary, to think of the Highest One as supernatural is the worst form of idolatry: 'the very ideas of religion as essentially supernaturalist, and of God as essentially a supernatural being, are idolatrous conceptions' (39). 'The Highest One = the outpouring of Existence Itself by way of its exemplification in ordinary existents for the sake of the self-disclosure of Existence Itself' (116). This process of outpouring, Johnston says, 'seems well suited to command total affirmation by one's will. It is a process that makes all of reality, and, arguably, to affirm this process and thoroughly identify with it is to truly love God' (116). Be the latter as it may, Johnston's essentialist conception detaches religion from almost all of its historical expressions and the religious impulses of most of humanity. Apart from a roomful of people who may share Johnston's views, all, starting with the Pope, are idolators. 'After idolatry is purged, not every "religion" will actually be a religion, and little in the way of "religious doctrine"

will be religious. Few will actually have had a religion, as opposed to a simulacrum of one' (37). The student interested in *religion as it is* will not waste much time on such proposals. How religion – something recognizable as religion – could be or should be is another thing altogether.

Part I

Theory

Chapter 1

The advent of spirits and the birth of religion

Spirits and religion

My intention in this chapter and the next is to give a persuasive account of how the concept of *spirit* or *spiritual being* entered the human imaginary. As we shall see, there is not one such concept, or perhaps it would be better to say that many different kinds of thing fall under the one concept. But since it is tedious to keep pluralizing I will speak of *the* concept in the singular. All, or nearly all, religions have some such concept and it is fundamental to them. The account that I will give of the invention of the concept is naturalistic in that it is in terms of human psychology and cultural processes that do not presuppose supernatural or non-natural interventions or conceptions. In so far as it succeeds, it is a step towards naturalizing religion, that mixed class of complex constellations of beliefs, practices and institutions.

We know that spirits entered human life some time in the Palaeolithic era, probably quite late in the Upper Palaeolithic, and that in the course of time there emerged many different and elusive conceptions of what they are, and that eventually some became gods – powerful supernatural spirits who are worshipped. Monotheistic world religions evolved and, as philosophical (and theological) and scientific ways of thinking came to bear on them, the gods and spirits and the notions of the supernatural with which they were associated became very abstract and abstruse indeed. I do not wish to suggest for a moment that there was anything like a linear progression from primitive religions associated with spirits and multiple gods to superior ones, as if it were a single stream steadily building over the ages toward monotheism, and sending out occasional rivulets. I believe something like the opposite. But it is important to know that there was a very long time when no people believed in spirits; a later time when some people in some places started believing in spirits of various sorts and related to them by way of supplication and propitiation; a later time when many people started *worshipping* very exalted and powerful spirits – gods; and then a relatively short period over which monotheism

DOI: 10.4324/9781315519814-3

8 Theory

and other world religions like Buddhism became ascendant. These situations overlapped and today of course all four situations obtain. Each of these situations generated, and was very likely generated by, specific changes in human psychology and cultural possibilities. We shall use these situations or eras to structure the argument that follows.

The concept of spirit is discussed in more detail in later chapters but some preliminary bearings will be helpful here. Demons, ghosts, gods, angels, souls, sprites, spectres, elves, goblins, fairies and many similar things traditionally fall under the concept. The ethnographic data, and inferences to prehistorical societies from it, suggest that spirits have been minimally conceived since earliest times as elusive, often imperceptible, anthropomorphic agents with extra-human or supernatural abilities.[1] They are often considered to inhabit or be immanent in things like rocks, animals, rivers, plants, the wind and the sky; and, as individual human souls, they animate human bodies. The entities on the list differ in important respects, of course, and even in small and simple cultural groups there is diversity of opinion about the kinds of entities that should be recognized and about the natures of such as are recognized, just as there is today in large literate technological cultures. To get some sense of this diversity consider the *kwoth* of the Nuer people. The *kwoth* cannot be perceived by the senses and are indeterminate and intangible except in relation to their effects. What a *kwoth* is like in itself, the Nuer sensibly claim not to know. 'We are simple people, how can simple people know about such matters?' they say.[2] At another extreme are spirits almost of the same order as human beings. The Kalabari of the Niger Delta recognize three categories of religious beings:

> the first two are seen as existing "in spirit" only, while the last, like human beings, have both bodies and spirits: unlike Deads and Village Gods, they can be seen, heard, touched, and smelt by anyone who happens to cross their path in the rivers. They are not like the wind: they can be talked of inhabiting definite localities as the Deads and the Village Gods cannot. Many other gods of primitive peoples could be cited as resembling the Kalabari Water-People in their thoroughgoing materiality.[3]

Gods, who probably arrived with the establishment of chiefdoms and kingships, are generally powerful spirits who seek devotion and are worshipped.[4] Some eventually become all-powerful. But the gods of many tribal peoples and indeed of the Classical pantheons have many evident limitations and foibles. *Souls* are usually conceived as embodied human or animal spirits; unsurprisingly, since the spirit conception may well have evolved from the conception of the soul. Over the years, conceptions of the spiritual world have undergone many variations and elaborations but it seems to me that the vast majority of religious people today still hold anthropomorphic conceptions of spiritual beings not very different from those that are sketched here. Because of their immense diversity, I shall generally use the phrase 'gods and spirits' to sweep up the whole family of supernatural folk. So much by way of introducing spirits.

A neat definition of religion as belief in spirits was proposed by the father of cultural anthropology, Edward B. Tylor.[5] In his view, the earliest religion, animism (as he named it), is essentially a quasi-scientific scheme invented by the earliest 'savage philosophers' to explain an enigmatic range of phenomena – dreams, human agency, death, but also the agency of animals and causation of natural phenomena. Tylor's view is, for evident reasons, often referred to as a form of intellectualism. The spirits of animism function as kinds of theoretical entity but Tylor makes it clear that that is not all they are. They are entities sufficiently resembling humans, especially in terms of understanding and agency, to enable interaction with them on the model of human-to-human relations.[6] So, anthropomorphic agency explains causation in the world and the disposition or movement of spirits explains phenomena such as dreams, death and illness. Religion, philosophy and rudimentary science are born.

During the last half of the last century the idea of animism as a primordial religion, and of belief in spirits as the core of all subsequent religion, at least as framed by Tylor and his adherents, fell under a cloud.[7] However, recent studies by cognitive anthropologists and evolutionary psychologists have resuscitated the idea and there is now substantial agreement among researchers that the essence of religion – without placing too much stress on 'essence' – is indeed belief, or at least a disposition to believe, in spirits.[8] The contemporary conceptions and arguments obviously differ in several respects from Tylor's, and in the next chapter we will explore the differences. Tylor based his views on the not-always-reliable ethnographic data available to him but he got a great deal right; on certain key points rather more right, in my view, than our contemporaries. He was surely right in believing that animism was alive and well in the superstition, religions and philosophy of his time; as it is in ours.

A belief in spirits, in supernatural objects, fleshed out in the way we have begun to do, and widely shared within a cultural group, is necessary but not sufficient to characterize the religion of the group. Religion is, as we said, a very complex phenomenon. The term denotes a vague concept, as philosophers say, so it is difficult to formulate a definition that captures the complexity and excludes borderline cases. The best definition I know is this:

Religions are passionate, communal displays, of costly commitments to the satisfaction of non-natural causal beings – e.g. gods and/or

10 Theory

ancestor spirits – and/or the overcoming of non-natural causal regulative structures – e.g. cycles of reincarnation, reward and punishment – resulting from evolutionary canalization and convergence of:

1 widespread belief in non-natural causal agents and/or non-natural regulative structures;
2 hard to fake public expressions of costly material commitments – offerings and/or sacrifices of goods, property, time, and/or life – to the satisfaction of those non-natural causal agents and/or the overcoming of, or escape from, those non-natural causal regulative structures;
3 mastering of people's existential anxieties – death, deception, disease, catastrophe, pain, loneliness, injustice, want and loss – by those costly commitments to the satisfaction of those non-natural causal agents and/or the overcoming of, or escape from, non-natural causal regulative structures; and
4 ritualized, rhythmic, sensory co-ordination of (1), (2), and (3) in communion, congregation, intimate fellowship, or the like.[9]

This definition captures most religions, those that recognize gods as well as those that recognize only lesser spirits and supernatural regulative structures such as reincarnation. It excludes would-be religions such as Scientology, assuming its religious objects are natural entities (extraterrestrial beings). It excludes ideologies such as communism because commitment to spiritual beings, such as is intrinsic to the ideology, is lacking. The most significant thread running through the definition is belief in supernatural agents or processes. This is pleasingly consistent with Tylor's view, the view that will be developed here. Arguably, there are borderline cases, Jainism and some forms of Buddhism for example, that are atheistic but count intuitively as religions.[10] These may prove the rule. But it is notable that in reality, rather than in the Ideal as mentioned in the introduction, the majority of devotees to these religions do invoke supernatural beings or processes. Belief in spirits, as diverse as these entities are across cultures, and as uncertain as the metric of belief or conviction may be, seems to be a definitive feature of every religion. If the reader's intuition protests at this restriction then the definition may be taken as prescriptive and the considerations that follow to apply only within its domain of application.

Religion in the Palaeolithic

Homo habilis who, as the name indicates, made tools is usually considered the earliest of the *Homo* genus and emerged over 2.5 million years ago. The earliest stone tools date to about 3.3 million years, however

The advent of spirits and the birth of religion   11

these were probably fashioned by non-human Australopithecines. *Homo erectus* made his way across Asia and down to South-East Asia and beyond at least 800,000 years ago. Further along the evolutionary track, large-brained *Homo heidelbergensis*, probably the immediate ancestor of both *Homo neanderthalensis* and *Homo sapiens* – modern humans – is evidenced in Africa and Eurasia at least 500,000 years ago. Modern human fossils dated to almost 200,000 years ago have been uncovered in several parts of Africa, and some North African fossils considered to be of archaic sapiens are perhaps more than 300,000 years old. The earliest evidence of modern human excursions into Eurasia are a jawbone and teeth dated between 177,000 and 200,000 years old found in the Misliya Cave in Israel, but the early forays of modern humans beyond Africa appear to have petered out until more than 100,000 years later.[11]

Some anthropologists have suggested that religion originates as far back as 300,000 years ago, in the Middle Palaeolithic era, or even earlier, well before the entrance of modern humans.[12] These religious ancestors, the argument runs, buried their dead deliberately, cared for the disabled, performed group rituals and may have used musical instruments. The putative facts are supposed to show that pre-modern ancestors were capable of ritual organization required for group worship, experienced elevated 'spiritual' states of mind, and entertained beliefs about an afterlife. Other anthropologists provide much later dates, though usually for modern humans in the Middle Palaeolithic; a few have claimed to find elements of religiosity in Neanderthals. We will look briefly at some of the evidence for early expressions of religion but ultimately accept the sceptical conclusion that there is no good reason for supposing that any activities recognizable as religious appear earlier than the cultural florescence conjectured conservatively to have occurred around 40–45,000 years ago. Some proto-religious features such as ritualistic behaviour certainly appeared earlier, but taken on their own do not amount to religion. The argument that follows presupposes the high bar for religion defined above, and proceeds in the main by casting doubt on the inference from the available evidence to belief in spirits.

The dating of prehistoric religious expression is difficult. One looks to evidence of similarities with historical religious practices and thought. In the historical period, we find prayer, worship, sacrifice, propitiation, public rituals usually involving dressing up, music and singing, the ritualization of birth, coming of age, death and the regulation of sexuality and gender roles are particularly prominent. Dead are frequently buried with durable markers but may be disposed of in other, less commemorative, ways. These activities are usually (but not always) supervenient on communal beliefs about spirits, souls, supernatural processes and some form of posthumous survival. Now, the evident difficulty of interpreting our prehistoric ancestors is that these kinds of beliefs and activities have

12 Theory

to be read off from their practical achievements: tools, musical instruments, burials and art objects. Even where the external contours of the earlier activities – playing music, burying the dead and so forth – bear close similarity to known religious practice, it remains uncertain what significance the ancestors attached to them. Thought can only be read from actions, but determining what *actions are being performed*, especially when they have no obvious practical significance, requires knowledge of the beliefs and desires that motivate them. Is adorning a corpse with precious artefacts a spontaneous expression of tenderness or grief? an act of propitiation? an extravagant display of wealth and status? the sign of an ideology of post-mortem existence? We can't really know unless we know what the agents were thinking. This essentially sceptical thought hangs its shadow over the following discussion.

Complex or 'symbolic' burial practices are often taken to indicate religious belief because they express concern for the dead and, possibly, belief in post-mortem existence; this belief is usually assumed to imply some form of disembodied existence although that doesn't strictly follow. There is evidence that Neanderthals and archaic modern humans deliberately buried at least some of their dead, though the significance of the interments is contested. Chris Stringer says that 'there is sufficient evidence of some level of ritual behaviour in the later Neanderthals at least, including infants being buried with simple grave goods.'[13] The oldest known uncontested symbolic burial, 'an early modern man interred clasping the lower jaw of a massive wild boar,' was found in the Shkul cave in Israel and dated to about 115,000 years ago.[14] In Qafzeh Cave near Nazareth a child is interred covered by huge deer antlers. The site is dated to 100,000 years ago. The meaning of these depositions, however, is unclear. But 'once we get to 40,000 years ago,' writes Stringer, 'we can certainly infer the existence of rituals and ceremonies to mark the death of individuals.'[15] At Lake Mungo in Australia, two people were stretched out and covered with hematite pigment perhaps originally applied to their bodies or hides. Ten thousand years later at Sungir in present-day Russia, a boy and a girl 'were interred head to head, accompanied by long spears made from heat-treated mammoth ivory, ivory carvings, hundreds of pierced arctic fox canines, and some ten thousand ivory beads that must have been sown onto their perished clothing. The spears probably took weeks to make and the beads many months in total, so these children were highly valued by their group, even in death.'[16] From the care lavished on these corpses, from the elaborate dress, ornamentation and sumptuous grave goods, it is tempting to infer that some form of religious ideology, perhaps even belief in an afterlife, motivated the bereaved. The evolutionary psychologist Robin Dunbar leaps to this conclusion. He details the rich contents of the Sungir site and concludes that the interment of the children 'only makes sense if those who buried them believed that they would continue to live in another world.'[17] What else, if not religious ideology about an afterlife, could explain the sacrifice of these precious goods? The inference is too swift. Unless these children were imagined to be going to a ball in the afterlife, in their finest and most impractical attire, there is almost nothing in the grave of conceivable use to them. The only exceptions are the ivory spears that vary in length from 18 inches to eight feet. It is possible that these spears were intended for use in a future hunting ground, but to my mind they are more suggestive of precious gifts to a growing child.[18] Alternative interpretations of the interments, with more emotional plausibility and unconnected to religious ideology, are not hard to find. If archaeologists 100,000 years hence dug up a skeleton dressed in Sunday best, set in a gilded coffin, with a bag of expensive golf clubs placed carefully inside, they might still not conclude that the dead man's people believed golf was played in the afterlife. E. R. Dodds once remarked in another context about the use of feeding tubes in ancient burial customs, that they showed not *thought* but the absence of it. I believe he meant that the practice reveals, not a structured religious ideology about an afterlife, but the spontaneous humanity of the bereaved: the swell of grief and tenderness, the urge to continue the relationship with the lost one. The gift of precious objects, especially objects once dear to the deceased, are typically human expressions of love. Atheists also bury and memorialize the dead with ceremony. And of course it seems probable that displays of disposable wealth on funerary occasions indicated high social status, as they do today. So there are several other plausible explanations of the interment which diminish warrant for the conjecture about posthumous existence. And even if we grant that the Sungir people believed in an afterlife, we simply do not know whether they conceived of it in spiritual terms; after all, the idea of a bodily existence in the afterlife is not unknown, and later exercised many a Christian theologian. The inference to religious ideology on the basis of burials is a stretch, even from Sungir, which is a fairly late site.

It has been said that the capacity for aesthetic appreciation is a sign of advanced intellectuality or spirituality. Sometime between 300 and 400 thousand years ago, Heidelbergs living in Essex and Germany crafted beautiful spears of yew and spruce.[19] Jean Clottes describes an interment dated about 400,000 to 460,000 years ago that contains 'a spectacular hand axe in pink quartzite rose, of exceptional quality and entirely unused that could represent a funerary offering and hence provide evidence of a belief in a world beyond.'[20] According to Bruno David, some stone tools produced by Neanderthals 'have aesthetic properties that imply an incipient artistic appreciation.'[21] If the artefacts were beautiful to their creators, the argument runs, then perhaps they had advanced not just to aesthetic spirituality but to religiosity, as Clottes seems to believe. Of

14 Theory

course, we have no way of knowing for certain whether the artefacts were shaped for their aesthetic qualities. We are not the best judges of utilitarian purpose. In fact it seems likely that these early makers did possess something like aesthetic sensibility, but even so, it is clear that there is no obvious passage, conceptually or developmentally, from aesthetic sensibility to all but the fluffiest understanding of the religious.

Well before 75,000 years ago, perhaps as early as 100,000 years ago, modern humans occupying a place now known as the Blombos shelter on the southern coast of South Africa collected lumps of ochre which they used to stain beads, cure animal skins and decorate themselves.[22] Excavation provided a rich cache of tools and engraved objects that appear, by the lights of some archaeologists, to have symbolic significance of a higher order than the merely decorative or the social signifier. On the narrow edge of one flat, palm-sized piece of ochre someone

> engraved a neat, symmetrical series of crosses with a line through the middle of them. Around them he or she scratched a containing line. . . . It seems that the whole "composition" was a carefully balanced, bounded *unit*, not a mix of unrelated marks.[23]

The pattern appears to be purposeful and religious significance has been attached to what may be the earliest uncontested example of portable art.[24] Archaeologist David Lewis-Williams, for one, finds several features potentially of religious significance. He conjectures that the soft red ochre may signify blood since blood is a polysemic symbol in many religions, past and present; the focused activity of engraving patterns seems to reveal a mentality capable of abstract reflection elevated beyond immediate practical needs; and the penetration of the surface seems to be directed at something that was inside the ochre, perhaps some spiritual power or entity. He says: 'We may have here an early hint of an important component of religious thought: immanence. Gods and supernatural powers can be *inside* statues, mountains, lakes, seas, nature itself, and of course people.'[25] This last is an important conjecture. But in truth the matter as it relates to Blombos is undecidable. The miniature engraving seems a rather private affair and odd when contrasted with the massive caves and geographical formations that, as we shall see presently, served for communal worship and as containers of spirits at a later age.[26] It is possible that those patterns in the ochre, like Henry James' pattern in the carpet, may have no meaning at all. And here it must be emphasized that although archaeological use of the term 'symbolic' is rather flexible there are critical differences between the patterned, decorative material found at Blombos and the representational, figurative and narrative work of the Upper Palaeolithic that we shall shortly discuss.

So the evidence for early (Middle Palaeolithic) religious belief considered so far has not been decisive. A cave in Bruniquel, France, contains broken stalagmites, some burnt, some stacked one on top of another, arranged in two large circles. These formations, which appear to be more than 170,000 years old, suggest that Neanderthals displayed modern behaviour, artistic and religious – or at least ceremonial – well before the arrival of modern humans in Europe. Archaeologist Tom Higham wonders whether the site was a meeting place for shamanic rituals or a site for funerary activity.[27] It seems to me that indications of ritual behaviour do not tell us a great deal about the presence of religious belief. Ritual behaviour has biological roots and is very likely a development from play, as conjectured by Johann Huizinga.[28] The young of all mammals play and there is much neurobiological evidence to support Jaak Panksepp's theory that play – PLAY – is one of the seven basic emotional command systems hard-wired into the mammalian brain.[29] In humans play and playfulness continue into adulthood. We can easily imagine in the earliest stages of social life adult play continuing children's make-believe and role-playing. Our ancestors would have enacted roles, imitating and identifying with prey or feared animals, parents and bigshots. The enactments would in time solidify into fixed rituals, used perhaps to (magically) invoke and control such objects. With the advent of spirits (down the track), they too would become objects of ritual.[30] All that is easy to imagine because it is present in the religious practices of people today, often in undisguised forms. Make-believe, repetitive or formalized actions and dressing up are the rule in most religions and, if dance and music were also part of early ritual, there would be a reasonable analogical case for inferring an antique age for religious expression.[31] Moreover, it might be thought as many have thought, that the experiences undergone in these activities brought to a pitch by rhythmic dancing and chanting or trance-inducing agents would *ipso facto* manufacture religious experiences or mystical states characterized by encounters with spirits (See Chapter 2).

But this also is too swift. Many ceremonial and ritualized activities do not involve religion, and if the origin of ritual is indeed primarily play then this should be unsurprising. So affirming that Middle Palaeolithic rituals of the sort we are speculating about *must* be religious merely supposes that which should be proved. In particular, it is important – and this is a theme that will recur in several contexts – that for an experience to be a *religious* experience it must be given the stamp of the relevant concepts. Even if the rituals reached a trance-like or hallucinatory pitch, they do not 'off their own bat' create religious concepts such as the rich and necessary concept of *spirit*. Hallucinatory, ecstatic or 'spiritual' experiences may, as we shall see, contribute as objects of enquiry in the formation of such concepts but only once they are subjected to a

16 Theory

high level of abstract thought requiring sophisticated language.[32] To this claim we now turn.

Language and spirits

Not so long ago it was generally agreed that a cultural revolution took place in Europe with the arrival of modern humans about 40,000 to 45,000 years ago.[33] In addition to complex tools and a huge variety of decorative objects the pioneering Aurignacian culture (43,000–26,000 years ago) produced carved portable objects and spectacular rock painting and engraving – art that was for the first time not just decorative but figurative, sometimes narrative and imaginative. That this efflorescence was exclusively associated with the European branch of modern humans is increasingly contested, and many researchers argue for an earlier cultural acceleration, perhaps 80,000 to 100,000 years ago in the African homeland. 'What is clear,' says Bruno David, 'is that once modern humans arrived in the land of the Neanderthals close to 45,000 years ago, they came with an artistic package that was already in full bloom.'[34] Whether this *is* in fact clear turns on the meaning of 'full bloom.' There is reason to qualify David's contention and it has to do with language.

I have been urging that without an underpinning of religious ideology concerning spirits practices are devoid of religious content. I have cast doubt on the evidence of early burials, aesthetic accomplishment and ritual as strong warrant for religious ideology. Anthropologist Richard Klein argued that the first clear and undeniable proof of an ideological system occurs no earlier than about 45,000 years ago.[35] Only about then, according to Klein, is there a consistent pattern of increasing diversity of tools, undoubted art, symbolism and ritual. If we take 'symbol' to mean an object (a picture, a word, a thing) that is *intended* by an agent to mean or represent some other object, then we should agree that it is only through representational or symbolic art that we have reliable access to ideology, to a people's beliefs and perspectives on the world. If decorative activity, such as was identified at Blombos, is also symbolic then it is entirely opaque to us. It is plausible, perhaps necessary, to associate the emergence of representational, narrative art with the emergence of language. Pictorial narrative structure is evidence for stories thought out and told; language is a necessary condition for such structures. Stories about spirits, of inspirited animals, of creator beings and so forth, are evidence of religious ideology.

So when did humans acquire language? A case for a very early date is made by Daniel Everett.[36] He argues that *Homo erectus* possessed language at least 1.9 million years ago. These ancestors, according to Everett, manufactured bone and stone tools, including backed knives,

The advent of spirits and the birth of religion   **17**

used pigments and made wooden artefacts and proto-iconic art; built shelters and settlements; hunted in organized groups; travelled far and wide using sea-faring vessels to spread 800,000 years ago to what is now Indonesia and, possibly, to the remote island of Flores with its diminutive human 'hobbits.' To do all this, Everett argues, *Homo erectus* must have possessed a sophisticated means of symbolic communication – a language. Not all archaeologists accept this list of practical achievements, but even if *Homo erectus* did manage them it is not self-evident that they require language. Chimpanzees learn how to make tools by watching, wolf packs don't have conferences before hunting, many animals decorate themselves and groups of animals have been known to be transported to distant shores by tsunamis and the like. And there is a telling difficulty with Everett's story. If *Homo erectus* and presumably his African representative *Homo ergaster* possessed language 1.9 million years ago, communicative ability beyond signalling alarms, moods and intentions in the here and now, why did so very little of moment happen in the cognitive sphere over the next 1.8 million years compared to the extraordinary and rapid development of human culture in the last 45,000 years? Cultural attainments may be lost, and regress as well as progress is to be expected, but the yawning gap in prehistory entailed by the early language hypothesis is seriously damaging to it.

Chris Stringer writes:

> From my perspective, modern human language probably evolved out of growing social complexity over the last 250,000 years to bolster mind reading and communication. . . . The Neanderthals must have been highly knowledgeable about the world in which they lived, too (for example, about the materials from which they made tools and the animals that they hunted). But in my view their domain was largely in the here and now, and they did not regularly inhabit the virtual worlds of the past, the future and the spirits.[37]

Rudimentary forms of language may have sparked up rather as Stringer supposes. The critical transition that concerns us here is from the rudimentary to language complex enough to express propositions about supernatural, impalpable objects such as spirits, and the personal inwardness and social arrangements that could sustain belief in them. Klein (and others) argue that about 50,000 years ago fortuitous genetic mutations in modern humans suddenly enhanced certain brain functions producing changes in language capacity and cognition. These mutations did not affect brain size, which peaked around 200,000 years ago, but brain organization. The abruptness of this development is supported by the observation that despite the morphological modernity of the more than 100,000-year-old Shkuhl and Qafzeh skulls and of some

18 Theory

early African fossils, the artefacts associated with these sites are typically Middle Palaeolithic, comparable to those made by Neanderthals. This mutation hypothesis is not easy to confirm or defend. On the one hand there is no direct evidence for the posited genetic mutation; on the other hand there is the accumulating evidence for higher cultural achievement at earlier dates, for example in the African Middle Palaeolithic. However, if there *was* a quantum leap to modernity about 45,000 years ago, a cultural florescence, then the acquisition of complex linguistic ability would go a long way towards explaining it. And Klein's hypothesis is supported by other considerations. The anthropologist Ian Tattersall, approvingly quoted by Noam Chomsky, says:

> it is becoming increasingly clear that the acquisition of the uniquely modern [human] sensibility was . . . an abrupt and recent event. . . . And the expression of this new sensibility was almost certainly crucially abetted by the invention of what is perhaps the single most remarkable thing about our modern selves: language.[38]

Tattersall dates this acquisition to between 50,000 and 100,000 years ago. The statement fits with Chomsky's influential views on language. Chomsky has long held that natural languages share an underlying universal grammar embodied in a fixed nucleus or brain module that is a recent biological endowment, the result of a sudden and unique genetic mutation.[39] If these thinkers are right, then some light is shed on what does appear to be a remarkable cultural florescence at the dawn of the Upper Palaeolithic.

Enter spirits

I will come to the artistic evidence for the cultural explosion in a moment but I want first to briefly set out a hypothesis that may in part explain it: the synchronous development of language complex enough to refer to and describe supernatural objects, and representational, narrative art.[40] We have said that without a religious ideology of spirits or gods, there is no religion; the notion of spirits must be understood broadly, as explained above, and by 'ideology' is just meant a web of more or less organized beliefs. Then it will be evident that without language of very considerable complexity there can be no religious belief. To entertain beliefs about supernatural objects that may float free and be independent of material objects and so, in a quite ordinary sense be abstract and abstruse, requires mastery of very complex language skills. Reference to them requires not only names but substitutable definite descriptions and operations with identity, as well as rafts of beliefs supporting definite descriptions. What I mean is this. We can imagine

The advent of spirits and the birth of religion   19

a human tribe with a simple gestural and spoken language capable of naming material objects by ostension. But with immaterial objects, invisible and intangible, reference is tricky. Identification of spirits that are hidden in material objects, or entirely free of them, requires the use of definite descriptions substitutable for their names, over repeated varied occasions. To see this, consider one who is asked whether the local spirit called X is the same as the spirit named Y (of an adjacent group perhaps). The bare names cannot provide an answer; nor can the question be settled by pointing to a physical location. Even if the spirits inhabit the same rock formation, spirits, like members of the Trinity, resist easy individuation. To resolve the issue of identity requires knowing definite descriptions of X and Y: X is the one who is the master of animals, for example, or is the one who heals. To reach this point of conceptualization requires the capacity for keeping in mind what is not present to the senses but only described, together with rafts of subsidiary beliefs expressed in sentences (about animals, power, healing), and operations for identity on definite descriptions: the master of animals *is* the one who heals. This demanding complexity is one reason why I propose that representational art, especially parietal art that identified spiritual beings in natural formations, emerged, as it seems, so abruptly. To come to terms with experiences that would subsequently be regarded as spiritual, and the growing awareness of the need to explain the phenomena of death, dreaming and so forth, required language adequate to identify and describe spiritual beings. The best metaphysics available. But with the as-yet rudimentary character of the linguistic apparatus portable and parietal art was employed to aid in locating and describing the spirits, providing points of material reference and character. Language enabled the development of representational art and that art abetted the development of language and the earliest metaphysics. This proposal, if sound, would provide some reason to believe that the origin of natural language rich enough for reference to the spiritual was indeed roughly coeval with the origins of representational art. They developed hand in hand. That's the hypothesis. But does the artistic record provide any support at all for a consilience of language capable of handling abstractions, representational art and religion at the dawn of the Upper Palaeolithic?

It does. In the deep caves of Europe for a period of some 25,000 years, from the Aurignacian era to the end of the Magdalenian, parietal and portable art objects appear to reveal a religious ideology on a pan-European scale.[41] Thousands of wall paintings, engravings, charcoal drawings, stencils, figurines, engraved bones and stone plaquettes have been uncovered. From perhaps as far back as 36,000 years ago in the Chauvet-Pont-d'Arc Cave in the south west of France artists covered the walls with depictions of prey and predators: horses, aurochs, mammoths, lions, leopards, bears and rhinoceros.[42] In one group the artist(s)

20   Theory

having picked out outlines in the rock surface completed a painting of four beautiful horses' heads, each of which 'seem to show a different mood or character, as though depicting the passage of time or some inner narrative.'[43] There are no complete human figures in the cave but there appears to be a therianthropic (human/animal), 'shamanic' figure with the body of a bison and a human leg; and there is another Aurignacian composite figure, the Venus of Chauvet, with a clearly depicted vulva attached to incomplete human legs and a bison head above them giving the impression of a Minotaur figure or a mounting, perhaps the earliest expression of the widespread mythological theme of mortal women having sex with spirits in animal form.[44] Venus figurines, not all with the well-known and exaggerated anatomical features, became relatively common in the Gravettian period. There are also panels of red ochre hand prints and hand stencils and many abstract markings.

In the Magdalenian site of the connected caves, *Enlene* and *Les Trois Freres*, in southwestern France, after passing through the *Enlene* antechambers with prolific deposits of broken plaquettes and parietal insertions, and then some convoluted and illustrated passages and chambers, one eventually reaches the deep 'Sanctuary.' On the right-hand wall, four metres above the floor, is the famous image of the therianthropic 'sorcerer,' or *Le Dieu cornu*. Engraved and painted, the figure 'has antlers, a horse's tail, seemingly human genitals but set back as on a feline, bear or feline paws, large owl-like eyes, what appears to be a beard, and human legs and feet.'[45] Being situated on a high ledge it would have been visible to a large group, perhaps as a climax to their visit, and is distinguished from many other of the depictions in these caves which are accessible to one or very few persons at a time. According to Lewis-Williams, the elevated therianthrope suggests belief in a powerful being whose transcendence of the human/animal dichotomy people emulated in altered states.[46] Just below this imposing figure is another of a human with a bison's head possibly playing a nose flute. Some researchers have identified this figure as a representation of a shaman. There are relatively few of these shamanic figures in Magdalenian parietal art but considerable interpretive weight has been placed on them. The *Enlene* cave contains a huge array of bone fragments deliberately wedged into crevices in the chamber walls. Although the walls are riddled with fractures the insertions preponderate around the paintings on the walls. The practice has familiar religious resonance. Clottes writes:

> The basic motivation is a desire to go beyond everyday life, to pierce the veil of physical reality, and gain access to, in one form or another, supernatural powers, either through an offering – even a symbolic one – or by touching them directly. Very frequently, for example, when Orthodox Jews go to pray before the wailing wall in Jerusalem

and deposit rolled pieces of paper with their supplications in the crevices between the stones, they come one step closer to approaching a divinity at a site regarded as sacred.[47]

Elsewhere in the cave are scattered many stone plaquettes engraved with animals, mostly horses and bison, often scratched and broken. These activities are also strongly suggestive of sacrifice, of symbolic offering. There is much evidence also of apparently plaintive attempts to contact supernatural powers immanent in the cave walls. The proliferation of hand prints and stencils (created by blowing paint onto the hand covering the surface) can be seen in this light. Although most group activity discernible in the larger theatres of the caves is of adults, there is evidence of an adult lifting a child to leave prints on a high ceiling where he or she could make concrete contact with spiritual beings.[48] Finally, the celebrated Lascaux cave complex contains thousands of figures, including many hundreds of animal depictions and geometric figures including a kind of colour field of rectangles of yellow, grey, purple and red reminiscent of abstract art. Of particular interest to us are the spindly drawings of a dead man with a bird's head and possibly an erection located just above the figure of a bird-like head stuck on a wand.[49] The man appears prone, perhaps killed by a speared bull with its intestines spilling out. Fifty kilometres to the west at Cougnac cave in the Dordogne there appear three multiply speared anthropomorphic figures, 'the wounded men,' interspersed with animals in different parts of the caves.

These few examples must be taken as representative of a vast array of depictions. Now at last in the middle Upper Palaeolithic the lineaments of religious ideology are clearly discernible. Some of the representations suggest narrative, stories of events in time and place, of the sort that require significant achievement in language. The conjunction of the 'bird-man,' above the bird stave, confronting the dying bull irresistibly suggests a narrative, especially when viewed in the light of later mythology and ethnography; and the 'wounded men' appear to be telling a story of war or sacrifice. Public narrative suggests in turn the presence of fixed sets of beliefs or something like myth, doctrine or ideology to which all can relate. The deliberately broken plaquettes and wall insertions certainly suggest sacrifice and propitiation and the images of outstretched palms speak to us of desire to commune with, to beseech, the powers within the walls. The human/animal figures suggest, of course, shamanism.

Spirits and shamanism

With narrative, representational art indicating advanced linguistic ability, with strong indications of sacrificial activity and supplication, and with depictions of figures reminiscent of shamans, there appears very

22 Theory

solid ground for religious belief and practice in the Upper Palaeolithic. But what are the focal religious objects? Does the evidence point conclusively to spirits? After all, the most striking fact about Palaeolithic art is the predominance of animals. How is that fact to be linked to the entry of spirits? Several hypotheses have been framed to explain the predominance of animal depictions. Compelling is the idea that the representations were part of magical-religious rites to render animals easier prey, more plentiful or less fearsome. The theory gains support from the widespread use of sympathetic magic in the past and present. But it does have a telling limitation. Frequently, neither the most hunted animals nor the most fearsome, the ones that would call for the most energetic magical exertions, are the most depicted; in fact, sometimes expectations are reversed, as at Niaux, where the majority of representations are of bison though ibex, not bison, were the main prey. Moreover, the employment of sympathetic magic doesn't easily account for the preponderance of hand prints and stencils and abstract designs. Another less plausible theory is to the effect that we are witnessing the *sui generis* impulse to create art intrinsic to our kind. Somewhat damaging to this 'art for art's sake' theory, however, is the fact that many of the depictions are found in deep, dark and inaccessible areas of normally uninhabited caves; for also intrinsic to our kind is the need to exhibit. A third hypothesis posits a kind of fetishism or zoolatry in which animals are admired and worshipped, *before* concepts of spirit had entered the human imaginary. The animals most often depicted are powerful, swift or fertile (though there is at least one depiction of a grasshopper), and they are often depicted as magnificent – one is inclined to say *reverentially*. It is not difficult to imagine how important animals were to the ancestors, how deeply immersed they were in the total animal ecology. A fundamental affinity with, and reverence for, animals and nature remains a feature of known hunter-gatherer and other primitive societies. That affinity is based on reverence for the animating spirits or souls of animals, but we can imagine an earlier state when this was not so.[50]

It seems likely, or at least not implausible, that all these motives – magical control, animal reverence and aesthetic impulse – were effective, together or separately, perhaps in different times and places. To discount them altogether, as Jean Clottes does in favour of the shamanic hypothesis, is probably overreach.[51] But his hypothesis is certainly important. Clottes calls attention to two conspicuous features of parietal art. The first he reckons the most important feature of all Palaeolithic parietal representation: 'the constant utilization of natural contours, that is to say multiple reliefs of the wall: hollows, bumps, fissures.'[52] A hollow resembling a stag's head is completed with antlers; a natural relief is transformed into a horse; a small stalagmite serves as penis, and so on. The feature may be an artistic convenience but it is especially illuminated in

The advent of spirits and the birth of religion 23

the light of a religious conception: belief in the immanence of spiritual beings in the cave walls. It is as if the artists discerned the lineaments of animals – and here we must say of animal *spirits* – inhering in the rock, and sought to locate and bring them into relief. It is plausible to suppose that this – perhaps together with the Blombos engravings – is the first stage of an animist series that later locates spirits in rivers, lakes and mountains, statuettes, idols, tabernacles and temples. This understanding also illuminates the second feature Clottes draws attention to: the profusion of hand images, probably produced in ritual contexts. The extended palms imprinted on or near spirit representations may be understood as attempts to commune with spirits. Touching a saint's relic, a sacred wall, a cross or icon, are still means of establishing contact with spiritual objects. These observations certainly suggest that the spirits have arrived and are immanent and accessible in natural features like caves that are entrances to a spiritual realm. The therianthropic depictions reinforce the idea that at least by the Magdalenian period shamanisn, still widespread across continents, had become a distinctive religion. As Jean Clottes says, all clues point to a religion of shamanic type. The shaman is, above all, a master of spirits who can leave their body, fly to the spirit world to encounter other spirits often in animal form, rescue souls and battle evil shamans. Shamans are the mediators between the social world and spirits. Shamanism undoubtedly is religion, predicated on animism and a belief in spirits.

We have now glimpsed how spirits may have entered the human imaginary or basic conceptual scheme of our ancestors. But we have not considered how the very conception of spirit may have arisen in the first place. That is the subject of the next chapter.[53]

Notes

1 There are differences and overlaps between the spiritual, nonnatural, supernatural, extra-human, preternatural, paranormal and related notions. I am, however, rarely going to distinguish between them. A comprehensive notion of the supernatural has become so deeply ingrained in ordinary usage that there is little expository gain in departing from it, except where it leads to evident confusion. Distinguishing between the natural and supernatural is especially difficult in considering primordial and primitive groups which have no conception of nature, certainly nothing like the contemporary naturalistic-scientific one. Our world view does not serve to order the world of spirits. Wind, breath, light, for example, which we do not think of as supernatural, are regarded in many primitive societies as spiritual phenomena. The term 'primitive' is loaded with unhelpful associations but it still seems useful to describe the condition of humanity that, though it may have undergone immense changes,

24 Theory

is still in all likelihood closer to the primordial, to the cultures of early ancestors. Moreover, the term is so common amongst the early anthropological writers I discuss that it would be tedious to replace it. It will be evident from my text that no moral valuation of these cultures is intended. On naturalism and religion see Oppy 2018.

2 Quoted in Horton 1997, 24. The classic work on Nuer religion is Evans-Pritchard 1956.

3 Horton 1997, 25.

4 I follow Bellah who argues that spirits or powerful beings emerge as objects of veneration and worship, and therefore as gods, only after egalitarian band societies graduate to more rigid hierarchical chiefdoms and kingships. Thus, in transitional pre-missionary Tikopian society 'for the first time, and not entirely clearly, one can detect along with numerous powerful beings still present in the land, beings that can tentatively be called gods. . . . [T]he praise, thanksgiving, and requests for blessings offered by the chief acting as priest are what allow us to speak of these rituals as worship and the objects of these rituals as gods' (Bellah 2011, 185–186).

5 Tylor 1873/2016.

6 Robin Horton states that the 'great value of Tylor's definition is that it leads us to compare interaction with religious objects and interaction with human beings' (Horton 1997, 26).

7 In the 1960s E. E. Evans-Pritchard was able to say that the speculations of the first generation of cultural anthropologists were as dead as mutton (Evans-Pritchard 1965, 100). So-called 'symbolist' or 'expressivist' views took the field, partly under the influence of Wittgenstein and Peter Winch 1979. See for example Tambiah 1990. The views were not universally shared and anthropologists such as Robin Horton critiqued these views effectively and made important advances along the Intellectualist line of things.

8 Guthrie 1993, 2007a; Barrett 2007; Whitehouse 2007; Bering 2011; Dunbar 2022. But whereas Tylor viewed the doctrine of spirits as involving a kind of intellectual construction devised to explain certain mysteries they see the disposition to belief in spirits as the product of various evolved cognitive modules. Interestingly, in philosophy panpsychism has also risen from the dead. See e.g. G. Strawson 2009, 2018.

9 Oppy 2018, 31. See also Martin 2007, 217ff. The definition is perhaps imperfect. Some religions do not involve passionate or costly displays. There is also a reasonable question about whether fetishism involving worship of animals in the absence of a conception of *spirit* (if indeed there was such a thing) should count as religion. See below.

10 Martin 2007.

11 Throughout this chapter I rely on a number of authorities, amongst them: Lewis 2003; Lewis-Williams 2010; Stringer 2012; Clottes 2016; David 2017; Condemi and Savatier 2019; Higham 2021; Dunbar 2022. The field of paleo-anthropology is in flux and new discoveries emerge almost daily. An attempt at undue precision on my part is likely to be quickly rendered obsolete.

12 Roughly: Lower Palaeolithic: 3.3M – 300k; Middle: 300k – 50k; Upper: 50k – 12k years ago.
13 Stringer 2012, 154.
14 Stringer 2012, 130.
15 Stringer 2012, 137.
16 Stringer 2012, 137.
17 Dunbar 2022, xii–xiii; 150.
18 It is worth contrasting these funerary objects with the abundance of truly practical aides found later in Egypt. By 5000 years ago Egyptians were equipping tombs with food supplies, weapons, replicas of boats, various statuettes and so forth. The replicas 'were believed to have the innate properties of the originals, including the ability to become full-sized, and, once special rituals had been carried out, it was expected that they would be able to serve the owner in his afterlife' (Rosalie David 2002, 21). The utilitarian nature of these goods suggests they were not just personal possessions or expressions of grief, tenderness or fear.
19 Stringer 2012, 109.
20 Clottes 2016, 32.
21 David 2017, 103.
22 David 2017,118–133; Lewis-Williams 2010, 12ff.
23 Lewis-Williams 2010, 12.
24 A number of figurine-like objects have been claimed to have greater antiquity though whether these are human productions is contested. See David 2017, 97–100.
25 Lewis-Williams 2010, 171.
26 Much later, *massive* geographical formations in which they recognized images of their gods still guided both Sumerians and Egyptians in locating sites of worship and settlement. See Kriwaczek 2012, 25.
27 Higham 2021, 40; David 2017, 102–117. Higham also contends for 'possible abstract art' in Gibraltar that is at least 65,000 years old and so must be attributed to Neanderthals.
28 Huizinga 1949. It is often argued that the major *function* of ritual is facilitating social bonding and group cohesion (e.g. Dunbar 2022, 131–148). That may be, but that happy outcome does not provide a causal explanation of ritual's *origins*.
29 Along with SEEKING, RAGE, FEAR, LUST, CARE, PANIC/GRIEF. See Panksepp and Biven 2012, Chapter 10.
30 The role of identification with spirits is discussed in Chapter 4.
31 The oldest known musical instruments are four beautifully crafted flutes found in the Hohle Fels cave in Germany. They are dated at 35,000 to 40,000 years, but the exquisite craftsmanship suggests more antique forerunners.
32 As Kant says, thoughts without content are empty, intuitions without concepts are blind.
33 On the early Out Of Africa model the major dispersal of modern humans from Africa occurred about 55,000 to 60,000 years ago, while recognizing earlier transitory movements into the Middle East. Recent discoveries suggest earlier enduring dispersals. Higham

26 Theory

(2021) proposes that there were at least two enduring movements occurring between 60,000 and more than 160,000 years ago. There is evidence for modern humans in the Arabian Peninsula as early as 85,000 years ago and in Sumatra 65,000 years ago. The dating of modern human arrival in Europe has been pushed back but not substantially, so far.

34 David 2017, 117. There is evidence of significant advances in tool-making, the use of colourants and beads and geometric or patterned art-work; but there are few shelters or deep caves in Africa and the climate is not conducive to preservation of parietal art.

35 See the discussion in Stringer 2012, 125–129, 212–213.

36 Everett 2018.

37 Stringer 2012, 163.

38 Quoted in Chomsky 2018, 3.

39 Language in his view is primarily an instrument of thought, a computational faculty. Its role in communication is secondary. The theory of universal grammar embodied in innate features of the brain plausibly explains a range of important characteristics of language acquisition and creativity. The evidence is compelling. For example: language centres in the brain light up when exposed to artificial languages constructed with universal grammar but not to artificial languages without it; young children acquire any human language with astonishing rapidity and ease, but not if unstimulated at critical times for language learning; they produce and understand new sentences and syntactic constructions independently of previous exposure or association. Whether any competing theory can explain these characteristics as successfully as Chomsky's remains moot. This innate base need not have arisen anew and assembled suddenly 50,000 or a 100,000 years ago. But nor would it have required gradual construction, in the sense that there must first have appeared brain structures geared to proto-languages (used perhaps by *Homo erectus*) that progressively evolved into the neurobiological base of modern human language. That scenario is possible but not necessary. An analogy: a car without spark plugs is not any kind of vehicle at all; it does not move or convey though it may have other uses. But with the plugs it suddenly becomes a means of conveyance, something altogether different. So, some brain structures previously devoted to other functions, or entirely inert, may have undergone simple and abrupt genetic mutations producing the capacity for structured thought.

40 Many theorists have discussed the levels of intentional complexity required to hold religious beliefs, in the context of 'mentalizing' or 'theory of mind'. They are right to do so. Something of the order of fourth level complexity is surely necessary: 'A believes that B believes that spirit S exists and will forgive C.' See e.g. Dunbar 2022. But there is a prior and more fundamental issue: the acquisition of the abstract concept of *spirit*.

41 Roughly: Aurignacian: 45,000–30,000; Gravettian: 30,000–22,000; Solutrean: 22,000–17,000; Magdalenian: 17,000–12,000. Excellent

The advent of spirits and the birth of religion **27**

photographs of all the objects and locations I mention are available on many internet sites.

42 There is considerable dispute over dating of these sites; David (2017, 148–158) concludes that some of the finest charcoal depictions may indeed be Aurignacian.

43 Stringer 2012, 120.

44 Clottes 2016, 147ff.

45 Lewis-Williams 2010, 218–219.

46 Lewis-Williams 2010, 220.

47 Clottes 2016, 136.

48 Clottes 2016, 129. A significant number of these hand prints have missing fingers. Burkert has suggested that finger sacrifice on the principle *pars pro toto* appears to be the most plausible explanation (Burkert 1998, Chapter 2).

49 The figure of the bird may be highly significant since throughout Asian shamanism and indeed early Greek shamanism the shaman's soul is represented by a bird, obviously associated with free flight. See Dodds 1951, 141 and fn.38.

50 The carefully wrapped and buried animals in Egypt from the early Badarian period is evidence of animal veneration. Whether the animals were regarded as inspirited seems unclear, as also why certain animals and not others were objects of veneration. Whether fetishism or zoolatry preceded belief in anthropomorphic divine beings also remains controversial (Rosalie David 2002, 51–52). By the end of the pre-dynastic period most divine powers were represented or worshipped in animal forms. If there did exist such pure forms of fetishism then totemism is a likely development from them. It has been suggested that the Palaeolithic animal depictions represent clan totems, or sexual or social group configurations now obscure to us. One objection to this account, though not a decisive one, is that animals that might have been considered the most plausible of totems, such as bison and lions, are sometimes depicted quite irreverently as speared or dying. It may be noted that fetishism would be incompatible with the ideas of cognitive anthropologists explored in the next chapter.

51 Clottes 2016, Chapter 2. Clottes discusses several other theories and, it seems to me, successfully disposes of them.

52 Clottes 2016, 117–118; also David 2017, 164–165, 179–182.

53 A comprehensive study of extant hunter-gatherer groups supports the view that shamanism was a development from earlier animism (Peoples et al. 2016). These authors deny, however, that either animism or shamanism qualify as religions. According to them, animism is not a religion or philosophy but a by-product of cognitive processes, a widespread way of thinking among hunter-gatherers. This view of animism is refuted in the next chapter. Why the authors deny that shamanism is a religion or set of religions, while acknowledging that it supervenes on belief in spirits and is highly correlated with belief in an afterlife (only one exception in there sample) is a mystery.

Chapter 2

Mysticism, intellectualism and the poverty of cognitivism

Sorting out

In the previous chapter we accepted that belief in spirits or supernatural beings (or supernatural processes) is a necessary though not sufficient feature of (most) religions. The belief is not sufficient because religion comes with a panoply of practical and institutional features besides a bare commitment to the spiritual. Spare 19th-century spiritualism, for example, does not count, though species of it may of course be attached to one religion or another. We accepted that the belief was necessary because although there are borderline cases such as Jainism or austere forms of Buddhism that appear to be atheistic, and religions such as pantheism that are problematic for other reasons, in practice the vast majority of religious people believe in spirits or gods of one sort or another. Belief in spirits typifies religion. We conjectured that the emergence or invention of the concept of spirit was underwritten by the evolution of language sophisticated enough to manage abstract concepts of the immaterial and invisible, and the interdependent development of representational, narrative art. But the question of why exactly the concept (or concepts) of spirit was formed and entered the human imaginary was deferred. What was it in the experience of our ancestors that instigated them to take this remarkable metaphysical leap? This chapter addresses that question.

To my knowledge, at least four different types of answer have been given to the question. The first observes correctly that human creatures have experiences that can suitably be called mystical or ecstatic (or psychedelic) in that they seem to transport their subject to a realm freed from material coils. It then posits that these anomalous experiences give rise to the concept of spirit. This view has considerable ancestry. The second answer is quite recent and is based on experimental as well as somewhat speculative work in cognitive psychology. I will refer to this view – or perhaps more accurately set of views – by the omnibus term 'cognitivism.' It is probably true that cognitivism is the received view in

DOI: 10.4324/9781315519814-4

Mysticism, intellectualism and the poverty of cognitivism 29

current thinking about the origin of the spirit concept in the anthropology of religion. Cognitivism posits the operation of sub-personal cognitive mechanisms or modules that generate the experience of independent agencies taken to be spirits populating the world of the animist. A striking feature of this view, distinguishing it from the others, is that animist belief is altogether detached from experiences of the self and self-agency. The third view we have already touched on. It is Tylor's Intellectualism according to which the invention of the spirit concept was a philosophical achievement of the first 'savage philosophers,' devised to explain enigmatic phenomena such as dreaming and death. The fourth view to be considered is in many ways a development, or rather supplementation, of Tylor's view by Sigmund Freud in *Totem and Taboo*. I will briefly criticize the first three approaches and then ultimately defend a version of the fourth.

The mystical path to spirits

Mystical, ecstatic or trance states have an important place in many historical and contemporary religions and the idea that religion arose from such experiences is compelling. Our primordial ancestors are likely to have experienced ecstatic states and would have tried to make sense of them once they had the conceptual equipment to do so. Ecstatic states are tantalizing and mostly pleasurable and there are multiple ways of inducing them more or less at will. Fasting, induced fatigue, extended rhythmic dancing and chanting, isolation and various other privations are still practised. Psychotropic agents have been widely used. The use of betel nut has been traced as far back as 11,000 BCE and the hallucinogenic effects of some mushrooms may have been discovered much earlier. In a recent study Robin Dunbar says that 'with or without the help of psychoactive drugs, the mystical component, with its strong emotional overtones, underpins all religious behaviour, no matter how sophisticated the religion. It is the motor of religiosity.'[1] By 'mystical component' Dunbar means 'a feeling of divine transcendence that comes over an individual from time to time, sometimes spontaneously, sometimes as a result of deliberately engaging in ritualized activities. It is variously referred to as ecstasy or enthusiasm.'[2] Having these experiences, his account runs, leads directly to a belief in the existence of a transcendental or supernatural dimension where spirits in various guises are encountered. The mystical experience *is* an encounter with the supernatural, and the supernatural realm is populated by spirits. This is the origin of religion. Similar views have been expressed by other thinkers over the years.

Of course, not all individuals who profess religion enter into mystical states. But somewhere along the line, I think Dunbar means, the

30 Theory

religions they profess are anchored, historically or conceptually, in the experience of individuals who have had contact with spiritual beings. Our spaced-out ancestors to begin with, and then shamans, prophets, mystics and televangelists who have the privilege of encountering the supernatural regularly. Ordinary people also claim to occasionally have religious experiences.[3] The question is left hanging, however: granted that mystical or trance-like experiences are unusual and transformative, and like dreams and some psychotic states appear to be of a world quite other than the poor quotidian one, how precisely do they lead to a *spiritual* world? Anomalous experience requires interpretation in terms of concepts *already* in the social imaginary or conceptual scheme. A contemporary atheist and friend of psychotropics having a psychedelic experience is unlikely to infer encounters with spirits.

David Lewis-Williams gives a detailed and persuasive answer to this question. Like Dunbar after him, Lewis-Williams believes that entry to supernatural realms in altered states of consciousness is the foundation of religion. And he provides a genealogical account by linking these states to the Palaeolithic ancestors' experiences of parietal art in deep caves. His argument can be reconstructed like this. Lewis-Williams points out that descent into deep, serpentine caves under the glare of torchlight can cause profound hallucinatory states, a phenomenon that has been noticed by more recent visitors to such caves. Since all modern humans have the same neurological structures any recurrent themes that occur in hallucinatory states are likely to be hard-wired into the human brain and therefore universal. So the themes that have been documented in shamanic cultures from the arctic, Siberia, Africa, Amazonia and South-East Asia, amongst Western spiritualists and psychedelic enthusiasts, will be themes shared by the ancestors. These apparently pan-human themes are: sensations of leaving the body and flight as a disembodied self, descent into a tunnel or seeming to travel through a vortex, meeting spirits and animals and being seized by them and, so, gaining access to a supernatural realm.[4]

> Upper Palaeolithic people probably took entry into the caves as equivalent to entry into an underworld. Then, bearing in mind the hardwired vortex experience, we can suggest that they probably saw the passages of the caves in terms of the vortex – the tunnel – that leads underground and into *deep*, hallucinatory states of consciousness.[5]

These hallucinatory experiences, in particular the experience of flight and vortex travel 'lead inevitably to beliefs about a tiered cosmos,' that is to say, to beliefs about a supernatural world.[6] This seems on the face of it quite plausible. Moreover, the notion of a supernatural world and vortex travel also lead in another direction, that of immanence in material things, of hidden spirits located in cave walls, lakes, the sky and mountains. However, it remains problematic that none of these neurologically determined experiences of vortex travel, flight and so forth precipitated by the hallucinatory conditions induced in illustrated caves, taken singly or together, lead directly to the definitive stuff of religious belief, the belief in spirits. Notably, Lewis-Williams does not explicitly say that the experience of spirits is hard-wired.

He is mistaken, I believe, in supposing (as do others) that an ideology of spirits simply piggybacks on anomalous, unusual, ecstatic experiences. So, for example, he says, that the meditation of the Kundalini yogi and the ecstatic dancing and hyperventilation of the Kalahari San shamans 'activate the nervous system in such a way as to produce similar *religious experiences.*'[7] We can assume that the shaman's experience involves encounters with things that will eventually be recognized as spirits. But these experiences are not *intrinsically* religious, they are not stamped as religious until the things encountered are recognized or conceptualized as spirits. The San conceptualize their experiences through the prism of their spiritual concepts and beliefs. *We*, for example, would not conceptualize them as such. Experiences without concepts are blind. A concept not already available in the social imaginary or conceptual scheme cannot be used to give experience significance. So how, once again, did the ancestors stumble across those various concepts of *spirit* with which they made sense of their unusual experiences? The mystical path comes to a dead end.

Cognitivism

The cognitivists are largely concerned (as we are) to determine how conceptions of supernatural beings or spirits are acquired. Once that is settled, the accumulations of the rest of religion, the diverse ideologies, practices and so forth, are thought to unfold naturally. To this extent they agree with the Intellectualism of Tylor and his followers. But the recent researchers have at their disposal advances in biology and cognitive science enabling them to cast their proposals in forms quite different from those of their forerunners. To explain the human tendency to believe in spirits they invoke cognitive mechanisms, systems, devices or modules, supposed to have evolved either as direct adaptations to specific environments or as accidental by-products of other adaptations. So the proposals come in two flavours. In the direct *adaptationist* form, usually associated with group selection, religiosity is an adaptive trait that improves cooperation and cohesion within human groups, advantaging them in competition with non-religious groups. In the second form, religiosity is not itself adaptive, it has no survival value on its own; it is a *by-product (or spandrel)* of evolved dispositions that are

32 Theory

adaptive.[8] The second form is the most plausible and influential so that is where our discussion is focused.

In the typical religion-as-by-product explanations religion is said to piggy-back on hard-wired perceptual and other cognitive systems selected for advantage in our primordial past. The universality of the cognitive systems – and not the universality of human experience – is supposed to explain the universality of animistic and anthropomorphic religious conceptions. The most important of the systems are the automatic *agency detection device* (ADD) and *theory of mind* (ToM). An innate agency detection device that rapidly notices animate movement is a very useful thing for both hunters and prey. On the principle that it is better to be wrong than sorry such a device is likely to become hyperactive, become an HADD. And (so the story goes) HADD is likely to detect not only the leopard in the bush but the enemy therein and, ultimately, the spirits lurking there. Similarly, the capacity to 'read' other minds in your group, to grasp their moods or intentions, to be able to adopt 'the Intentional stance,' to have 'a theory of mind' or capacity to 'mentalize,' is an obviously useful social accoutrement to enhance genetic fitness. ToM in high gear is likely not only to induce animism but to dispose to belief in invisible minds with purposes, minds much like ours, minds indeed that know our purposes – powerful spirits and gods. These cognitive systems, then, produce as by-products the tendencies to manufacture focal religious objects – spirits – that are basic to all religions.[9]

Many other cognitive 'systems,' 'tools,' 'devices,' 'mechanisms' and 'modules' have been proposed. Barrett also records: Naïve physics, Naïve biology, Naïve psychology and Intuitive Morality modules.[10] To fill out the basic requisites for religious ideology and practice Whitehouse invokes a 'violence inhibition mechanism,' a 'hazard precaution system,' a 'security motivation system' and several others.[11] Indeed, according to Thomson, to believe in a god 'our mind bounces off no fewer than 20 hard-wired adaptations evolved over aeons of natural selection.'[12] Some systems mentioned by Thomson, such as those that underlie the disposition to transference (in the psychoanalytic sense) and the attachment system first described by John Bowlby and extensively elaborated since, have strong evidential support and clearly do play a crucial role in the genesis of religiosity.[13] (Attachment theories are discussed in the next chapter.) These, however, tend to be ignored by cognitive anthropologists and evolutionary psychologists. Whether there is a case for the existence of the other modules – other than the appearance of conveniently filling functional holes – is controversial.[14] Examination of the scientific evidence for their independent existence is beyond our ability, but we can certainly enquire whether they achieve what is claimed for them viz. the universal tendency to posit spirits and gods and the devotional emotions attached to them.

S. E. Guthrie, a pioneer of the cognitivist line of thought, famously asked why people tend to see human faces in clouds. He swiftly dismisses what he calls the 'wishful' or 'comfort' theories according to which we unconsciously project human faces and benign spirits to make our life-world a more friendly place. The spirits and gods are as often dangerous and vindictive as they are benevolent, he correctly observes, and the wishful theory can't explain them. His own suggestion is that imagining anthropomorphic beings in our environment is in part the consequence of the operation of HADD: from the evolutionary perspective detecting agency, especially the complex agency of our fellow humans, is the most important task for survival in a perceptually ambiguous world.[15] The more such modules operate the better a creature's survival chances. Now, the evolution of a hard-wired agency-detecting system is plausible. By itself of course it doesn't quite get us to the detection of human life. It may generate alarm: there is something alive in the bush! It will stoke what I'll call the 'haunted-house effect': *something* horrible is there! But to arrive at *human* agency requires ToM, the propensity to attribute to an object beliefs and intentions like our own. Yet even ToM doesn't get the theorists to the place they wish to go. They need to go beyond human agency to explain the emergence of supernatural agency. So, what is the passage from human agency to supernatural agency, to spirits as we have come to broadly understand them? There is, after all, a winding way from the rustle in the bush, to unseen predators and human enemies, to the immaterial spirits and gods inhabiting the ideologies of most religions. A disposition in humankind to anthropomorphic attribution or projection can scarcely be doubted. We do see faces in clouds and carpets and, as we shall see, we often project much of ourselves into others. But that the tendency to attribution is the result of innate cognitive modules operating before and independently of a cache of imbricated concepts – language dependent and pre-linguistic – can indeed be doubted. No attribution, no interpretation of sense experience, can be made in the absence of appropriate concepts. Suppose I see a bush and imagine it is a burglar; I come to believe, that is, that the bush is a burglar. But I could not believe that the bush is really a burglar unless I already had the concept of *burglar*. It follows that ToM may dispose us to infer human presence only on condition that relevant conceptual content in belief or intention is available to its inferential machinery.[16] It cannot take us from the rustle in the bush to supernatural beings without the prior existence in our social imaginary or conceptual scheme of some such concepts as *spirit, powerful being* or *god*. And it scarcely needs saying that it cannot explain the emotional investments in such beings that are the hallmark of religiosity.

It is evident that the concept of spirit, even in the relatively unadorned sense that we have introduced it, as comprehending the

34 Theory

anthropomorphic objects of supplication and propitiation towards which our ancestors extended their palms, cannot be the immediate and exclusive product of any set of cognitive systems. Spirits are the product of invention, imagination and culture. It may be granted that the systems produce the anxious feeling of the haunted-house effect and, via ToM, the presence of human agency. But that is scarcely an advance in the anthropology of religion. To bridge the gap between anxiety, human agency and the ontology of spirits some anthropologists have taken a desperate step. They propose that the concepts of *mind, immaterial spirit* and *soul* are innate, and are therefore available to modules for immediate attribution.[17] The chasm is leapt in a single bound:

> According to the new cognitivism . . . theory of mind leads us unconsciously, and incorrigibly, simply to assume agency in whatever phenomena we can. Mind, the essence of agency, is . . . conceived as invisible and intangible . . . that the mind survives death is our default assumption. The assumption is produced neither by wishful thinking (as in Freud) nor by the need to explain particular phenomena (as in Tylor), but by a kind of cognitive economy.[18]

The idea that infants are born dualists with innate conceptions of immaterial minds that survive death is, to put it mildly, highly implausible. Yet there appears to be some experimental support for these remarkable ideas and cognitivists have drawn on it. Some of the most cited experiments were conducted by Jesse Bering and collaborators.[19] The experimenters showed children a puppet play in which an alligator swallows a mouse and the mouse is affirmed to be 'not alive anymore.' The children are asked questions that distinguish physical and mental attributions. Would the baby mouse still want to eat? Would the baby mouse still want to go home? An 'overwhelming majority of the youngest children' (five- to six-year-olds) professed that the mouse could no longer eat, but most of the three- to five-year-olds 'still attributed thoughts and emotions to dead baby mouse.' Bering interprets this result as demonstrating an intuitive conception of a mind-body split and predisposition to 'endorsing' (believing? wishing?) continuity of mind after death, and therefore an afterlife. He writes:

> Rather than simply being inculcated by religious adults, the default belief in young children is that mental capacities survive death, albeit in some vague, unarticulated way . . . young children are best envisioned as being naturally prepared to endorse the concept of an afterlife because it matches their own intuitions about the continuity of mind after death.

Those intuitions, Bering thinks, arise from ToM's role in generating notions of agency, projecting selves or spirits as we might say, even in the absence of material agents. That is why '[p]eople in every culture believe in an afterlife of some kind or, at the very least, are unsure about what happens to the mind after death.'[20]

I cannot comment on the detail of the experiments; nor do I believe that it is necessary to do so. By the age of five or six, children have sophisticated linguistic skills and are well on the way to induction into the Intentional idiom of the tribe, including religious ideology which often enough is inculcated soon after infancy. Bering himself notes that children brought up in Catholic schools were more likely to 'reason in terms of psychological continuity.' Moreover, wishful and emotion-laden trends dominate the younger child's thoughts, especially on issues as momentous as not going home (losing mother). Why would the baby mouse want to go home? Because the child would. How could the child think *that* if he was no longer alive? *Not* because children have a positive conception of an immaterial afterlife for themselves but because they cannot entertain their own material non-existence – which is quite a different thing. (Children can have a dread of annihilation, but that too is quite a different thing.) Bering's contention that belief in an afterlife is universal because innate and therefore present early in life is contradicted by ethnographic studies and history. For example, a study of the Vezo people concludes that

> the realization that some sensory, cognitive and emotional faculties survive after death appears to grow with age. This finding . . . contradicts the claim put forward by Bering and his collaborators that young children have a natural disposition to make these attributions . . . a disposition which weakens with age as children learn to construe death as a biological process.[21]

We saw in the previous chapter how late in coming were conceptions of spirit to the human imaginary – a circumstance that would be remarkable if they were innate or the operational consequences of evolved cognitive modules such as HADD. We know that dualistic conceptions of mind/spirit and matter even in historical times are uncertain and tenuous. In the Old Testament *Sheol* does not promise individual existence. The shadowy spirits who descended to Hades were not quite immaterial. The ancient Greeks did not imagine their gods were immaterial. In the Platonic-Christian tradition the idea of a mind-body split and the issue of just what was resurrected after death was a muddy affair. In many cultures it was believed that only kings, chiefs or aristocratic orders had the privilege of an afterlife. This was so in early Egypt and other parts of Africa and Asia. In some cultures there is no belief in an afterlife at all.

36 Theory

These facts defeat the claim that conceptions of soul and spirit and post-mortem survival are innate and universal, and place a stern question mark over the cognitivist contentions we have been examining.

Before I summarize some of the larger difficulties with cognitivism I want to briefly expose Bering's own account of the origins of religion. It is, I think a *reductio ad absurdum* of one direction that cognitivism can take, but not untypical of it. Like other cognitivists Bering dismisses the 'comfort' or 'wishful' accounts of religion: 'I don't think these types of answer are entirely intellectually bankrupt actually' he condescends, 'but I do think they beg the question. They're perfectly circular, leaving us scratching our heads over why we need to feel like there's something bigger out there or to have a sense of purpose to begin with.'[22] He also rejects the accidental-by-product views advanced by most other cognitivists. According to Bering, 'religion – and especially, the idea of a watchful, knowing, reactive God – uniquely helped our ancestors survive and reproduce.'[23] The argument, in outline, is as follows. A critical development in human evolution was the capacity for ToM. Special neural systems are dedicated to this capacity. Once ToM starts cranking it becomes indiscriminate and we are disposed to see intentions, beliefs, signs and purposes everywhere. An overactive ToM not only over-detects animacy, it can't help applying the Intentional stance promiscuously. Overactive ToM explains our inferences about supernatural minds, the belief in an afterlife, the tendency to believe that life has a purpose and the origin of natural theology. God, Bering declares, 'was born of theory of mind.'[24] This is familiar, but Bering injects a twist by accepting a premise: 'regardless of the particular religion one subscribed to, the central gods were envisioned as possessing a deep knowing of people as unique individuals – of their "hearts and souls".'[25]

The premise is mistaken. Some religions have no inquisitive supernatural beings, others do not have gods. Some have high creator gods who are often remote and care not a whit for what goes on in the hearts and souls of humankind. Village or local gods or ancestors usually have access, not to hearts and souls, but to socially consequential information such as who urinated where, stealing and lying.[26] As a rule, these beings have only limited powers and knowledge; some may be downright stupid or easily fooled. It seems likely then that in the prehistoric period in which Bering supposes that ToM was busily creating religion the spirits were limited beings with limited knowledge. Bering's thesis is predicated on an untenable projection of monotheistic conceptions of omniscience backwards in time where they have no purchase in fact. Yet much depends precisely on the universal knowingness of gods:

> For many, God represents that ineradicable sense of being watched that so often flares up in moments of temptation. . . . In other words,

Mysticism, intellectualism and the poverty of cognitivism   37

the illusion of a punitive God assisted their genetic well-being whenever they underestimated the risk of actual social detection by other people. . . . By helping to thwart genetically costly but still powerful ancestral drives, these cognitive illusions pried open new and vital arteries for reproductive success, promoting inhibitory decisions that would have been highly adaptive under the biologically novel, language based rules of natural selection. The illusion of God, engendered by our theory of mind, was one very important solution to the adaptive problem of human gossip.[27]

Since gossip can ruin reputations and reproductive success, persons with a tendency to religiosity i.e. belief in omniscient gods, are selectively advantaged. Thus, 'God (and others like him) evolved in human minds as an "adaptive illusion" one that directly helped our ancestors solve the unique problem of human gossip.'[28] With this final illustration of cognitivist theory we can turn to summarizing objections to it.

First, the theories fail to provide a plausible account of the origin of the concept of spirit which is basic to their understanding of religion. It is likely that systems such as HADD and ToM are part of our evolutionary heritage, primed in the infant-mother matrix and refined in social interaction. But it is a long stretch from the operation of these systems to the ontology of spirits, let alone the complex doctrinal and ritual content of religions. The systems may be involved in the tetchy predisposition to populate the environment with unseen animals and human enemies but they don't deliver concepts of spirit (or soul) recognizable in any ethnography. At best cognitivism explains superstition or propensity to superstition, not spirits as the historically contingent creations of reason, imagination and will; and of course they explain nothing of the immense variety and distinguishing markers of religions.[29]

Second, they fail to explain why the mental systems appear currently to be inactive. What motivates people to religious observance today? If HADD or ToM were still active then it is remarkable how few sightings of gods and spirits we have; though every now and then Jesus is discerned in a potato chip and a statue bleeds. It is evident that systems such as HADD, rewarding as they may have been in the jungle and savannah play practically no part in the genesis or acceptance of theistic belief today. There is, to be sure, no dearth of superstition but it is difficult to see it subtending from the cognitive systems as these have been deployed.[30]

Third, cognitivism ignores fundamental features of religiosity, such as the yearning for emotional attachment and communion. To adapt the wonderful saying about behaviourism, cognitivists feign emotional anaesthesia. We saw that the idea of being watched is important for Bering's account. At one point he observes how hard it is to shake off the

38 Theory

sense that someone or something is watching you and cares.[31] *Cares?* There is little in the operation of the cognitive systems to suggest that they render other minds caring about us, and nothing at all that recognizes the significance of reciprocal emotional investment in relationship to gods and spirits. Bering tells the story of how, after his mother died, he felt her trying to communicate a gentle message in the quiet harmony of jingling wind chimes.[32] He discerns the play of ToM. But why is it his mother returning in this way, and not some burglar or god? Bering was probably experiencing grief. The jingling chimes likely revived traces of his mother in his unconscious attempt to restore emotional touch with her; that is what explains the *particularity* of his experience – not a hyperactive ToM. Many people do have that sense of being watched over, but innate cognitive mechanisms do not explain it. Deeper psychological accounts such as psychoanalysis, which explain this sense of being watched by the activity of a partially dissociated aspect of the self identified with internalized parental images (Freud's 'superego'), readily explain it in the context of an overarching theory. But such accounts cognitivists reject, which leads us to:

Fourth, the cognitivists' failure to seriously consider alternatives to their hypotheses. They are disdainful of psychoanalytic and other psychodynamic explanations. Since the remainder of this and subsequent chapters will be tracking along psychoanalytic lines it will be useful to disarm the cognitivist objections here: objections to the so-called 'wish-fulfilment' or 'comfort' theories of religion. Guthrie says that the wish-fulfilment theories of psychoanalytically orientated anthropologists are mistaken because many religions 'have features for which no-one is likely to wish. The deities of some are cruel and angry, and often complemented by devils or frightening ghosts. In others the after-life is either absent or fleeting or is a Hades or other unpleasant place.'[33] Boyer avers that many religious ideas are anything but comforting: if 'religious concepts' are 'solutions to particular emotional needs [they] are not doing a very good job. . . . A religious world is often far more terrifying than a world without supernatural presence.'[34] We have seen that Bering thinks that such theories are circular or question-begging. Richard Dawkins and Daniel Dennett think the same.[35]

These objections are muddled and superficial. To begin with, wish-fulfilment theories are not circular or question-begging. Suppose I am asked why I am not hungry and explain that I just ate a hamburger. It could be insisted that the fact that a hamburger extinguished my hunger raises further questions about why this organism, my person, should be such that hamburgers extinguish its hunger. But it doesn't follow that my explanation is circular or question-begging. It follows only that further questions of a different order may arise. One might reasonably ask the cognitivists why they think that the evolutionary explanations of religious belief are ultimate as opposed to ones in terms of molecular biology or physics, since the evolutionary explanations obviously raise questions about processes germane to these disciplines. Adequacy of explanation is relative to context. Further, the argument that 'wishful' theories of religion are false because gods are often cruel and religions have nasty or less than comforting features is ignorant of the psychoanalytic theory it is supposed to refute. On the theories in question gods have human characteristics because they are coloured by human projections, some of them wishful. Humans have cruel, sadistic, destructive and self-destructive wishes and they frequently enter into masochistic relationships. The inner world that is projected contains demons as well as angels. It is not surprising that the religious enterprise, which as we shall see is in many ways a continuation of relationships with internalized parental representations and dissociated aspects of the self, generates terrifying scenarios and vicious and vindictive supernatural beings, as well as loving and protective ones.

In general, cognitivism ignores the emotional and social aspects of religiosity, the ways in which religious beliefs and practices are sustained by, and sustain, unconscious dependence on parents; and it ignores the ways in which character – the narcissistic, hysterical and obsessional dispositions among others – enter into the formation of focal religious conceptions. But all this remains ahead. I will argue that emotional and orectic (wishful) factors are far more significant for understanding the origins of religion, including of course the origins of the spirit concept, than the cognitivism currently endorsed by many anthropologists, philosophers and psychologists. The cognitivist accounts, like the ways of the mystical path, come to a dead end. It is tempting to surmise that cognitivism in the field of anthropology represents a triumph for puritanism and, in paradoxical concert with most religions, an assault on insight. Discussing sub-personal cognitive systems or modules, or the economics of memes, is safer than recognizing with psychodynamic theorists the orectic, sexual and emotional currents shaping religions. The step forward is to return, initially, to the Intellectualism of Edward Tylor.

Tylor revived

You will recall Edward Tylor's minimal definition of religion as belief in spiritual beings, and his claim that this belief constituted the earliest religion as well as 'the ancient savage philosophy of humankind.' The philosophical breakthrough was first about souls and then about spirits, which are rather like souls. Tylor had accumulated a vast amount of ethnographic data from the reports of travellers and missionaries and thought it reasonable to project backwards into the human ancestors the features of what, in the fashion of his times, he judged to be primitive

40 Theory

cultures. Despite these limitations he managed some good guesses. Generalizing from his data he found that the soul was mostly thought of in these cultures as

> a thin unsubstantial human image, in its nature a sort of vapour, film, or shadow; the cause of life and thought in the individual it animates; independently possessing the personal consciousness and volition of its corporeal owner, past or present; capable of leaving the body far behind, to flash swiftly from place to place; mostly impalpable and invisible, yet also manifesting physical power, and especially appearing to men waking or sleeping as a phantasm separate from the body of which it bears the likeness; continuing to exist and appear to men after the death of the body; able to enter into, possess, and act in the bodies of other men, of animals, and even of things.[36]

With these conceptions a great deal fell into place for the savage philosophers:

> For as the human body was held to live and act by virtue of its inhabiting spirit-soul, so the operations of the world seemed to be carried on by the influence of other spirits. And thus animism, starting as a philosophy of human life, extended and expanded itself till it became a philosophy of nature at large.[37]

The conceptions that Tylor distilled from his ethnographies have, of course, been sophisticated and elaborated by philosophically minded thinkers over the millennia. And there is diversity of opinion about them, amongst the philosophers, between religions and factions within religions and individuals within factions. But by and large the vast majority of the globe's religious population still conceive of these matters much as Tylor describes them. The animism Tylor describes so far would not quite qualify as religion in our earlier definition. In the absence of an emotional relation, of supplication, sacrifice and ritual, we have a merely intellectual edifice, an explanatory system or set of beliefs. Whether there ever subsisted such a minimal form of animism is an open question. In any case, we saw that by at least the Magdalenian period some religious attitudes were present, as the evidence of sacrifice clearly shows.

How did the first philosophers discover or invent the soul? Tylor suggests that they were arrested by conspicuous differences between several conditions: between living bodies and dead ones; between being awake and being asleep; and between perceiving in ordinary circumstances and perceiving in dream experience. The difference between the first and second of each pair could be explained by the presence of a thing with agency, perception, thought and feeling. That thing was soul. When a body is alive the soul animates it. In sleep the soul may temporarily leave the body and the presence of phantasms in dreams could be explained by the ingress of other souls into the dreamers' mind. Perception, thought, feeling and action do cohere in such ways as to make it natural to think of the soul or self as a unity and scene of inner life, and from these facts the notion of a substantial soul inhering in but separate from the body plausibly follows.[38]

The activity of animals and natural processes could also be explained by the differential presence of soul or soul-like agencies. Human agency is in certain respects the model of causation: we can bring about (some) changes at will and intervene in the course of nature. It once again seems plausible that the early philosophers should have reasoned that nature operates along the same agential lines as they do. As Hume remarked, 'There is an universal tendency among mankind to conceive all beings like themselves, and to transfer to every object those qualities with which they are familiarly acquainted, and of which they are intimately conscious.' Tylor quotes this remark and makes a very astute comment on it: 'Our comprehension of the lower stages of mental culture depends much on the thoroughness with which we can appreciate this primitive, childlike conception, and in this our best guide may be the memory of our own childish days. He who recollects when there was still personality to him in posts and sticks, chairs and toys, may well understand how the infant philosophy of mankind could extend the notion of vitality.'[39] We have seen good reason to believe that the ancestors felt, and shamanistic cultures still feel, less differentiated, less apart, from the environment than the mostly alienated members of modern societies. Tylor believed that this was a function of primitive thought being infantile. He was in a certain sense quite right. He was wrong only in believing that people of his time and class were less infantile and susceptible to primitive thought. But I leave this theme to Chapter 4.

We now have at last the beginnings of a cogent answer to the unanswered question of the previous chapter: How did the conception of spirit enter the human imaginary? Spirits are not, in the first instance, the inevitable inference from mystical or ecstatic states. They are not, as cognitivists maintain, the spontaneous product of innate cognitive systems. They are, at least in the first instance, akin to theoretical entities invented to fill explanatory gaps. First, is the realization of the soul as an entity coherently organizing experiences (perceiving, feeling, thinking, willing) and linking them to action. Then characteristics of the soul are extended to the realm of non-human spirits, supernatural agency and the animating forces of nature. These are easy, almost inevitable steps. This process of discovery or invention may be viewed as the evolution of a theory, proto-science or explanatory scheme.[40]

42 Theory

An important feature of this account should be underlined. The theory explains why humans are able to relate profoundly to spirits. It is because *in essentials they are just like us*. One of Tylor's great achievements as Horton observed was to enable us to see the interaction with gods and spirits as modelled on interactions between human beings. Religions are revealed as extensions of the human social world into a non-human or supernatural dimension. But at this point we become aware of a gap in Tylor's intellectualist account, one of which he was aware but failed to remedy. 'Again, the intellectual rather than the emotional side of religion has here been kept in view,' he writes. 'Even in the life of the rudest savage, religious belief is associated with intense emotion, with awful reverence, with agonizing terror, with rapt ecstasy when sense and thought utterly transcend the common level of daily life.' How do we get from the proto-scientific role that spirit plays in the explanatory scheme of the pioneer philosophers to recognizing the intense emotion and 'most sober and serious conviction' which the spirits inspire, 'the terror of the souls and the dead and harmful spirits' which he says are typical of savage tribes?[41]

And Freud

Freud was a close reader of the anthropological work of his time and in *Totem and Taboo* (1913) he largely agrees with Tylor that the doctrine of spirits was a kind of theory, a solution to a problem, specifically the problem of differentiating life from death. But he did not think that was the main problem. Freud added an important dimension to Tylor's scheme. Typically, Freud focuses on the emotional conflicts that he thought must underlie encounters with spirits. Tylor and many of Freud's contemporaries were particularly impressed by the preponderance and centrality of *evil* spirits in the cosmologies of primitive cultures, a preponderance that continues in some contemporary religious ones. Freud writes that he agrees with those who say that:

> the first born spirits were evil spirits, and who derive the idea of the soul from the impression made by death upon the survivors. The only difference is that we do not lay stress on the intellectual problem with which death confronts the living; in our view the force which gives the impetus to research is rather to be attributed to the emotional conflict into which the survivors are plunged.[42]

This passage marks an advance. What is the conflict Freud had in mind? At the time he was writing *Totem and Taboo* Freud was preoccupied with trying to understand the obsessional neuroses, and he was convinced that primitive man shared with obsessional neurotics the heightened ambivalence and belief in the omnipotence of thought that are striking features of that condition.[43] Because the obsessional is extremely ambivalent and dominated by the omnipotence of thought he exaggerates the potency of his ambivalence. Confronted with the loss of someone he loves, and therefore also hates, he projects his hostility in order to keep the conscious memory a loving one. So it is, Freud reasoned, with primitive man. He believed, with Tylor and all his contemporaries, that primitive man thought primitively. For Freud that meant being under the sway of the primary process modes of wish-fulfilling or omnipotent thinking. And so in the primitive's case the projected hostility is onto the ghost or spirit of the departed which is then experienced as angry, threatening, demonic and in constant need of propitiation. This idea of ambivalence playing a significant part in the formation of the demonic spirit explains much of the mode of interaction with evil spirits, the need for sacrifice and propitiation, ancestor worship and so forth. It does not occur to Freud at this stage that the anger projected onto spirits does not derive entirely from ambivalence. He has not yet sufficiently explored the phenomenology of mourning and envy. The anger at being abandoned by loved ones, the fear that the dead may be envious of the living and may return vengefully, as the multitude of vampire and werewolve folktales remind us. Moreover, the dead do not disappear with the death of the body. Their felt presence looms over everything and testifies to their lingering reality. Longing and searching, as John Bowlby has so movingly shown, continue in bereavement.[44] Many facts of this sort could be adduced to fill in details of the landscape of our emotional relations with the spirits of the dead. In focusing on the *emotional* problem confronting the savage philosopher Freud for the first time allows us to see questions about spirits and religion in the context of the ineluctable need for human relationship.[45]

Notes

1 Dunbar 2022, 48.
2 Dunbar 2022, 25.
3 James 1901–1902/1971 is the classic study. A sceptical discussion of these states is Ostow 2007.
4 Lewis-Williams 2010, 147–154. Elsewhere, however, he says 'it is only the basic notions of a tiered cosmos and immanence that are widespread: their details are filled in or elaborated, in specific cultures' (2010, 173).
5 Lewis-Williams 2010, 210.
6 Lewis-Williams 2010, 170.
7 Lewis-Williams 2010, 151, 153.

8 Theorists such as Dawkins 2006 and Boyer 2001 also offer evolutionary accounts of the *transmission* and survival of religious conceptions and practices. The question of transmission is not directly relevant to our interest in origins, but a few passing remarks seem apt. Dawkins is the most famous proponent of the accidental by-product view of religion but in *The God Delusion* he is mostly concerned with transmission. The right kind of explanation for religious belief, he argues, must lie in evolutionary biology because others, such as 'psychological explanations to the effect that people find some belief agreeable or disagreeable are proximate not ultimate explanations' (168). One proposal he examines is religion as a by-product of the tendency to fall in love, which he says is a kind of 'irrationality mechanism' built into the brain, conferring advantages in mating (185ff). Religion is a result of 'love misfiring', choosing a wrong, indeed non-existent, target. There is, as we will see, something to this, but Dawkins' account is thin. In many religions there is not so much love as fear of the supernatural folk who are supposed to be the objects of misfiring love. And of course we don't yet have an explanation for how the supernatural folk get into the picture in the first place. Another account he considers sees religion as a by-product of innate gullibility: 'Natural selection builds child brains with a tendency to believe whatever their parents tell them' (176). Credulousness in the young is indeed a useful attribute for vulnerable social creatures. 'But the flip side of trusting obedience is slavish gullibility' (176); it is because children are gullible that they easily accept the 'religious nonsense' they are taught. But then, it may be asked, why in the apparent absence of evidence do adults continue to believe? Dawkins appeals to the power of indoctrination. How does it operate? Why are indoctrinated religious views so immune to rational considerations? The weakness in Dawkins' story is that it doesn't have a conception of indoctrination into unquestioning faith that goes beyond learning doctrine. But learning cannot yield the quality of religious conviction that resists rational considerations and change of view. A cogent account of religious conviction must explain its tenacity and profound significance for its subject. These features cannot be explained by appeal to gullibility or indoctrination as Dawkins conceives it. There are in fact psychological and social explanations for these features of religion that we will consider, but they are not of the sort Dawkins considers scientifically respectable. Having officially dispensed with psychological theories that may have filled this gap, he embarks on his account of transmission: meme evolution, the selection of ideas in the environment of other ideas, on the model of natural selection. 'Some religious ideas, like some genes, might survive because of absolute merit . . . [others] survive because they are compatible with other memes that are already numerous in the meme pool . . . memetic natural selection of some kind seems to me to offer a plausible account of the detailed evolution of particular religions. . . . Simple memes survive

Mysticism, intellectualism and the poverty of cognitivism   45

by virtue of their universal appeal to human psychology' (201). 'The idea of immortality itself,' Dawkins adds, 'survives because it caters to wishful thinking.' This is not news. It is just a fancy way of saying that some ideas do better than others because they gratify human wishes. So despite officially denouncing psychological theory as only proximate Dawkins is compelled to smuggle in rudimentary common-sense psychology to rescue the meme theory.

9 Dennett 1989 introduced the notion of the intentional stance that spawned the family of related conceptions. In psychology, the notion of a theory of mind was extensively absorbed. See, for example, Boyer 2001; Barrett 2007; Bering 2011. For mentalization see Fonagy et al. 2004.

10 Barrett 2007.

11 Whitehouse 2007.

12 Thomson 2011, 33.

13 Bowlby 1969; Kirkpatrick 1999; Panksepp and Biven 2012; Granqvist 2020.

14 See the discussions in Whitehouse and Laidlaw 2007.

15 Guthrie 2007b, 37. See also Guthrie1993, 2007a; Barrett 2004.

16 What concepts are; whether any concepts, beliefs or intentions can be held in the absence of language; these are not questions I propose to go into here. Much of my thought is guided by Davidson 1974 and 1982. But clearly the concept of spirit is language-dependent.

17 Guthrie 2007b, 45ff.

18 Guthrie 2007b, 51.

19 As reported in Bering 2011.

20 The quotations are from Bering 2011, 124, 124, 113.

21 Astuti 2007, 173ff.

22 Bering 2011, 5.

23 Bering 2011, 7.

24 Bering 2011, 190.

25 Bering 2011, 190.

26 Boyer 2002, 178ff.

27 Bering 2011, 192.

28 Bering 2011, 7.

29 Laidlaw 2007 for persuasive argument to this point.

30 Proponents such as Justin Barrett (2007) argue that HADD and ToM continue to be instrumental in the formation of religious belief today, just as they explain our belief that the computer is deliberately trying to frustrate us, that light patterns on a television screen are real people, that a wisp of mist is a ghost or spirit. As Laidlaw 2007 (237ff) points out, the assimilation of these diverse phenomena involves deep confusion. In the same article Barrett moderates his view: 'It might be that HADD rarely generates specific beliefs in ghosts, spirits and gods by itself, and hence does not serve as the origin of these concepts. Nevertheless, HADD is likely to play a critical role in spreading such beliefs and perpetuating them' (192). Quite a difference. It seems to me that although many people today do claim

46 Theory

to have religious experiences, as in Pentecostal and charismatic services, these have little or nothing to do with the cognitive modules evolved for quite other purposes.

31 Bering 2011, 159.

32 Bering 2011, 88ff.

33 Guthrie 2007a, 288.

34 Boyer 2002, 23.

35 Dawkins 2006, 168. Dennett 2006, 102.

36 Tylor 1873/2016 Vol. I, 429. 'But beyond this, if we consider the nature of the great gods of the nations, in whom the vastest functions of the universe are vested, it will still be apparent that these mighty deities are modelled on human souls, that in great measure their feeling and sympathy, their character and habit, their will and action, even their material and form, display throughout their adaptations, exaggerations and distortions, characteristics shaped upon those of the human spirit.' (Tylor 1873/2016 Vol. II, 247–248)

37 Tylor 1873/2016 Vol. II, 184–185.

38 Galen Strawson 2009 lists seven ways that the self is thought of: as a thing; as specifically mental; as a subject of experience; as single; as a distinct thing; as an agent; as having a character or personality. Those are the ways in which we *do* think of the self, and they were very likely arrived at early in the human story.

39 Tylor 1873/2016 Vol. I, 477–478; cf. Freud 1913, 77.

40 Some would object that the explanatory schemes of 'savage philosophers' could scarcely be regarded as theoretical, let alone scientific. Call it 'proto-science' if you wish. For my part, I am with Tylor and Horton in being impressed by the similarities between the schemes and science, not the differences. They are based on observation and were attempts to explain a broad range of phenomena in terms of a few basic entities (souls/spirits), a point powerfully made about some African religious systems by Horton 1997. They explain causation in terms of personal agency, a mode of explanation still with wide currency. As the anthropologist I. M. Lewis wrote in his sober study of spirit possession: 'whatever else they are, spirits are certainly hypothesis used to explain what we would regard as psychological states' (2003, 172). There is reflective criticism in at least in some of the schemes relying on spiritual agency to explain what we would call natural phenomena, even if they do not *systematically* challenge their assumptions in the manner of modern science. I do not discuss here in any detail the views of those schools of anthropology referred to as expressivist or symbolist that hold that the primitive schemes are not intended as explanatory at all but merely evince attitudes to the world, attempts to achieve transcendence, indirectly express social structures or politics and so forth. I believe that these views, if taken to expose the central aims of the primitive religious/scientific schemes and not just contingent features of them, are transparently mistaken. On these matters, see Horton 1997 where the intellectualist perspective is extended and the symbolist interpretations are decisively refuted.

41 Tylor 1873/2016 Vol. I, 359, 111.
42 Freud 1913, 92–93.
43 This is discussed further in Chapter 4 and the Appendix.
44 Bowlby 1980/1998.
45 In addition to the phenomena of death, sleep, dream and mourning, the ancestors must have been impressed by madness, trance and dissociative experiences. They were vulnerable to starvation, predation and separation and therefore probably to traumatic dissociative states. Their lives were, after all, nasty, brutish and short.

Chapter 3

For the love of gods

Explanation and communion

This chapter will advance the idea that the modes of achieving communion with gods and spirits are essentially the same as the modes available in human-to-human relationships, including, importantly, narcissistic relationships. A sketch of the psycho-historical evolution of the concept of a single, omnipotent and caring god will show how that development made intense attachment and communion with the deity possible. That leads to a discussion of contemporary attachment theory which has made attachment needs central to its understanding of religiosity. The theory is appealing but can be shown to be wanting in critical respects. In particular, it skirts the defensive (in the psychoanalytic sense) uses of relating to an omnipotent being in sustaining the economy of narcissism, specifically of self-regard and self-esteem. The next chapter then takes up the role of narcissistic processes in individual and group religious beliefs and behaviour. The following chapters explore their pernicious consequences.

You will recall Tylor's intellectualist conception of animism as explanatory, as proto-science or philosophy, and his belief that animism was at the core of all religions and indeed of philosophy. Tylor regretted that he had kept only the intellectual side of religion in view and had ignored the 'intense emotion' and 'rapt ecstasy' involved in relations to spirits. We saw that Freud made an important advance by taking up some of these emotional factors. He argued that evil spirits are the ghosts of the dead disfigured by the projected hatred inherent in the ambivalence of primitive man to his love objects. The relation to the spirit is a veiled continuation of earlier relationships. But apart from influencing pioneering psychoanalytic anthropologists such as Geza Roheim and Abram Kardiner, Freud's views had little lasting resonance.

In a limited respect the neglect was repaired by the anthropologist Robin Horton. Horton introduced a distinction that greatly facilitates the understanding of religion.[1] He observed that all religions have two

DOI: 10.4324/9781315519814-5

variable poles or aspects: on the one hand, *explanation, prediction and control* of the actions of the gods and spirits and, therefore, the course of nature presumed to be controlled by them (EPC, I will say). In early papers Horton referred to this aspect as the *manipulative mode* of religion, and this term in some ways better characterizes it and sets the proper contrast with the second aspect of religion. This is *communion* (C), in which intimate relationship is sought with gods and spirits because such relationships with wiser, more powerful beings are 'valuable in themselves,' not for, or not only for, instrumental gain. The fact that spirits are anthropomorphic makes it possible that interactions with them should be modelled on human-to-human relations, and thus makes communion possible.

To explain, predict and control the actions of spirits humans must use the same interpretative and practical devices that they use among themselves. In the effort to understand and predict supernatural behaviour beliefs, desires, and emotions are attributed to the spirits; in the effort to control them humans beseech, bargain and propitiate, just as they do among themselves. EPC clearly overlaps the C aspect of religion and every human-to-god relationship can be placed on an EPC/C scale; to the extent that one is emphasized the other tends to be reduced. The Nupe people, for example, have 'religious systems characterized by an extreme emphasis on manipulating the gods as tools for the achievement of health, wealth and issue.'[2] Interest in communion is scarcely present. Other societies, like our own at least since about the 17th century when the scientific revolution began to erode the EPC credentials of religion among the educated, tend to emphasize communion, devotion and closeness to the divine without (overtly) seeking other benefits. From these two aspects taken together it follows that 'religion can be looked upon as an extension of the field of people's social relationships beyond the confines of purely human society . . . with the exclusion of pets.'[3] Assertions, such as those by Rudolf Otto about the *sui generis* character of religion, in fact have little anthropological support. Indeed, all vigorously flourishing religious traditions include a strong emphasis on EPC, and on manipulating the gods and spirits. Where a strong sense of ordinary objectivity, a 'sense of thereness,' of the divinities is lacking, the possibilities of communion evaporate.[4]

Horton does not consider the C aspect as scrupulously as he does EPC, however he suggests that the most promising path for further understanding is likely to be psychoanalysis.[5] This is unsurprising since his view is consilient with what might be expected to spring from psychoanalytic object relations theory, attachment theory and other lines of psychological investigation exploring religion through the lens of interpersonal relationships. Given his field-anthropological focus, Horton elaborates on the *overt* similarities between human-to-human and

50 Theory

human-to-god relationships. In this book I will focus (as I did in Pataki 2007) on the unconscious significance of these relationships. One reason for this is as follows. Gods and spirits are not the kinds of entity one encounters in the normal run of things, not for most people anyway. It is however clear that they *can* be objects of attachment and intense emotion. This is a remarkable trait of humankind. We become emotionally attached to things imperceptible to the senses: gods, spirits, fictional characters, ideologies and other abstract conceptions. How is this incontestable fact possible? The matter doesn't strike most theorists as seriously problematic; for them it is just so, it happens.[6] My underlying thought, one that would perhaps be widely shared by psychodynamic thinkers as well as religious sceptics, is that in the human-to-god relationship there must at deeper levels be projections of the representations or images of real parental objects and aspects of the self to which we are still attached – which are still unconsciously cathected, as psychoanalysts say.[7] If that is so, then we can go on to discuss two levels of engagement with religious objects. On one level, there is engagement with them *as objects defined by their culturally attributed characteristics*; on another level, as *representatives of internal objects or aspects of the self*. If that thought is true then we need to examine religion from both perspectives and attend to the way their lines intersect. We should expect that attachment to religious objects as well as providing social and religious identity, moral guidance and so forth, would also serve many unconscious defensive functions; including the narcissistic defences that appear so conspicuous in Abrahamic religions and, as we shall see, animate much of the intolerance and violence with which they are associated.

Anthropomorphism

We have been insisting that the gods and spirits are conceived anthropomorphically, at least in so far as they can be included in the circle of human communion on the model of human-to-human relationships. The idea that the gods and spirits are sufficiently anthropomorphic to be used for the regulation of self-esteem on the model of human-to-human solicitude is central to the argument of this book. But the premise of anthropomorphism is often challenged. It is necessary therefore to turn to the anthropological and historical evidence, bearing in mind that our interest in religion is *as it is*, not as it could or should be in some ideal figuration.

In Chapter 1 we encountered the images of outstretched palms in caves and shelters which appear to speak of appeal or propitiation in ways familiar between one human being and another. We noted some of the general characteristics of gods and spirits as conceived by hunter-gatherers, pastoralist peoples and ourselves. Spirits and souls are different from sticks and stones: they can be disembodied, travel swiftly from one place to another, or be at several places at the same time. Spirits and gods are often wiser and more powerful than humans, though occasionally more stupid: Agouti of the Kalapalo people of central Brazil is 'a sneak and a spy' and Jaguar is 'a violent bully who is easily deceived.'[8] They can take on the form of animals and possess humans. They may be imperceptible except to trained religious specialists. They may be omnipotent and omniscient. They are ontologically highly diverse. They are, however, *always* anthropomorphic or person-like in key respects. They have human-like emotions, understanding, intellection, concerns, animosities and so forth.

According to the Akkadian *Atrahasis*, before humankind there were only gods. Hence the gods had to do all the work of digging canals and building dikes. This led to a strike of the younger gods against their seniors, especially against Enlil the acting chief. Fortunately, the cunning god Enki found a solution to the troubles. Together with the mother goddess he created men to do the toil the gods had been obliged to do: henceforth 'they shall bear the burden.' But soon men multiplied and became clamorous and disturbed the gods who decided to destroy them by sending a flood. Enki, however, ever resourceful and solicitous of men, directs the good man Atrahasis to build an ark. . . . It is wrong to believe that this is mere poetic elaboration on a more abstract divine reality to which these ancients subscribed. In the forerunners to contemporary theistic traditions an almost iconic anthropomorphism prevailed. 'Mesopotamian religion was always strongly anthropomorphic,' says Beaulieu.[9] The Olympian deities 'are human almost to the last detail' says Burkert.[10] and 'Ahura Mazda is a god in heaven, no doubt, but clearly conceived as a person in acting and reacting.'[11] It is the same in traditional and tribal religions around the globe. Of African religions Olupana writes:

> Stories across the continent depict the deities as anthropomorphic beings or impersonal spirits who share numerous characteristics with their human devotees. Gods and spirits are made in the image of humans. They speak, are heard, endure punishment, and attain rewards just like human beings.[12]

As one would expect the social arrangements of the polytheistic pantheons are modelled on human arrangements:

> Divine constellations reflect the fundamental order and elementary structure of human society – husband and wife, brother and sister, mother and son, mother and daughter, father and son, . . . lover and beloved, lord and slave, hero and enemy and so on.[13]

52 Theory

Despite the redactions of many generations the old anthropomorphic god remains visible in the Old Testament. In *Job* and elsewhere God calls an assembly of his children, where Satan famously challenges Him. In *Genesis* Adam and Eve hear the 'Lord God walking in the garden in the cool of the day' and later God (El) wrestles with Jacob. As late as the 8th century BC, and probably much later, the goddess Asherah was worshipped as Yahweh's wife.[14] Little changes in the Christian era or with the advent of Islam. As well as believing in a supreme anthropomorphic deity – albeit incorporeal, unchanging, omnipotent – primitive Christians also believed in a vast array of other spiritual anthropomorphic beings. Origen and Augustine believed that the pagan gods were real, though they thought them demons or fallen angels. The pagan Porphyry offered sacrifice to angels as a token of goodwill, and presumably as a cheap hedge.

I must add here that I do not for a moment wish to invidiously contrast these tales of anthropomorphic beings with a supposedly superior understanding of divinity today. On the contrary, I believe that the shift from the straightforward anthropomorphism of animism and polytheism with their predominantly EPC mode of relating – unimpressive as that may be – to a more abstract monotheism with its predominantly C form of relating is a regression, a slide towards more delusional modes of thought and feeling. Here I merely wish to emphasize the near ubiquity of anthropomorphic conceptions of the gods and spirits. In an extraordinary passage David Hume asks:

> Where is the difficulty in conceiving that the powers or principles, whatever they were, which formed this visible world, men and animals, produced also a species of intelligent creatures, of more refined substance and greater authority than the rest? That these creatures may be capricious, revengeful, passionate, voluptuous is easily conceived. . . . And in short, the whole mythological system is so natural, that, in the vast variety of planets and worlds, contained in the universe, it seems more than probable, that, somewhere or other, it is really carried into execution.[15]

The conception of such beings is more defensible than the abstruse and de-personified conceptions of Abrahamic deities.

To be sure, at least since Xenophanes philosophers, theologians and mystics have evolved conceptions of deity that purpose to avoid the inherent difficulties in the anthropomorphic notions. Xenophanes complained that men make the gods 'have clothing, voice and body just like them.' 'If cows and horses had hands,' he said, 'they would draw their gods in the shape of cows and horses.' We do not know what Xenophanes thought the gods were like. I will pass over the tracts of mystical,

For the love of gods 53

apophatic, allegorizing and metaphysical de-anthropomorphizing because I deny that these efforts have in any fundamental sense altered the thought of the ordinary believer, nor indeed of many of the learned. The sophisticated may discard the crude anthropomorphic notions of the 'simple' believer (Aquinas' term), but the vast majority who take a religious tradition seriously, perform its rituals, pray and seek communion with the deity, do not share the learned conceptions. Simple believers may not expect that prayers will be answered, sacrifices rewarded or sins punished, but they do expect to be heard and understood by their deity. It is essential to every religion that their gods or spirits have intellection, emotion and agency and be capable of reciprocation. It is unsurprising therefore that in almost every significant historical expression of religion the gods and spirits, whatever other unfathomable characteristics they may have, manifest distinctly human traits. That is the condition upon which the possibility of religiosity as communion rests. Moreover, if the psychoanalytic argument I develop below is sound then it may be expected that even the most abstract conceptions of gods are experienced unconsciously in a concrete manner, along the lines of parental introjects, and hence as at least partly anthropomorphic.[16]

Monotheism as progress towards personal communion

We now leap over millennia of polytheistic realism about the gods and spirits and enter the age of increasing abstraction and unrealism. The consensus among historians and archaeologists is that the Biblical account of the origin of Israelite monotheism is insupportable.[17] In all probability the early Israelites crystallized from an indigenous Canaanite or West Semitic population, probably in the course of the 12th to 10th centuries BCE, and ancient Israelite religion was 'in the main an outgrowth of and part of Syro-Canaanite religion.'[18] The exact details of its evolution remain vague. It seems that early in the first half of the first millennium BCE the high Canaanite god El becomes identified or transliterated with Yahweh, a Semitic storm god arriving perhaps from the Midian south, and comes in the north to be associated with the legend of exodus from Egypt. In the process of transliteration Yahweh acquired El's wife Asherah as consort, and there is evidence that she was widely worshipped. At this time worship in both Israel and Judah, as in the rest of the Middle East, was polytheistic, with certain gods, perhaps household gods, receiving favoured cult. Injunctions to the exclusive worship of Yahweh, combined with severe denunciations of all other gods, though not yet explicit denial of their existence, appear in the Prophetic literature from the 9th century BCE onwards when the northern kingdom was under intense pressure from the Assyrian superpower that was soon to destroy it. In any case, by the end

54 Theory

of the 7th century BCE Yahweh had acquired a following in elite circles in the southern Judean kingdom. At this point several dramatic political, historical and psychological developments rapidly converge. King Josiah's politically motivated suppression of Canaanite deities and his efforts to centralize the cult of Yahweh in Jerusalem were significant steps towards forging monotheism. The Babylonian exile following the destruction of the Jerusalem Temple exposed Judean intellectuals to the abstract conceptions of Persian religion and, very probably, to Mesopotamian and Egyptian literature. They were also confronted with the political and psychological trauma of the destruction of their nascent state, the subordination of their god and the humiliation of defeat and deracination. Whether it was the effectiveness of Josiah's brutal advocacy; the collision between Israelite monolatry and the religious conceptions of older, more powerful, polities; or, perhaps, the logic of humiliation and narcissistic rage; or very likely the sum of these and other factors[19]; it was on the return of some of the exiled elite to Jerusalem that a definitive monotheism was declared. Second Isaiah proclaims: 'There is no God but I.' The existence of other gods is denied, their worship is declared an abomination, and all religions but one are declared false and wicked. Israelite religion gave birth to a unique conception of a god that was revolutionary, complex and baleful.

The advent of monotheism complicated religious sensibility. Two of these complications are of particular significance. Monotheism opened the possibility of a more intimate and intense communion with the god. As Freud observed, once 'god was a single person, man's relation to him could recover the intimacy and intensity of the child's relation to his father.'[20] Second, the prospect of intimacy with an omnipotent god introduced a new range of narcissistic relations. The relationship to a mostly caring, parent-like god becomes a major means of regulating distress and self-esteem. Before looking at these developments in detail it is fascinating to observe their prefiguration in Egypt and Mesopotamia. A verse of the late third millennium BCE *Instruction for Merikare* goes:

> Humans are well cared for,
> the livestock of god:
> he made heaven and earth for their sake,
> he pushed the waters back
> and created the air so that their nostrils might live.
> His images are they, having come forth from his body.
> For their sake he rises to heaven;
> it is for them that he has made plants and animals,
> birds and fish,
> so that they might have food.
> If he killed his enemies and went against his children
> this was only because they thought of rebellion.
> For their sake he causes there to be light.

To see them he travels [the heavens] . . .
When they weep he hears . . .
God knows every name.[21]

Notice the contrast with *Atrahasis* where humans are created to serve the gods, to lift *their* burden. These verses, anticipating Biblical cosmogenesis and anthropocentrism, present the novel idea that creation is for *humankind* and fashioned for *its* needs – and, still more remarkably, because the gods *care*. The further idea of an unmediated personal and salvific relationship makes its appearance in Egypt during the second millennium BCE and even earlier at various times in Mesopotamia. Now each human being may have a personal god among the lesser gods who intercedes for them with greater gods. An Egyptian hymn from around the 1330s BCE illustrates the relationship.

You are Amun, lord of the silent,
who comes at the call of the poor.
I called you when I was in sorrow,
and you came to save me.
You gave breath to the one who was imprisoned,
and you saved me when I was in bonds.
You are Amun-Re, lord of Thebes,
you save the one in the netherworld.
You are the one who is gracious to the one who calls on him,
you are the one who comes from afar.[22]

In Israel, in prophets such as Amos and Hosea, the human-to-god relationship undergoes a further transformation. It becomes libidinized or sexualized. God is not only a benign and loving lord, a shepherd to the flock, a deliverance from afar (the parent who comes to rescue the child). The familiar tropes are complemented with that of a betrayed, jealous and resentful God.

When Israel was a child, I loved him,
and out of Egypt I called my son.
The more I called him,
the more they went from me;
they kept sacrificing to the Baals
and burning incense to idols.
Yet it was I who taught Ephraim to walk,
I took them up in my arms;
but they did not know that I healed them.
I lead them with cords of compassion,
with bands of love . . .
and I bent down to them and fed them.[23]

56 Theory

We have arrived at an entirely new concept of a god intimately concerned with individual human needs and expecting in return, not only cult, but love. The gods of polytheism occasionally intervened in human affairs but their solicitude for mortals was bounded. Reciprocally, although devout respect and fear of the divine were common, there was little in these religions which could be called 'love of god.' The author of the Aristotelian *Magna Moralia* wrote: 'It would be eccentric for anyone to claim that he loved Zeus.' Yahweh intervenes not occasionally but unceasingly. The other gods had domestic lives and cosmic responsibilities; human affairs were a distraction. Yahweh seems entirely invested in humankind and in their reciprocated love and loyalty. As the god sheds iconic form and human limitations and becomes less anthropomorphic, religion becomes more *anthropocentric*, a triumph of human narcissism. The human moves to the centre of the cosmos, the centre of God's attention and unwavering if severe love, just as God is idealized and abstracted beyond comprehension and the reach of envy.[24] And as the god is idealized and rendered omnipotent and limitless so by means of identification the capacity for human megalomania is enlarged.

Monotheism decisively shifted the model of religion as principally providing EPC towards its second pole, that of communion. The residues of animism and polytheism, the endeavour to manipulate the gods through prayer, sacrifice, magic ritual and so forth are not relinquished (see next chapter). But with monotheism the idea of communion with a single, personal, loving being graduates to the centre. It is a costly graduation with two momentous consequences.

First, divine functions, previously distributed amongst the family of deities, are invested in one all-powerful object of intense emotional attachment upon whom *everything* depends. No Enki can rescue humankind from the anger of Enlil. Now there is nowhere to turn but God, and so to love 'the LORD your God with all your heart, and with all your soul, and with all your might' is the first principle of the new tradition. If such personal attachment is profound, failure to live up to divine demands is to risk abandonment. But dependence so complete engenders hatred and despondency, and since hatred of God must be repressed it will tend to be turned upon the self or projected. There is in fact some historical evidence suggesting that the growth of a personal relationship with a favoured god leads to depressive anxiety in the form of religious despair. Beaulieu writes that in the Middle Babylonian period, in the latter half of the second millennium BCE:

the worship of the personal god reached full maturity. The insistence on the intimate relation between worshipper and god favored the blossoming of a pervasive notion of sin, while anxiety created by the frequent absence of divine response and support led to a growing awareness of the remoteness of the gods and unfathomableness of their will.[25]

By and large, pervasive guilt and self-loathing were rare among pagans but became a dominant malaise of Christian Late Antiquity.[26] Guilt towards God, as Nietzsche observed, becomes a new instrument of self-torture. Religious persecution, unknown before monotheism, becomes as common as rain. Religious despair and persecution are for the first time engraved into humankind's imaginary.

Second, idolatry, as paganism is now derided, is not only error; it is infidelity and immorality. The Egyptologist Jan Assmann has familiarized the notion of the *Mosaic distinction*. Revolutionary monotheism (as opposed to evolutionary monotheism, the final stage of polytheism) is 'based on the distinction between true and false gods, between one true god and the rest of forbidden, false, or non-existent gods.'[27] Polytheistic religions are concerned mainly with public actions such as the correct performance of rituals. Monotheism is concerned with orthodoxy, correct belief and sincerity of commitment. Monotheisms have in common an emphatic and exclusionary claim to revealed truth and are not based on the empirical evidence of divine activity in nature, as were the earlier religions. Natural evidence and reason are disparaged as seductions 'luring people away from eternal truths into the traps and pitfalls of the false gods.'[28] From claims to incontrovertible truth the monotheisms draw their antagonistic energy. Religious intolerance, hatred and violence enter a world that had been innocent of them: the hatred of the Elect directed at pagans, heretics, apostates and sexual non-conformists who threaten the Elect's certainties, and the retaliatory hatred of those who are excluded and maligned. To polytheists, monotheism's claim to exclusive truth was simply atheism, a contemptuous denial of *their* gods. The insistence on a special relationship with a single all-powerful god, on being the sole owners of religious truth, leads inexorably to feelings of superiority and difference, to engraving ethno-religious markers and to erecting fences lest the pure and holy religion be contaminated by the impure heathen or heretic. Marks of election lead to exclusivity, and exclusivity was, then as now, attractive to some people and anathema to others. So mutual hatreds have rippled through contending sects within the Abrahamic religions and between them, from Antiquity to the present. But hatred is not reserved only for the stranger or pagan but also for the heretic within. The Mosaic distinction 'cuts right through the community and even through the individual heart, which now becomes the theatre

58 Theory

of inner conflicts and religious dynamics. The concept of idolatry becomes psychologized and turned into a new concept of sin.'[29] Another avenue for self-hatred is bequeathed to humankind.

The Christianity that spread in Late Antiquity differed from other oriental cults in its intolerance and refusal to grant value to other forms of worship. It cut through the bewildering mass of alternative religions, mystery cults and philosophies that cluttered the period. The misery of the third century provided the conditions for the rise of Christianity as the urban centres of migration could no longer provide the security of family, lineage, clan and locality. People in a lonely and impersonal place were ready to accept 'a peculiarly intense parental relationship with a spiritual being – a relationship that had no real parallel in the locally based cults in their earlier lives.'[30] In this 'age of anxiety' a crucial development is the paranoid figuration of demons as agents of evil to be constantly defended against. The Christian stood alone with his God and manned the barricades in an invisible battle with the demons. 'To sin was no longer merely to err: it was to allow oneself to be overcome by unseen forces.'[31] There seems to be an episodic association between social insecurity and misery and the yearning for a personal relationship with a single omnipotent god that even antedates Christianity. The attempt to construct a bond between man and deity appears to peak in times of social distress when ordinary human relations are disrupted. The search for communion seems to have arisen in Egypt and Mesopotamia during times of social dislocation, as in the latter half of the second millennium BC. In Greece eras of political and social discord gave rise to mystical movements in the 6th century BCE (Pythagoras, Orphism); the aftermath of the Peloponnesian war (Plato); the 1st century BCE (Poseidonius, neo-Pythagorism); and the 3rd century CE (Plotinus). The pagan philosophy of Later Antiquity reflects this longing for personal communion. 'The soul should be continually directed towards God,' wrote Celsus.[32] Our times appear to be another such of social dislocation, confusion and misery.

In my view, this desire for communion with an omnipotent – and by now an extremely vague – god is degenerative from both the quest for communion with anthropomorphic gods as a means to control the material world and from magical control (an aspect of EPC) in the purely instrumental sense. But the very opposite has been asserted and more frequently assumed. It is said that the establishment of a profound relationship with one god represents an achievement of integration superior to the fragmented condition of polytheism or, of course, the abandoned state of atheism. It is supposed that god-directed guilt is an advance over the alleged fragmented (or paranoid-schizoid) relationship to many gods or spirits.[33] This argument mistakes the nature of the earlier religious attachments. Intense attachment relationships are rarely formed with

For the love of gods 59

more than a very few persons or objects. But only rarely in polytheist religions is the human-to-god relationship intense, let alone fanatical. The cooler, reserved and dispersed relationships with the spirits and gods of the earlier religions could scarcely support the intense psychological demands of the monotheisms. Monotheism does not integrate what one might call the manifold of divine possibilities; it tries to annihilate all but one of them (the false gods, the devils, the heathens), and with them possibilities of more realistic relationships with the human world.

Communion and attachment

I have been sketching elements of the psycho-historical evolution of the concept of a god that made intense communion (or dependence or attachment) with the god possible. The term 'communion' was used to designate the relationship that evolved between human and god in parts of the world, not everywhere and for everyone, in preference to 'attachment' or 'dependence' because the word suggests a relationship that is intimate, sincere and open to merger or identification. The idea that the human-to-god relationship mirrors human-to-human relationships is not new. It is implicit in some early Greek thinkers and Feuerbach's famous version was known to Sigmund Freud. Freud injected into this large frame a new element: his novel developmental model of the mind. The relationship between human and god is shaped by and perpetuates that between child and father.

> When the growing individual finds that he is destined to remain a child forever, that he can never do without protection against strange superior powers, he lends those powers the features belonging to the figure of his father; he creates for himself the gods whom he dreads, whom he seeks to propitiate, to whom he nevertheless entrusts his own protection. . . . The defence against childish helplessness is what lends its characteristic features to the adult's reaction to the helplessness which he has to acknowledge – a reaction which is precisely the formation of religion.[34]

In this view, religion is essentially object-relational and wish-fulfilling. In their psychical origin 'religious ideas . . . are illusions, fulfilments of the oldest and most urgent wishes of mankind.' These wishes relate in the first instance to being cared for and protected by the father. Although Freud increasingly appreciated the significance of maternal relations, and the maternal aspects of divine figures, he never quite coordinated this with his chief statements about religion. An *illusion*, as Freud uses the term, is a wish-fulfilling belief engendered by a wish. It may be true despite its provenance. *Delusions*, in his framework, are engendered by

60 Theory

wishes, contradict reality and are immune to rational change. Freud's considered view is that religion is delusional, or delusion-like. Religion 'comprises a system of wishful illusions together with disavowal of reality, such as we in an isolated form find nowhere else but in amentia, in a state of blissful hallucinatory confusion.' He then adds, 'these are only analogies, by the help of which we endeavour to understand a social phenomenon; the pathology of the individual does not supply us with a fully valid counterpart.'[35] Freud often compares religion to obsessional neurosis, but also says that religion may obviate, or perhaps disguise, neurosis – because of its mass-delusional character. Religion has the effect of

> depressing the value of life and distorting the picture of the real world in a delusional manner – which presupposes an intimidation of the intelligence. At this price, by forcibly fixing them into a state of psychical infantilism and by drawing them into a mass delusion, religion succeeds in sparing many people an individual neurosis.[36]

Religion, then, is *delusion-like*, it involves something approaching a psychotic divorce from reality. We shall see that this account is close to the mark in the case of religious fanatics.

Having laid out some elements of Freud's account we need to note a significant ambiguity in the main passage quoted above. It is unclear whether unconscious *infantile* wishes, whose object is parental solicitude, are being allayed in the life devoted to gods, *as well as* the adult's quite realistic dependent needs and anxieties, unrealistically directed at powerful, protective (albeit illusional) deities. The extent to which gods unconsciously represent parental objects, and hence provide substitutive or symbolic satisfaction for infantile unconscious wishes, is, it seems to me, muddy in this text (See Appendix). The difference between infantile wishes preserved in the unconscious, and conscious adult wishes to be loved and protected which are similar though realistic, is not explicitly recognized. But in a later passage he states that the effective strength of the child's mnemic image of his father combines with the persistence of his need for protection to 'jointly sustain his belief in God.'[37] So it would seem that gods unconsciously *represent* parental objects and symbolically satisfy unconscious infantile wishes for protection *at the same time as* allaying adult dependent needs and anxieties.[38]

Much of the subsequent psychoanalytically orientated work on religion, of attachment theory and, indirectly, of other psychological approaches (such as terror management and coping theory) can be seen as variations on, or critiques of, the Freudian ideas, with the role of the father replaced by mother as primary caregiver or significant object. In my reading, the ambiguity just noted points to a significant divergence between the psychoanalytic and other approaches. The direction of psychoanalytic thought is that supernatural figures unconsciously *represent* parental objects and symbolically satisfy unconscious infantile wishes; and so to that extent involve a fixation to, or revival of, early object relations. The past is dynamically alive in the present. Attachment theory, initiated by John Bowlby in a brilliant series of publications, is currently the foremost account of childhood development. In many respects attachment theory is an evolution from psychoanalytic object relations theory. However, over the issue of the revival of early object relations in religiosity, the differences between psychoanalytic and attachment approaches are stark. As a leading attachment theorist, Per Granqvist, says: 'Unlike Freud . . . attachment scholars do not tend to view attachment behaviour in adults as manifestations of regression or unhealthy dependency.'[39] Whether that dependency should be characterized as unhealthy we will at this stage leave moot; more to the point, attachment theorists don't see the earlier relationship as still alive in the later one; most psychoanalytic theorists do.[40]

Bowlby described an innate behavioural system with the basic aim of maintaining the infant's proximity to the parenting figure who provides the infant with a secure base and safe haven. The neurological and behavioural evidence for such a system is very strong.[41] Its evolutionary advantages in slow-developing primates are evident. Suffice to say that endeavouring to maintain attachment to a protective parental figure and to its various incarnations throughout life is a fundamental need, and its failures are immensely consequential. The psychologist Lee A. Kirkpatrick describes some of the ways in which attachment needs are mirrored in religiosity.

> To achieve the objective of establishing physical proximity, infants engage in a variety of behaviors such as crying, raising arms (to be picked up) and clinging. With increasing cognitive abilities, older children are often satisfied by visual or verbal contact, or eventually by mere knowledge of an attachment figure's whereabouts. This latter observation opens the door to the possibility of a non-corporeal attachment figure with which actual physical contact is impossible. Religious beliefs provide a variety of ways of enhancing perceptions about the proximity of God. A crucial tenet of most theistic religions is that God is omnipresent; thus one is always in 'proximity' to God. God is frequently described in religious literature as always being by one's side, holding one's hand, or watching over one. . . . [V]irtually all religions provide places of worship where one can be closer to God. In addition a diverse array of idols and symbols – ranging from graven images to crosses on necklaces to painting and other art forms – seem designed to continually remind the believer of God's presence.

62 Theory

The most important form of proximity-maintaining attachment behavior directed toward God, however, is prayer.[42]

The reason why there are similarities between the infant's attachment behaviour and the religious adult's behaviour is that the primary attachment behavioural system is active in both. It operates especially when safety or emotional dysregulation are threatened. As well as securing a safe base, some theorists also see the attachment system as serving 'mentalization' or ToM, the capacity to understand others in terms of Intentional states. In terms of developmental outcomes, there is an array of attachment possibilities along a secure/insecure spectrum. Here we need not go into the overall formative details. In the case of religious objects, a variety of studies suggest that the vicissitudes of attachment history significantly influence a person's representations – 'internal working models' (IWMs) – of God and other supernatural figures. Broadly, people with secure attachment and with positive IWMs of themselves and others will tend to view God positively as a secure base and safe haven. People with insecure attachment, who are preoccupied/ambivalent or avoidant, are likely to have corresponding views of God as ambivalent or rejective and harsh. In a major work, Granqvist notes that these findings are borne out by cross-cultural studies:

> In cultures where parenting is typically harsh and rejecting, people tend to have corresponding representations of God or gods as wrathful and punitive. In contrast, in cultures where parenting is typically warm and accepting, people tend to have a corresponding representation of God or gods as loving and accepting.[43]

But there is an important exception. Where parental attachment figures are unsatisfactory or worse, divine figures may become surrogates. Relations to such figures may compensate for insecure attachment and provide the kind of secure attachment relationship denied with one's parents or other primary attachment figures. At the centre of this picture, and simplifying somewhat, are causal arrows from {benign or malign parenting} to {secure or insecure attachment} to {corresponding IWMs of parents and others} to {corresponding *or* compensatory IWMs of God}.

The empirical findings of the attachment theorists are of the first importance though they can scarcely be done justice to in a short space here. However, their conclusions are open to objections in some respects and fall short in others, and these can be briefly examined. Overall, they are inadequate to the complexity of religious phenomenology. I will note some particular difficulties with the approach with a view to exploring in the next chapter a richer psychoanalytic account, specifically of the narcissistic aspects of religion which go missing in attachment theory.

For the love of gods **63**

We have seen that for most of the historical record, and very likely in prehistory, religion does not have a prominent communion or emotional attachment aspect. Religious observance before monotheism is mostly at the EPC pole. The beseeching, prayerful, manipulative aspect of religiosity may, of course, be a part of EPC relating. If a shaman sought contact with his principal, or a Roman priest sent up a sacrifice, it was to achieve some material end. Love of deity is often said to be central to most religious belief systems but historically speaking that is simply not so. Rather it would seem, as Freud observed, that only when a people lose confidence in their ability to influence the spirits do they abandon manipulation, the use of magic and imprecation, and seek communion.[44] Many religions scarcely have a communion aspect at all but are marked by cool pragmatism.[45] This fact is obviously inconvenient to the broad application of the attachment model. The capacity for EPC, as Horton said, is the basic sustainer of a religion's life because it creates a sense of the reality of its religious objects. *Mere* communion, so to speak, with a non-corporeal object presupposes a loss of a handle on reality, as wobbly as that handle may be. The fact that historically EPC has been the dominant mode of religious expression is not only inconvenient to attachment research but raises the question of what it is about humanity that has made EPC the default position.

Although the attachment literature contains vague references to the way in which adult 'religious standards' are formed on the basis of the standards of the attachment figures of childhood, there appears little discussion of the direct role of *religious ideology* – of the specific character and conceptions of a religion – in the formation of the child's IWMs of deity, and their impact on individual religious dispositions. This omission leaves a significant hole in the attachment theoretical study of religion: although it captures some schematic elements of religious phenomenology it fails to capture much of its definitive content; a fact acknowledged by Granqvist.[46] We know that the mind of the preschooler and early schoolchild is extremely receptive to religious and spiritual ideas, and parents and teachers regard this period as particularly opportune for inculcating their brand of religious ideology. The interaction between parent and child significantly shapes the child's IWMs of gods and spirits, and the parent's religious beliefs and IWMs of deity enter into that interaction. But the details of religious ideology and practice to which the child is exposed, and the way these are *interpreted* by the child – an interpretation that may depart markedly from the parent's beliefs – are also significant. Such details are treated as extrinsic to the main lines of attachment research. In the next chapter we will show their intrinsic significance.

Finally, religious profession and affiliation spreads over a broad spectrum. On one side of a mild centre are people whose identification with a

64 Theory

religion has little psychological resonance. It may be a part of the 'social scene,' it may be habit. On the other side of the centre, the resonance may be profound indeed. Here are people referred to as fundamentalists and fanatics. They are the clamorous representatives of a larger group who are driven to religion by needs not well described as emerging from the correspondence or compensation pathways of the attachment crucible. The attachment-orientated research, although focused on monotheism, scarcely touches on what in my view is most distinctive about it. In the essential structure of its ideology and emotional impress, monotheism *is* fanatical. Given the opportunity it quickly reverts to its principal tendencies: intolerance of difference, persecution, violence and hatred of mind when thought challenges its illusions. It has been so since Antiquity and is evident today wherever religion has political influence: in Russia, Eastern Europe, Israel, many Muslim nations and the United States. Of course, many people, even those who know the historical record and acknowledge these tendencies, see them as incidental, as perversions of True Religion. I contend that these are *intrinsic* features of monotheism. That is a proposition we will pursue in the following chapters and we can begin to see how it might be true by now turning to examine further aspects of the role of narcissism in religion.

Notes

1 See his collection Horton 1997.
2 Horton 1997, 42.
3 Horton 1997, 32.
4 Horton 1997, 372.
5 Horton 1997, 42ff, 369–372.
6 Granqvist 2020, 39–46.
7 That is to say charged with interest of a libidinal or aggressive character. See Pataki 2014, 35–42. The fact that spiritual objects are in fact fictive, as I believe, underlines the significance of the unconscious aspects of the relationship to them.
8 Bellah 2011, 136ff.
9 Beaulieu 2007, 165.
10 Burkert 2004, 183.
11 Burkert 2004, 123.
12 Olupona 2014, 20–21.
13 Assmann 2007, 19–20.
14 Collins 2007, 182.
15 Hume 1757/1992, 151.
16 Attempts to evade anthropomorphic conceptions often result in farce. Terry Eagleton's (2006) attempt to satirize Richard Dawkins' characterization of God as some kind of omnipotent 'chap' is a case in point. Eagleton patiently explains that theologians do not believe that God is 'either inside or outside the universe. . . . His

transcendence and invisibility are part of what he is. . . . For Judeo-Christianity, God is not a person in the sense that Al Gore arguably is. Nor is he a principle, an entity, or "existent": in one sense of that word it would be perfectly coherent for religious types to claim that God does not in fact exist. He is, rather, the condition of possibility of any entity whatsoever.' After a short space, during which the reader is to contract amnesia, Eagleton continues: although not an entity, God has 'revealed himself' in Jesus, 'and sustains all things in being by his love.' God created the universe 'out of love rather than need,' though 'God might well have come to regret his handiwork some aeons ago.' God is 'free of any neurotic need for us and wants simply to be allowed to love us.' The person of Jesus has revealed 'the father as a friend and lover rather than a judge.' The obvious lesson from this muddle points to the difficulty of conceiving God without human predicates.

17 E.g. Dever 2006, 2020; Collins 2007; Bellah 2011.
18 Wright 2007, 178.
19 Robert Wright (2010) discusses the resentment towards the oppressive regional powers expressed by the prophets of the time. 'In the end . . . the logic behind monotheism was pretty simple given the natural mindset of Israel's exilic intellectuals. Yahweh's honour, and Israels' pride, could be salvaged only by intellectual extremes. If the Babylonian conquest didn't signify Yahweh's disgrace, if Yahweh wasn't a weakling among the gods, then he must have orchestrated Israel's calamity – and orchestrating a calamity of that magnitude came close to implying the orchestration of history itself, which would leave little room if any for autonomy on the part of other gods' (180–81). 'Monotheism was amongst other things the ultimate revenge': the oppressors who tormented Israel are deprived of their gods and they must acknowledge Israel's superiority on both a political and theological plane (178).
20 Freud 1927, 19.
21 Quoted in Assmann 2007, 22.
22 Quoted in Bellah 2011, 245.
23 Hosea 11 quoted in Bellah 2011, 302.
24 Hume noticed the other side of the coin. Where deity is represented as infinitely superior to mankind, the human mind sinks to submission and abasement and the monkish virtues of mortification, penance, humility and passive suffering. 'But where the gods are to be perceived only a little superior . . . we are more at ease in our addresses to them, and may even, without profanneess, aspire sometimes to a rivalship and emulation of them. Hence activity, spirit, courage, magnanimity, love of liberty, and all the virtues which aggrandize a people' (Hume 1757/1992, 149). It was possible to envy the polytheistic gods for their beauty and immortality, as did the Greeks, but in the Abrahamic religions envy is defended against and disguised by pathetic idealization. On the defence against envy by idealization see Klein 1957. Agnes Petocz has noted how the need to

66 Theory

disguise God by abstraction becomes more urgent as religious need regresses to its origin in the human need and helplessness of the child (private communication).

25 Beaulieu 2007, 169.
26 Dodds 1965, 28ff; Brown 2018, Chapter IV.
27 Assmann 2007, 28.
28 Assmann 2010, 29.
29 Assmann 2007, 30.
30 Horton 1997, 374–375; See Brown 2018, 62 ff.
31 Brown 2018, 53.
32 So prevalent had this view become that to 'the man in the street the term "philosophy" came increasingly to mean the quest for God' (Dodds 1965, 92, 100ff.)
33 Freud seems sometimes to be of those who believe that monotheism was an integrative advance in intellectuality and spirituality (Freud 1939, 88, 111–115). He instances Jewish antipathy to magic. But there was no such antipathy. On Temple magic and sacrifice see Goodman 2019, 206–210.
34 Freud 1927, 20.
35 Freud 1927, 39.
36 Freud 1930, 84–85.
37 Freud 1933, 163.
38 Substitutive satisfaction is discussed in more detail in the next chapter and the Appendix. See further Pataki 2014, 2019.
39 Granqvist 2020, 88.
40 There is a range of interesting views within a broadly psychodynamic framework. Rizzuto 1998; Meissner 1984; Faber 2004; Ostow 2007 are representative. I single out only two interesting variations for contrast. Ostow argues that the covenantal relation to God 'provides both horizontal [to the group] and vertical [to God] attachment to a divine entity. I would guess' he continues, 'that this dual attachment provides the major motivation of religious affiliation' (84). Religion, he says, is 'psychologically based ultimately on the updated yearning for the earliest infantile experience of the mother's comfort' (53). Religious experiences are reactivations of childhood and adolescent experience. Thus experiences of awe reproduce experiences recorded implicitly as memories of the contours of the mother's body and voice; penitence represents the child's attempt to regain parental good-will, and so forth. However, the force of 'updated' in the quoted passage is unclear. Ostow says: 'The need to reach out is so strong that it extends to animals and upward to virtual companions, spiritual entities, the images of ancestors, and even at times to mythological spirits' (127). Quite so. But it is unclear whether the need to reach out is the need of the infant within or of the adult who harbors it, or both. Martin Faber's carefully elaborated account of religious attachment is different to both Freudian and attachment theory. Faber rightly emphasizes the repeated maternal ministrations and rescues that are encoded in the infant's mind

as implicit memory. These, he argues, are state-dependent memories i.e. are likely to be recalled in similar circumstances. Repeated activations structure neural circuits. 'As the child finds his way to the supernatural divine, he discovers a sphere that bears a striking, uncanny resemblance to the experiential world in which he has been dwelling right along through his pre-subjective interactions with the caregiver. . . . The religious realm, in two words, *corresponds implicitly* to the child's mind. It is a realm that contains at its center an invisible parental presence who supports and sustains the child, *who gives him existence*, his being (the "Creator")' (36–7). For Faber, it is not a wish that goads the projection of the internal world but rather an external experience that elicits it. So, you are in a majestic church and told that God loves you. The experience awakens past ministrations and encounters which are transferred onto the gods and angels. An obvious difficulty with Faber's model is its vulnerability to the sorts of criticisms levelled by cognitivists at Freudian wish-fulfilment theory: it fails to account for the negative aspects of religious experience. Both the experience of maternal care and the religious matrix into which a soul is cast may lack the angelic, providential quality that backdrops Faber's account.

41 See Bowlby 1969; Cassidy and Shaver 1999; Panksepp and Biven 2012; Granqvist 2020.

42 Kirkpatrick 1999, 806. Kirkpatrick assembled extensive survey data which supports a link between attachment needs and religious belief. For example, in a US national poll, when subjects were asked 'What comes closest to your own view of faith?' 51% of respondents said 'a relationship with God'; 19% said 'a set of beliefs'; 4% said 'membership of a church or synagogue'; and 20% said 'finding meaning in life'. In a US study of clergy, the most common response to the question 'How does faith help you in daily life?' was 'Access to a loving God who is willing to help in everyday life.' These statistics are more than 20 years old and since they were assembled religious and political polarity, paranoia and conspiratorial thinking have exploded in the United States. My guess is that. among the religious, even more people would rank their relationship with God as the most significant feature of their religion. That would be consistent with what was said in the preceding section about ages of anxiety.

43 Granqvist 2020, 139–140.

44 Freud 1933, 165.

45 Horton 1997, 373ff for examples.

46 Granqvist 2020, 267.

Chapter 4

Narcissism in religion

Shamanism and narcissism

I want to begin this chapter with a motley of examples from the cultural record where the internalization and identification with spirits is used to regulate self-regard (how one sees oneself), self-esteem (how one feels about oneself) and the conditions of security necessary for a continuity of self-experience. These are the principle components of narcissism, the capacity to love or think well enough of oneself, but which may in certain circumstances develop into hatred of oneself, or a grandiose sense of superiority to others and the need to devalue or destroy them. Most of the examples are of transient or permanent incorporation of spirits, of being possessed by them, and in every case there is a specific motive of mastery or self-esteem regulation. After those initial examples I will sketch the framework in which the terms used above find their home and explanatory value and, finally, with this infilling, turn to the development of narcissism in individual religiosity. The following chapters will show how several of the narcissistic aspects of religiosity are responsible for a large measure of the violence, moral perversity and irrationality associated with the monotheistic religions. Narcissism is a central motif in psychoanalytic and other psychodynamic theories and there is still considerable disagreement about its place in the development and constitution of mind.[1] My account will of necessity be selective and impressionistic, but I hope that it will suffice for our purposes and compel the reader's conviction.

The discussion of shamanism was left hanging at the end of Chapter 1. The word 'shaman' comes from the Siberian Tungus meaning 'spirit-inspired priest or healer.' 'A shaman,' says the anthropologist I. M. Lewis,

> is a person of either sex who has mastered spirits and who can at will introduce them into his own body. Often, in fact, he permanently

DOI: 10.4324/9781315519814-6

Narcissism in religion **69**

incarnates these spirits and can control their manifestations, going into controlled states of trance in appropriate circumstances . . . the shaman's body is a "placing" or receptacle, for the spirits. It is in fact by his power over the spirits which he incarnates that the shaman is able to treat and control afflictions caused by pathogenic spirits in others.[2]

An experienced shaman can master many spirits, including those sent by enemy shamans, but may have a somewhat Faustian contract with one special spirit. Communion with spirits may involve conversation and guidance, in which case the shaman may relate the spirit's revelations or directions to the community; but it may culminate in full possession when the shaman's personality is totally effaced in ecstasy, often with strong sexual connotations. In every case (Lewis argues) shamanistic possession represents an assertion that the powers that control the cosmos and the calamities they inflict on humankind can be mastered; for the shaman lives in the radiance of higher powers and occasionally can fully identify with them, much as some religious specialists and fanatics claim to do today. The shaman may acquire great prestige and wealth.

Spirit possession is not restricted to shamans. In his study of ecstatic religions (predominantly in East Africa), Lewis distinguishes peripheral possession cults from central possession religions. In the former, spirits are typically invasive, capricious and amoral; possession appears involuntary and is often temporary. Typically, the 'victims' are women in highly patriarchal societies, and subordinate males. The possessing spirit vocally expresses grievances, that happen to be the subject's, in socially acceptable form, and the victim's 'illness' may mobilize restorative action in the husband or master. Such possession may be viewed as transitory or hysterical identification serving self-assertion and as a means to compensation under oppressive conditions. That of course is not the official view within the culture, although it may be the suspicion. Central possession religions typically involve ancestor spirits and more autonomous deities, although they also recognize invasive demonic spirits, usually from adjacent peoples. In these religions, controlled and non-invasive i.e. non-demonic possession is usually the privilege of a religious elite who are sometimes chiefs but more often shamans. Possession in these religions, says Lewis, is a response to circumstances which people 'do not know how to combat or control, except through those heroic flights of ecstasy by which they seek to demonstrate that they are the equals of the gods.' 'What is proclaimed is not merely that God is with us, but that He is in us.'[3] To have God within, in the logic of the unconscious is to have eaten God, is to be God, is to be omnipotent. It is to be invulnerable and safe from harm.

70 Theory

We met the Kalapalo people earlier. They believe that powerful beings or spirits express themselves through music. So it happens that

> the powerful beings who are the focus of ritual life and their form of expression, namely music . . . provides almost the entire content of the [Kalapalo] rituals. . . . [B]y collectively performing music, they not only model themselves upon their images of powerful beings, but they feel the worth of those models by experiencing the transformative powers inherent in human musicality.

Through music and ecstatic evocation they do not worship, but identify, with the powerful spirit, and at the same time achieve an exalted group identity. Bellah also observes that amongst Aboriginal Australians 'The Ancestral Beings, like the powerful beings of the Kalapalo, are not worshipped but identified with in ritual enactment.'[4]

In the ancient world, transitory identification with a god is evident in the phenomenon of ecstatic prophecy. At Delphi the Pythia became *entheos*: 'the god entered into her and used her vocal organs as if they were her own . . . that is why Apollo's Delphic utterances are always couched in the first person, never in the third.'[5] The Biblical prophets also rely on the first-person trope. About the year 172 CE a voice, not his own, began to speak in Montanus: 'I am the Lord God Almighty dwelling at this moment within a man. . . . Look (it said) man is a lyre, and I play upon him like the plectrum.'[6] Lasting self-transformation through identification is also known at this time. A formula common in Gnostic and Neoplatonic literature of Late Antiquity 'I am Thou and Thou art I' suggests non-possessive mystical union but perhaps also identification, as in the remarkable passage from the *Ophite Gospel of Eve* quoted by Dodds: 'I am Thou and Thou art I: where Thou art, there am I also. I am disposed in all things: wherever Thou wilt, Thou dost assemble me, and in assembling me thou dost assemble thyself.'[7] It is said that every lover lives in the body of the beloved. Those who wish to identify with a god, to become the omnipotent mother, sometimes pay a high price. In her city, Pessimus, the priests of Cybele the Great Mother whose cult under many different names was immense and arguably still represented, were eunuchs initiated through self-castration. (They did better than Cybele's lovers who all came to a worse end.) There is strong reason to think that shamanism exerted a powerful influence on Greek conceptions of the soul and afterlife.[8] Orpheus and Pythagoras amongst other seminal figures clearly have shamanistic contours. And of course there is another shaman, a master of spirits, Jesus Christ, whose influence has been even more lasting.

The dynamic of narcissism and identification can be seen to play out transparently in the evolution of early Christianity and explains one of its fundamental doctrines. Following the account in Erich Fromm's *The Dogma of Christ*, in the early 'adoptionist' dogma, Jesus was a man adopted by God, elevated to Messiah, and become a god, the 'Son of God.'[9] If a man becomes a god he becomes equal to God. When the son is elevated to His father's side, the hostility to the father is diminished, since the power of the father over the son is abrogated. By unconscious identification with the Son, the believer's Oedipal desire of rivalling the father is symbolically satisfied: it will seem unconsciously as if the actual father *has* been rivalled (see below 'Narcissistic relations'). The hatred of the father is allayed but not eliminated. The residue of unconscious death wishes against the father are displaced onto the Son (who is now a god and father-like). And thus in the Son's suffering and death the early Christians could atone for their murderous wishes by identifying with the Son. They, too, are punished. Thus it is that Jesus's crucifixion expiates the guilt of all. But there is something psychologically deeper here that Fromm failed to see. If this tormented man can become a god, so we, too, who are also tormented, can become gods. The unconscious identification with the tortured man on the cross is the believer's path not only to absolution from guilt but to apotheosis. Nietzsche, in one of his many brilliant moments of insight, wrote:

> I recall again the invaluable saying of Paul: "God hath chosen the weak things of the world, the foolish things of the world, base things of the world and things which are despised": that was the formula. . . . Everything that suffers, everything that hangs on the Cross, is the divine. . . . We all hang on the Cross, consequently we are divine. . . . We alone are divine.

With the eventual triumph of the Athanasian doctrine in the fourth century different sets of unconscious wishes come into play. A man was not elevated to be a god, according to this doctrine, but God descended to become a man, and God and Son are of one substance. The unconscious import of this doctrine rests on the implication that rivalling and displacing the father is now unnecessary, since the Son had been equal to the Father from the beginning. It reflects the church's assumption of power: there is no need to rebel; the better attitude is to submit. Henceforth rebellion and hatred are sins and must be turned inwards and transformed into guilt. The foundation stone of the church's medieval hegemony is laid.[10]

Narcissism and identification

We have assembled historical instances where internalization and identification with exalted spirits or gods are clearly strategies for regulating conditions of security and self-esteem.[11] They may be direct, as in the

72 Theory

shamanic assertion of supernatural control over disease, enemies or a harsh environment. They may be indirect, as when oppressed or marginalized people are possessed by irresistible spirits and indirectly assert their claims for respect and recognition. The similarities between these primitive forms of spiritual possession and the practices sweeping Christian churches, described in the next chapter, will not be lost on the reader. We can now turn to the psychoanalytic framework in which the rest of the chapter unfolds.

The first generation of psychoanalysts noticed that children often identify with animals or identify their parents with animals, quite frequently with large frightening animals. That is, they imagine or pretend, and at a deeper level come at least transiently to believe – though the belief may persist unconsciously – that they, or other people, *are* animals. This fact is useful in psychotherapy with children since they readily dramatize their inner worlds and family constellations using toy animals. Such identifications are bread and butter for the makers of cartoons and curators of children's museums. The analysts also noticed that patients often identify with their therapists as part of what is known as transference and may begin to imitate some of the characteristics of the analyst, as they perceive them. Freud and other pioneering analysts also noticed a fleeting form of identification in mass hysterical contagions, much like transient possessions, some of them historically notable. And they noticed early on the role of identification in neurotic symptom formation. It was not until his 1910 discussion of Leonardo's homosexuality, however, that identification was brought clearly into relation with narcissism. Freud conjectured that Leonardo's homosexuality had its source in identification with his mother. Leonardo initially had an intense and exclusive relationship with her; when the bond was broken he represses his love for her and 'puts himself in her place, identifies himself with her and takes his own person as a model in whose likeness he chooses the new objects of his love.'[12] Subsequently, Leonardo's relationship with his love objects becomes one of self-to-self: in unconscious phantasy, Leonardo is at once his mother and his love objects. That is the basic structure of an important kind of narcissistic relationship acquired through identification. Already, two major classes of identification can be distinguished in the example of Leonardo. He identifies *introjectively* with his mother (internalizes, incorporates, eats her); it is for him unconsciously *as if* she was in him and he was her. But he also identifies *projectively*, as he projects (externalizes) his (ideal) self-images onto the boys he loves, and identifies with them. So it is he, Leonardo-identified-with-mother who loves boys-identified-with-Leonardo. He loves himself as he was loved by his mother (or wishes that he was loved by his mother) and the boys he loves represent his ideal self, perhaps the boy he felt himself to be when he was loved. In effect, he loves himself. Identification profoundly

Narcissism in religion **73**

affects self-regard and self-esteem. The narcissistic economy turns, one might say, on dispositions to love or to hate oneself; and how that goes is deeply affected by the objects with which one is identified – on who, ultimately, one sees or feels oneself to be. These early Freudian insights into narcissism have been hugely elaborated in later psychoanalytic work, and the concept of identification remains important to psycho-analytic and other psychodynamic theoretical and clinical thought. The conditions and processes that have been brought under these heads are complex, the crucial evidence is mostly clinical, and the psychoanalytic literature on them is vast. Only a few of the pertinent lines of develop-ment are described below.

Narcissistic relations

There is no need to be too specific about timing. From the beginning of awareness, infants want to feel good, to be free of pain, hunger and anxiety, and want their objects (mother in the first instance) to be per-fectly good by their own guiding lights. They want to live in the circle of an omni-benevolent world. The world is not so good, but various means of regulating both the 'inner' experiential world and the real caring en-vironment are available to the infant. The latter can be achieved by in-sistent protest, and the former by employment of various psychological mechanisms. Infants have the capacity to split off (or withdraw attention from) bad states or aspects of the self and bad aspects of their attach-ment objects. They can also project (usually bad and rejected) aspects of the self into objects and introject (usually good or desired) aspects of objects. These processes alter the distribution of pleasure and pain in the experiential world. Having introjected objects they can identify with them introjectively. Having projected aspects of themselves they can identify projectively. In the very early stages, it is not clear that we can speak properly of narcissism because although there are mechanisms for regulating self-feeling, for maintaining in Freud's phrase a 'pure pleasure-ego,' there is not yet a clear reflexive relation to the self: the self does not take itself as an object and (pace Freud) it seems inappropriate to attribute self-love to the earliest stages. The vehicle of introjection and projection is omnipotent (wish-fulfilling) phantasy: when some state of affairs is imagined or phantasized then, in certain conditions, it seems to be real and can substitute for reality, as do dream and hallucination; sometimes with lasting consequences. The child's mental life remains for quite some time under the sway of what Freud called 'the omnipotence of thought' and this experience of (quasi-)omnipotence eventually com-bines with a number of incidental affirmations of it.[13] The mastery of walking and talking and the new exhilarating love affair with the world affirm it. Parents usually are still satisfying the child's needs on demand

74 Theory

and may be felt to be extensions of his will. The conjunction of these circumstances elates the child and reinforces his sense of omnipotence and grandeur.

With the formation of a nascent self, it becomes appropriate to speak of the reflexive libidinal relation of narcissism. The maintaining of the omni-benevolent world now requires regard to the intricate relations one has with one's self. Although at first good states of the self or primitive self-esteem depend largely on feeling loved by others it increasingly depends on the capacity to value and love oneself. Where self-esteem cannot be gained through love, either another's or one's own, then the machinery of omnipotent phantasy may be invoked to compel love, to create an illusion of it, or to build a fortress against its absence. Also necessary for the feeling of security and self-esteem at this stage is the child's capacity to regulate its mother's presence. Disruption of the optimal ranges of attachment proximity provokes anxiety and panic. Once becoming aware of their relative helplessness and dependence children usually insist on the mother's continuous presence and will stretch their attachment repertoire to achieve it. Later, the child strives to *know* the mother's whereabouts. If the need to know is infused with anxiety it may be deformed into a need to know everything which, under the impress of omnipotence, may be transformed into an illusion of omniscience. The child may in phantasy become omniscient, or suffer desperately from the need to be so. It is striking that the attributes – omnipotence, omniscience and omnibenevolence – so necessary in the regulation of infantile narcissism are precisely the key perfections attributed to many a god. The unconscious need for omniscience, we will see in Chapter 8, forms a fateful combination with the revealed religions that know no uncertainty or fallibility.

Another important factor involved in the regulation of the narcissistic economy is the capacity for idealization of self and object representations with which the child may identify. Freud referred to the setting up of an 'ego-ideal,' by which he sometimes meant an ideal-self (and at others an ideal to be aimed at), that is 'a substitute for the lost narcissism of his childhood in which he was his own ideal' – a kind of rescue operation for narcissism. But children may also idealize themselves by identifying with their admired (and, often, feared) parental objects. If they are like (or better than) these objects then they too will be admirable and powerful. Being able to idealize themselves, children now possess another means to further idealize objects by projecting their own idealized conception of themselves into them, a manoeuvre of very great significance later in love relations, as it was with Leonardo. Significant figures needed for protection and security are often idealized by having their 'bad' aspects stripped away, or split off, so as to not contaminate their goodness and obviate the desired relation to them. The psychoanalyst

Narcissism in religion 75

W. R. D. Fairbairn particularly emphasized how the child in splitting the object may take badness upon himself, a process that leads to guilt and shame and self-abasement. He called this the 'moral defence.' The processes I have described are more or less normal developments. But in some circumstances, identification with the idealized objects and idealized self-representations can lead to the creation of unconscious grandiose conceptions of the self that dominate the entire personality.[14] One particularly malign outcome occurs when the self and object have been idealized for their aggression or destructiveness and the grandiose self that forms from the fusion of the ideal self and idealized object is suffused with aggression; a condition sometimes known as malignant narcissism, a condition discussed further in Chapter 7.

It is difficult to sustain childhood narcissism. Parents become progressively uncompliant, and the child's expanded understanding soon discloses his real dependency. Children's love of others and maturing moral sense render naked egotism painful. Various strategies are now available to keep a grip on self-esteem and omnipotent control. They may consciously surrender much of their own narcissism but reinforce the idealization of objects and form a kind of hero-worshipping incorporative bond living in the orbit or radiance of the great and adored one. The adolescent crush, unrequited slavish love, adoration of cult and political figures are descendants of this strategy. Idealized self-images can be projected into the parental figure, and then by re-identification restore what was earlier surrendered; unconsciously it then seems that they are the idealized incorporated figure. These and several other unconscious strategies undergird and decisively influence later religious belief, behaviour and sense of self.

The inculcation of religion

One good reason for believing that unconscious representations of real objects – of parental figures or the self – underlie relationships to divine objects subtends simply from the inescapable human need for *human* relationship. If suitable human objects can't be found then we humanize those objects that can be found. Faces in the clouds. If gods and spirits do not exist then that highlights the fact that the second term of the relationship, actually empty, must be filled and shaped by unconscious projections if there is to be a meaningful relationship at all. We go so far as to humanize the invisible, the hidden, the unreachable. Gods, spirits and movie stars may function as substitutes for real persons provided they are humanized and rendered less alien and remote. We know that the earliest love objects are never entirely surrendered; their representations remain preserved unconsciously, ready to be projected into friends, lovers, institutions and leaders to at least partly reconstitute the early

76 Theory

experiences of safety and wholeness at mother's breast. It would be astonishing if religions escaped this universal compulsion. In fact, the extraordinary feature of religion, from its earliest days when supplicants reached out to spirits immanent in cave walls to the theologically dense religions of today, is the extension of object-relational striving into a supernatural or spiritual dimension.

So there is good *a priori* reason to believe that in a human-to-god or spirit relationship that goes at all deep, unconscious projections into the divine figures of representations or images of parental objects and aspects of the self play a significant role. It is the resulting unconscious relationship that invests religiosity with its tenacity and poignancy. If that is so, then we are charged with examining the engagement with religious objects at the two levels previously noted. First, as engagement with *objects defined by their culturally attributed characteristics*; this is the level of most theological and philosophical discourse on the gods, social analysis of religion, political commentary and so forth. Second, as *representative or symbolic of internal objects or aspects of the self*; an aspect of the psychology of religion. It is the latter, compound engagements that are outlined below.

The inculcation of religion usually commences when children are still under the sway of infantile narcissism, the real and imaginary merge, and parents are believed unquestioningly. Ideas about supernatural figures fuse with representations of parental figures and rudimentary religious ideology is imbricated with internal object relationships. This process creates needs that religions later satisfy. Teaching about the goodness of God or Jesus or the Prophet is particularly appealing, for of course children want to live in a benign world and the religious figures take on a kind of reality in the child's mind.[15] To feel oneself at one with, or to bask in the radiance of, an omnipotent, kindly supernatural figure certainly heightens self-regard and feelings of security. The relation to a benign supernatural figure is likely to contribute to a benign sense of self. But if the child's world is not benign, if parents are harsh or supernatural figures are represented as punitive and unyielding, then there is likely to emerge a correspondingly harsh and punitive image of the self. Many religions, especially at the fundamentalist end of the spectrum promote the surrender of the child's narcissism and may recommend beating it out of them, as we will observe in Chapter 7.

A sense of one's goodness, importance and power is not easily surrendered, however. They may sometimes be surrendered on condition of being at least partly restored by identification with an idealized divine figure, as with parental figures, even if that figure is idealized for its aggression and cruelty. If narcissism is extinguished with threats or beatings, the image of the self, fashioned on the images of aggressive parents and the child's own angry projections, may be angry and punitive, and the corresponding image of God is likely to be wrathful, remote and un-yielding. Children brought up in a cold or crushing atmosphere are more likely to depend on supernatural substitutes to contain their narcissism, according to the compensation model discussed in the previous chapter. Their self-esteem is likely to be precarious and sustainable only through unremitting effort – prayer, sacrifice, self-abasement – to achieve emotional proximity to an uncaring God. If, in the effort to maintain a relationship with an unsullied divine object, children are driven to split their images of self and object, project the good aspects into the divine images and identify with the bad, as in the 'moral defence,' the result is a self that feels empty, sinful and dependent. Still, this dependent relationship with a divine being can provide a sense of security in a harsh world; and if the relationship graduates to identification, or to membership of a group for which the divine being is the Ideal, it can provide the illusion of power. But self-esteem achieved in this way is precarious. Underly-ing the divine images are dissociated images of the bad parents. So it is that criticism of religion, or 'religious discrimination,' is perceived as an attack on the child-parent bond and may provoke fanatical rage and violence. Even when religious ideas have been abandoned, or intro-duced only late in life, experiences of grief or hardship may reactivate the longing for the lost idealized objects and attach them to religious conceptions.

Finally, these narcissistic defensive measures can be repeated in rela-tion to the religious group. The group is idealized and the grandiosity conferred on it is incorporated through identification. Belonging to the Elect is a gratifying and effective way of retrieving lost narcissism: if the group you belong to is special, you must be special. The group may unconsciously represent the ideal object (God, the body of Christ etc.), and the idealized aspects of the self. The religious group is prone to be the instrument of narcissistic assertion and aggression that had to be suppressed in childhood. To be a member of an august religious group, to be a member of the Elect, is the perfect station for bullying. Having the power to compel others to think and act as you do not only con-firms the faith and eliminates challenges to it, but also nourishes gran-diose self-conceptions by testifying to your power. This dynamic can be expressed in several dramatic ways, as discussed in Chapter 7. But a frequent claim, that *any* group can be an instrument of narcissistic as-sertion and aggression, that religious groups are not exceptional in this respect, must be deflected here. Ethnic, racial and political rivalries, not to mention sporting contests, do involve obvious narcissistic investments and frequently descend into violence. It is true that other group identi-ties can serve as vehicles for narcissistic aggression. But religions are particularly well fitted because their ideological conceptions – commerce with the supreme being, membership of an Elect, moral superiority and

78 Theory

incorrigible belief – create and accommodate the conditions for such aggression.

Here then, in a word, is the critical feature of the course of narcissistic development that runs under the impress of inculcated religious ideology: *a developmental environment permeated by religion weaves religion into the very fabric of the individual's narcissistic economy.* Religion is imbricated with individual and group narcissism in the ways outlined above.[16] In these circumstances, religions may be thought of as repositories of narcissism. At certain points, difficult to locate precisely, the normal development of narcissism can be converted by religious conceptions (though not only by them) into pathological forms of narcissism suffused with rage and potential violence. Perceived loss of status and marginalization then painfully affect the religious person's self-esteem and identity. The sense that they are at the centre of their nation's ethos, of history, of the cosmos, is challenged. Then projection becomes defensive and, in the fundamentalist or fanatical mindset, fear precipitates paranoia and violence. We will turn to this development in ensuing chapters.

Freud on narcissism and magic

As we saw in the previous chapter Freud describes the attachment to the deity (and indeed the figuration of the deity in the image of the protective father) as resulting from dependent needs in the child and adult. The dependency, the sense of helplessness, is experienced as a narcissistic wound inflicted by unyielding reality. But, curiously, apart from such statements, he makes only light connections between narcissism and religion as compared to his treatment of magic. In his last book, *Moses and Monotheism*, he tells a convoluted and unpersuasive story about the origins of monotheism. Moses was an Egyptian aristocrat who by force of will imposed on the early Israelites then dwelling in Egypt the austere monotheistic religion of the pharaoh Akhenaten, the worship of the sun-god Aten. After the exodus from Egypt, the Israelites rebelled and ungratefully killed Moses. Then a kind of cultural repression and latency set in, after which, with the return of the repressed, the austere god is revived and fused with both the image of the great man and the volcano god Yahweh. The reason that a single god became so compelling for the Israelites was that behind Yahweh stood the solitary figure of Moses and the remorse for killing him; and behind this killing lurked, atavistically, the archaic memory of the killing of the primal father of the horde, an event that Freud conjectured in several earlier works. So, Freud says: 'When Moses brought the people an idea of a single god, it was not a novelty but signified the revival of an experience in the primaeval ages of the human family which had long vanished from men's conscious memory.'[17] This ingenious argument has not had much traction for reasons not hard to see. Freud does, however, make some valuable passing remarks in *Moses* on the narcissistic aspects of the relation to God. He notes that circumcision, a covenant between God and Abraham, exulted the Israelites because it was a mark of specialness or, at the least, equivalence with the circumcised Egyptians. Freud says that 'the pride in God's greatness fuses with the pride in being chosen by him.'[18] Mosaic religion increased Israelite self-esteem because it allowed them to take a share in the exalted new God and asserted that the people had been chosen for a special destiny. He does not go so far as to say that people identify with God; it is more a case of basking in the radiance of God's greatness. The psychoanalyst Neville Symington wrote that 'Freud does not discuss the mechanism by which people rid themselves of their sense of helplessness through identifying with an omnipotent figure.'[19] The mechanism is indeed of the first importance but Freud did not entirely ignore it. In *Group Psychology and the Analysis of the Ego* Freud observes that members of a church may identify with Christ.[20] What seems to be lacking in Freud's treatment is an appreciation of the variety of ways in which the religious object may be idealized. In this he missed an important characteristic of the fanatically religious: God is not just an omnipotent spirit in whose natural radiance one may bask, or with whom one can identify; God is a repository in whom infantile and pathological narcissism may be banked without correction by reality.

Despite the thrift of these latter remarks, Freud has a great deal to say about magic which, in contrast to the anthropological discourse of his time, he does not trouble much to distinguish from religion; and his account of magic leans heavily on his account of narcissism.[21] Freud argues that primitive man, children under the sway of infantile narcissism and his obsessional patients appeared to have in common an overvaluation of the power of their thoughts.[22] He called this 'the principle of the omnipotence of thought.' The obsessional often fears his aggressive wishes will harm others; children believe, as Peter Pan says, that wishing makes it so; and 'primitive man had an immense belief in the power of his wishes.'[23] Although ambiguously expressed, Freud's main idea seems to be that if a person believed in the omnipotence of their thought then, for them, if they think (imagine, wish . . .) that something is the case, it will be the case. On the face of it, however, merely having this belief is neither sufficient nor necessary for omnipotent thinking. A person may believe that their thoughts are omnipotent and yet they may not be. And even without this belief, a person may be subject to wishful phantasies, delusions and hallucinations that are (quasi)omnipotently effective in that they are mistaken for reality. What really matters is not a belief *about* the omnipotence of thought but its efficacy: when thinking in the omnipotent mode it is for the person as if what they wish (or think) has come to pass.

80 Theory

Given his belief that omnipotent thought was a feature of infantile narcissism, obsessional neurosis and the magical thinking of primitive man Freud conjectured that there is an underlying identity of psychic structure in all three. When a magical rite is performed, a taboo obeyed, there is a current unconscious efficacious motivational state of the same kind as in the obsessional symptom of the adult and the wish-fulfilling phantasy of the child. In the case of primitive man, Freud thought, these states are present whenever magic is performed. Now this is pretty clearly wrong. The participants in a shamanistic séance, say, do not believe in the efficacy of the process *because* they then wish or hope for it, not even unconsciously. They already believe in it. They wouldn't be there otherwise. Belief in its efficacy was a given.

Still, it seems possible that despite the established structure of beliefs about magic, on special occasions of heightened emotional intensity such as may occur at a shaman's séance, people lose their grip on reality, regress and start thinking omnipotently. That may well happen but the phenomenon does not explain the belief in the efficacy of magic. The belief does not turn on inductive reasoning; it could not survive if it did. Suppose now it is urged that the reason that primitive man believes in *the entire system of magic* is because he *so wishes* magic to be efficacious. He wants his shamans and healers to be able to heal and defend against evil sorcery, and so forth. Such shared wishful states could hold the entire structure of magical beliefs in place. I think this gets things backwards. Children are educated into the ways of the tribe and learn the ways of magic; they have no reason either to doubt or to wish its efficacy, even if doubt were possible. Belief about the efficacy of magic is, one might say, immanent in the tribe's conceptual scheme or imaginary. Such beliefs are, in Levy-Bruhl's words, 'collective representations' of society. The systems of magic are detached from the sorts of motivational states presupposed in Freud's account of magic, and the latter just drop out. So it would appear, yet there does seem something right about the Freudian account.

This account of Freud's view could be recast, as Agnes Petocz does persuasively. All children share the early stages of (quasi-)omnipotence. However,

> the non-primitive child eventually comes to learn that wishing and magical gestures cannot make things so, and he "discards" those primitive views. Freud says: "we have *surmounted* these modes of thought" but they "still exist within us ready to seize upon any confirmation." So they remain in the background as magnets to regression, ready to resurface either momentarily during, say, experiences of the "uncanny" or in a more forceful and sustained way during mental breakdown (as in the Ratman's neurosis). The primitive child, on the

other hand, does not surmount those views via education (though obviously many experiences will contradict them) but instead finds a ready-made cultural package (the Lévi-Bruhlian "different conceptual structures") that corroborates (at least some) of them. But where have these conceptual structures come from? Are they not natural extensions of infantile modes of thinking in the face of environmental and inter-human situations for which alternative (scientific) explanations are not available? . . . If so, then the primitive's enculturated belief in magic itself is not entirely disconnected from his infantile wish-fulfilling modes of thinking, even though he is not responsible for creating his culture's specific set of conceptual structures.[24]

It may be that our (Western-style) education teaches children that wishing and magical gestures do not make it so. Though I rather think that all children, everywhere, learn this, painfully, in the conduct of their lives – but only up to a point: such things as prayer and religious ritual usually remain encouraged. More pertinent, however, is the question of whether primitive man, as the pioneering anthropologists conceived him, is in circumstances more favourable to the reactivation of the omnipotent modes of thinking that surely do remain in the background as magnets to regression, than the (Western) educated fellow. I doubt it, but I'm not clear how the matter might be determined. If the practice of magic in Africa today is taken as a test, there seems no more reason to invoke omnipotent modes of thinking in those practices than there is in the cool performance of a Catholic Mass. And it seems to me that educated Western folk in a Pentecostal service are no less susceptible to regression than the primitive.[25] Petocz notes that the primitive child is born into a ready-made package of cultural beliefs but wonders where this could have come from if not from an extension of infantile modes of thinking. Perhaps that *is* the source, though to rest the load there (and Petocz does not, or not entirely) is a far cry from Freud's view which requires the concurrent operation of infantile modes of thinking in every performance of magic. I don't think it is self-evident that these (magical) conceptual schemes *must* have evolved from omnipotent modes of thinking. We don't know much about how conceptual structures – embedded in languages and their logic – arise. But it is a plausible suggestion. It is not true that 'primitive man had an immense belief in the power of his wishes.' He has no such belief. He has a belief in the efficacy of magic. He doesn't draw an explicit connection between his wishes and magic. He would be crazy to, for the conjunction would unravel his putative belief. But there does seem something hugely wishful – hopeful – about magic and animistic thought – conceptual schemes – in general. This is no more surprising, perhaps, than that providential religion survives. Presumably, conceptual schemes develop to master an

82 Theory

environment. Where there is great practical helplessness and vulnerability in exacting environments it would seem likely that they will evolve along wishful, hopeful lines, along the lines of magic, sorcery and religious illusion. Whether they draw upon infantile omnipotent modes of thinking in their evolution appears to be moot.

Notes

1 The *locus classicus* is Freud 1914. Freud distinguishes primary from secondary narcissism and also an autoerotic stage of development but he vacillates in a long series of papers on how they relate to each other. Freud defines narcissism as libidinal investment in the ego (or self), though this leaves a host of questions unanswered about this strange reflexive relation. Already in 1914 he introduces many of the lines of subsequent study in relation to narcissistic pathology, the regulation of self-esteem, the nature of love and hatred, the internalization of objects and other germane matters. Within psychoanalysis, as within philosophy, there is a good deal of irresolution about the nature of the self, the nature of self-reflexive attitudes, and whether the self is an agency or an organized set of representations, that bear directly on the understanding of narcissism. Here such issues are largely bypassed. We will treat narcissism as a reflexive relation in which the self takes itself as an object of love or hatred. Important advances along the way include Klein 1952; Reich 1960; Kohut 1968/1978, 1972/1978, 1976/1978; Kernberg 1975, 2014, 2022; Rosenfeld 1987; Winnicott 1974. Useful collections of papers, some now classical, are in Sandler et al. 2012; Ronningstam 2000.
2 Lewis 2003, 45.
3 Lewis 2003, 30, 183. For an ancestor centred explanatory scheme Fortes 1959. For a recent, penetrating study of spirit cosmology and possession among the Yagwoia people of New Guinea see Mimica 2020.
4 Bellah 2011, 14, 153.
5 Dodds 1965, 70–71.
6 Dodds 1965, 63–64.
7 Dodds 1965, 73.
8 Dodds 1951, 135ff.
9 Fromm 1963/2004.
10 The theme of death and re-birth of the 'dying god' has ancient roots, certainly in the Near Eastern cults of Osiris, Attis and Adonis, possibly extending back to human sacrificial fertility rites in Neolithic times. The continuation of this theme from such antiquity attests to the depth of its psychological significance. Ian Suttie (1935/1960) pointed out that it also appeases our sense of injustice stemming from sibling rivalry: we are gratified at seeing another suffering privation and being demolished, as it seemed to us that we were demolished when supplanted by the younger, adored sibling.

11 Psychoanalysts usually distinguish between transient phantasies of incorporating an object; introjecting it, in which the object finds a more permanent place in the mind; and identifying with it in which case the self takes on some of the characteristics of the object. I will usually use 'internalize' to cover for the first two.

12 Freud 1910, 191. See also Ferenczi 1909, 1913.

13 The *locus classicus* for wish-fulfilment is Freud 1900, Chapter 7. The philosophical treatment of wish-fulfilment was greatly advanced in, amongst others, the work of Richard Wollheim 1971/1991, 1979, 1993; Hopkins 1982, 2012; Sebastian Gardner 1993 and Agnes Petocz 1999. Pataki 2000, 2014, 2015, 2019 discuss the clinical and theoretical issues involved in the notion of wish-fulfilment. Wish-fulfilment and the omnipotence of thought are considered in more detail below and in the Appendix.

14 See Kernberg 1975, 2004 passim.

15 Oral Roberts, the influential Pentecostal preacher, tells how in his childhood his parents prayed to Christ in such a conversational manner that 'I actually thought that Christ lived in our house, was a member of the family.' (Fitzgerald 2018, 211)

16 Where there are no gods or spirits as may be the case in some forms of Buddhism and Jainism narcissism is expressed in different ways, for example in seeking (illusory) independence from the world.

17 Freud 1939, 129.

18 Freud 1939, 112.

19 Symington 1998, 63.

20 Freud 1921.

21 A tradition in cultural anthropology robustly distinguishes magic from religion but Freud is not part of it. He does often remark in *Moses and Monotheism* that Mosaic religion forcefully rejected magic, perhaps to distinguish itself from Egyptian religion or as a manifestation of the higher intellectuality or spirituality (the German is ambiguous) that instinctual renunciation was supposed to achieve. The early Israelites did not of course abandon magic (see e.g. Goodman 2019, Chapter 8) but in any case even if they had that would hardly constitute grounds for the larger distinction. It seems plain that most contemporary religions retain magical practices, in prayer, oblations, renunciations and so forth. Petitionary prayer, to take one example, is in most religions a form of magical thinking. In Australia every year when there are droughts religious gatherings pray for rain. A typical Christian prayer goes:

> We name our simple need – rain for our thirsty land.
> Our tanks and dams are nearly empty,
> like our hopes for this season.
> Please, loving God, bring us rain
> to renew the ground, to replenish our dams,
> to bring some chance of feed,
> to bring the possibility of some reward
> to those who have toiled so hard.
> We turn to you in faith and hope.

84 Theory

Christians say that this kind of prayer is not magically instrumental in that it does not involve any expectation that God will deliver on the asking; or, alternatively, that it is not so much an asking but expressive of a desire to cleave to God's will. Prayer is to be distinguished, on this view, from magic which is understood as a technology or instrument for achieving ends. The Christian petitioner, however, has no expectation and does not conceive of his prayers as trying to achieve ends. Omnipotence is rejected. This distinction of petitionary prayer from magic is false, I think. The magician or shaman has no certain instrumental expectation either. He knows how often magic fails (and has good auxiliary explanations for failure) and how often the spirit he is beseeching will flatly reject his request. He and his congregants are trying to gain mastery over a predicament. They fluctuate between hope and expectation. As do, of course, the Christians who pray for rain. These issues are discussed often with brilliance in Wilson 1974.

22 If his patient 'the Ratman' 'thought of someone, he would be sure to meet that very person immediately afterwards, as though by magic. If he suddenly asked after the health of an acquaintance whom he had not seen in a long time, he would hear that he had just died, so that it would look as though a telepathic message had arrived from him. If, without any really serious intention, he swore at some stranger, he might be sure that the man would die soon afterwards' (Freud 1913, 86–87.)

23 Freud 1913, 83. 'If children and primitive men find play and imitative representation enough for them . . . [it] is the easily understandable result of the paramount virtue they ascribe to their wishes, of the will that is associated with these wishes and of the methods by which these wishes operate. As time goes on, the psychological accent shifts from the motives for the magical act on to the measures by which it is carried out. . . . It thus comes to appear as though it is the magical act itself which, owing to its similarity with the desired result, alone determines the occurrence of that result.' (1913, 84)

24 Personal communication.

25 See e.g. Evans-Pritchard 1965/2004 on the humdrum performance of magic and, interestingly, Naipaul 2010.

Part II

Polemic

Chapter 5

The new atheism and the new fanaticism

What is the new atheism?

I will start with the movement – if that is the right word – referred to as the 'new atheism.' It is a reaction, and we need to see what it is a reaction to. But before going there perhaps this is a good place to state my own attitude to atheism and to religion, in case this has not already become evident. In regard to atheism, I am in accord with the new (and the old) atheists. In my view, the proposition that there are no gods or spirits is indubitable but not incorrigible i.e. it is open to correction. In other words, I believe that there are no good grounds to doubt the non-existence of gods or spirits, but it is imaginable that there could be. This view is an instance of the fallibilism that is central to the scientific enterprise, and more broadly to the empirical stance, and most of the new atheists who are schooled in these quarters have acknowledged the possibility of error in their most careful statements.[1] My attitude to religion, however, is less uncompromising than that of the new atheists. I believe with Lucretius, Russell and so many others, that religions have caused immense harm to humanity. They are mostly dreadful afflictions. But religions are many and immensely diverse. They meet so many social and psychological needs that it is difficult to conceive what human life would be like in their absence. Even if religions are evil in the various ways that their critics have described it cannot be concluded that the world would be a better place without them. Religions may be harmful, but perhaps, for all we know, a world without them would be a much worse place than it is today. A resolution requires a prediction that is beyond our powers: we cannot compute all the relevant variables involved in an alteration as dramatic as the final departure of religion. Since I prefer the world to be a better place, this admission of ignorance moderates my considerable anti-religious sentiments and puts a hobble on enthusiasm for radical change.

Atheism has been around for a long time. Socrates was arraigned for failing to acknowledge the city's gods in 399 BC, and several of

DOI: 10.4324/9781315519814-8

88 Polemic

his near contemporaries – Anaxagoras, Critias, Diagoras, Democritus – were notorious for atheism.[2] On any traditional understanding of a personal god most of the major figures in philosophy since the 17th century have been atheists or Deists, usually secretly. It is often countered that most scientists before the 20th century were religious men. There is some truth in that but it is hardly surprising given that employment in universities required religious vows, and given the unlikelihood of a declared atheist surviving in such an institution or, until recently, even outside of one. In any case, since the Enlightenment much of the heavy lifting has been done. Philosophers refuted the theistic arguments, science provided ever-increasing understanding and control of the natural world, medicine diminished many of life's horrors, modern Biblical criticism and archaeology undermined the historical authority of the foundational texts, and religious authorities gradually lost their power to intimidate or eliminate their critics. As Bernard Williams aptly said, it is not so much that Hume and Kant broke up the furniture as that the world since then has drastically damaged the rooms in which it used to stand.[3] Although there is a revival of activity in the Christian universities, especially in the United States, for most professional philosophers and scientists today theism and the philosophy of religion are not compelling options. That, of course, is not true for the vast majority of the globe's population.

Given that atheism is scarcely new, it is incumbent to ask what, if anything, is new about the new atheism. The most striking aspect of it, perhaps, is the vehemence of the vanguard popular publications shaping it. It is a polemical movement. It may be sufficient to mention some of its leaders: Richard Dawkins, Daniel Dennett, Sam Harris, Christopher Hitchens and A.C. Grayling. Many of the new atheists are deeply influenced by evolutionary psychology and cognitive anthropology, some of which was discussed in Chapter 3. Although Dawkins had been advocating the incompatibility between religion and evolutionary theory since the 1970s, and Dennett since the 1990s, the new atheism didn't acquire polemical wings until the beginning of this century with the publication of trenchant books by these authors in the dark shadow of September 11, 2001, the intellectual depredations of the evangelical G. W. Bush administration in the United States, and the intelligent design controversies crystallized in the Dover decision of 2005.[4]

The books articulated what many people, at least in the West, opined about the association between violence and religious fundamentalism, particularly of Islamic fundamentalism, as well as the regressive influence of evangelical and other conservative Christian groups over a range of moral, educational and scientific issues in the United States and elsewhere.[5] Some of these regressive influences are discussed in subsequent chapters. Religious apologists and organizations responded by declaring

The new atheism and the new fanaticism **89**

what they thought about atheists, often in unchristian fashion, and their literary zeal proved even more prodigious than that of the atheists. The popular literature seemed, at least initially, to have little impact on academic professionals. This is unsurprising because in terms of argument or doctrinal content, as opposed to polemical posture, the new atheists provided little that was new. Some distinguished philosophers who are themselves atheists, such as Thomas Nagel and Philip Kitcher, rounded on the new atheists. And theists such as Alvin Plantinga and Charles Taylor, and crypto-atheists such as Mark Johnston, have chosen to be acid and supercilious.[6] Of course, that was all a decade ago. Since then, although the Islamic fundamentalist threat seems to have abated we have witnessed the startling recrudescence of aggressive Christian nationalism in Russia, Eastern Europe and South America, but nowhere more so than in the United States under the aegis of the Trump administration and, with it, unprecedented degradation of political discourse and contempt for truth in the service of religious power. To the port of these dire matters we shall shortly arrive.

But for now let's turn briefly to that which is new and urgent in the new atheism. It is, in the first place, evangelical and seeks converts with an alluring vision. In *The God Delusion* Dawkins says that one of his aims is to 'raise consciousness to the fact that to be an atheist is a realistic aspiration, and a brave and splendid one. You can be an atheist who is happy, balanced, moral and intellectually fulfilled.'[7] This kind of appeal cannot be found in the dour atheism of Camus or Sartre, or even Russell, or the bright dispositions of the Enlightenment. The earlier atheists offered epistemological self-respect and visions of moral progress, but neither joy nor salvation. Second, the new atheists are not intimately concerned with the detailed refutation of theism. That battle is taken to have been won, largely on the assumption that Darwin had rendered deity superfluous, and their ancillary philosophical reflections on the existence of deity are usually perfunctory. The new atheists' primary concerns are with religion's vices. The sub-title of Christopher Hitchens' bestseller says it concisely: 'How Religion Poisons Everything.' Religion, Hitchens says, is 'violent, irrational, intolerant, allied to racism and tribalism and bigotry.' It is contemptuous of women and coercive toward children, 'the accomplice of ignorance and guilt as well as of slavery, genocide, racism and tyranny.'[8] The other new atheists mostly agree. Dawkins focuses on religion's cultivation of the vicious condition of 'unquestioning faith.' The suicide bombers and Christian murderers of abortion doctors are motivated by what they perceive to be righteousness because 'they have been brought up, from the cradle, to have total and unquestioning faith. . . . Faith is an evil precisely because it requires no justification and brooks no argument.' And then, passing from the shallows to the mainstream, Dawkins concludes that 'even

90 Polemic

mild and moderate religion helps to provide the climate of faith in which extremism naturally flourishes.'[9]

This is vehement polemic. I believe it is generally justified. Discussion of religious aggression, manifested across almost the entire contemporary religious spectrum, we will defer to Chapter 7. Some of the intellectual vices and the evident conflict between science and religion – a profound conflict not only over what is to be believed but why and how it is to be believed – are discussed in Chapter 8, and some of the moral vices of religion are touched on in Chapter 6. However, the new atheists, it seems to me, are at bottom spooked by something more far-reaching connecting these vices: an assault on Reason that ranges across the entire fanatical and fundamentalist spectrum, but manifests most dangerously in the brew of Christian nationalism, theocratic hankering and contempt for truth that touched the seat of power during the G. W. Bush presidency and deformed rational politics in America during the presidency of Donald Trump and elsewhere, most notably in Russia and currently in Israel.

When I wrote *Against Religion* (2007) in the wake of the 9/11 atrocity I was still sure that the majority of religious people were neither irrational nor stupid, although, speaking globally, many obviously suffer from limited education and restricted world-views. Now I am less certain about the majority's rationality and more convinced about the irrationality of the fanatics, those who I then described as 'the religiose' and distinguished from the historical fundamentalists (see below). *Rationality* is a vague concept, of course, and this perhaps jaundiced estimation will depend on how it is understood; I will come to that in a moment, albeit without much light to shed. In the meantime, it is important to appreciate the nuttiness of the edges. What can one make of literate adults who think that the world is about 6000 years old or that hurricanes are produced by God's fist trembling over the oceans? What can one make of Jerry Falwell's statement two days after the Twin Towers came down:

> The abortionists have got to bear some burden for this because God will not be mocked. And when we destroy 40 million little innocent babies, we make God mad. I really believe the pagans, and the abortionists, and the feminists, and the gays and the lesbians. . . . I point the finger in their face and say, "You helped this happen."[10]

What can one make of people who believe that their televangelist prophets can revive the dead and cure cancer, who fervently believe that Donald Trump is a God-anointed Cyrus come to destroy the demon Hilary Clinton and save America?[11] To concede respect for such beliefs is to undermine the currency of thought. Some years ago in Israel the spiritual head of the Shas political party, Rabbi Ovadia Yosef, declared that forest fires in which 40 people perished were God's punishment for Jews failing to keep the Sabbath. When New Orleans was inundated by Katrina in 2005 Yosef agreed with the influential evangelical Pat Robertson and al-Qaeda that the devastation was divine retribution.[12] Robertson was encouraged by the destruction and subsequently beseeched the Almighty to send a hurricane to take out sinful Florida as well. These deranged pronouncements could be multiplied. The radical Islamists, Yosef and the televangelists are of course not representative – not quite yet – of the majority of religious believers, but they vividly illustrate the ignorance and irrationality that was gaining ground across segments of most major faiths. It has gained more ground since. To understand the combative tone of the new atheists it is essential to appreciate that they are reacting to a new, serious threat posed by religion in its fanatical registers, not just to the secular order or to free enquiry but, to repeat, to Reason itself.

The reaction may be understandable but in my view has lurched occasionally into excess. For many people, especially for those living in desperate circumstances where life is brief and with few pleasures, religion is the ground of security, self-esteem and hope. That is unfortunate because the ground is illusory, but it is nevertheless uncaring to try to deprive such people of its sustenance.[13] After all, the creed of most atheists, secular humanism, is inclusive: its benevolence, attentiveness and sympathetic understanding must rain on the irreligious and the religious alike. Religion, as I have tried to show in previous chapters, has deep roots in human attachment, love and despair, in sustaining self-esteem and defending the integrity of the self, often from the aggression of one's own mind. The new atheists, abetted by the evolutionary psychology and cognitive science criticized earlier, have only limited comprehension of the deep wells of need, deprivation and emotional privation from which much in religion springs. Misunderstanding religion they adopt scattered polemical measures that alienate the moderate centres of religion and are especially ineffective against those fanatical manifestations that really do need to be countered forcefully. I suspect that the elements of the new atheism that supervene upon cognitivism, as discussed in Chapter 3, represent a triumph for a puritanism in the social sciences that, in paradoxical concert with religion, is an assault on insight. The discussion of sub-personal cognitive systems and meme economics is less rebarbative than the exploration of unconscious object-relational configurations and emotional and sexual currents underlying religious ideology and institutions. In the works of the new atheists, as in the public arena framed by journalism, the absence of deep psychological insight allows the most superficial statements of religious believers about their motivations – putative concern for the unborn, fears over gender fluidity or homosexuality, for example – to pass unchallenged, as if these

92 Polemic

expressed their *real* motivations and were not just screens for various forms of hatred, envy and fear.

Fundamentalism and fanaticism

The term 'fundamentalism' has a well-defined meaning within the historical context of conservative American Protestantism. The fundamentalist movement emerged from roots in 19th-century millenarianism and grew in the early twentieth century, largely in reaction to upheavals threatening traditional social arrangements and values, especially the liberal scholarship challenging the literal truth and inerrancy of the Bible. A group of millenarians and like-minded evangelicals published a series of tracts, 'The Fundamentals: A Testimony of Truth,' intended to set out the fundamental beliefs of Protestantism. These were, in Malise Ruthven's words:

> the inerrancy of the Bible; the direct creation of the world, and humanity, *ex nihilo* by God (in contrast to Darwinian evolution); the authenticity of miracles; the virgin birth of Jesus, his Crucifixion and bodily resurrection: the substitutionary atonement (the doctrine that Christ died to redeem the sins of humanity); and (for some but not all believers) his imminent return to judge and rule over the world.[14]

In 1920 a conservative Baptist editor, Curtis Lee Laws, declared that 'Fundamentalists were those who were ready to do battle royal for The Fundamentals.' Since then the term has acquired promiscuous associations and is now used to designate an agglomeration of religious ideologies and attitudes, and even non-religious ones ('economic fundamentalism,' 'environmental fundamentalism'). In the media the term is applied to Islamic groups such as the Taliban, the Muslim Brotherhood, al-Qaeda, Isis and others. Within Christianity, in addition to the (historically) fundamentalist churches in the United States much of the amorphous conservative Christian right is included: many large evangelical, Pentecostalist and other charismatic churches, most Southern Baptists, as well as smaller cultish groups like Jehovah's Witnesses, the Amish, and the revealingly named Exclusive Brethren; radical movements such as Dominion and Reconstruction Theology, and Christian Identity must also be included; many rightwing Catholics are included, as well as numbers of Hindu, Sikh and Buddhist groups. Judaic fundamentalism includes the ultra-orthodox Haredi and within Israel various theocratically minded nationalist, supremacist and settler groups.

Clearly not all these representative groups are fundamentalist in the original meaning of the term which emphasizes doctrinal commitments that are scarcely common to them. Moreover, recent decades have

The new atheism and the new fanaticism   **93**

exposed a kind of alchemy of religious essence, a fusion with political, nationalist, racial or ethnic identities – an alchemy that in some cases was hiding there all along. So it now seems more appropriate to speak of political, nationalist and quasi-racial Christianity, Islam, Judaism, Hinduism and so forth. Indeed, religious identity gets racialized, as if there were distinctions of *physis,* of nature or immutable essence, separating the various confessions from those outside their religion.[15] Religious aims become congruent with those of nations, political or ethnic identities and pursued with the savage intolerance of fanatics.

But here I had better introduce some caveats: the picture painted in what follows is applied with a palette knife, not a fine brush. Many religious people are neither fundamentalists nor fanatics. Belonging to a religion, and having a religious identity, satisfies a *very* broad range of conscious and unconscious needs, including innocent social ones. Most religious people derive much satisfaction from engaging in their religious communities, enjoying the calendar of festivals, the ceremony, the occasions for gathering, the opportunities for charity, the sense of social belonging and of having a place in the cosmos. They find meaning in these things. Questions of theology or of personal relation to gods or spirits rarely engage them. On such matters they would perhaps be prepared to change their minds, should they confront persuasive evidence, and be interested in doing so, which they rarely are. Religious profession in such cases may be orthodox and sincere, yet fail to deeply engage the passions and inner world. One goes along, it is pleasant to do so.

But religiosity can appear in quite a different register. I want to distinguish a typical *fundamentalist mindset* that does not coordinate exactly either with zealous doctrinal fundamentalism or with the public representation of fundamentalism as militant extremism. In a distinguished work, Elisabeth Young-Bruehl contrasted a pair of useful concepts, the *ethnocentric* and the *orectic.*[16] Roughly, on her proposal, *ethnocentric beliefs,* including most religious beliefs, are acquired implicitly in the ethnic, religious or cultural group one grows up in: they are *learned* – though not necessarily taught – and held fast in the conceptual network common to the group. Parental models – especially the parental superegos – will be formative in the ways we have seen. But the parents themselves may not be tightly wedded to religion and that, and perhaps other factors, may mitigate the formation of strong links between internalized objects, religious doctrine and religiosity. Religiosity in such cases is only loosely linked to character. It is what we call a cultural thing. Religious beliefs and actions may be wish-fulfilling, but if they are it is only adventitiously: they are not *engendered* by unconscious wishes, fortified by them, or in their direct service. Thus, believing in life after death comforts, but the belief, or rather strong investment in the belief, may not arise *from,* say, the terror of death: it can be acquired as one acquires knowledge of geography.

94 Polemic

On the other hand are *orectic beliefs* engendered by and fulfilling wishes in more or less distorted shapes. Beliefs about racial or religious superiority, grandiose conceptions of oneself, self-serving conspiracy theories and so forth usually arise in this way. They can be more or less crazy. The Nazi Erich Ludendorff believed that Jews were at work behind Marxism, Catholicism and Capitalism, of course, that's run of the mill; but behind the Jews, he also believed, was the Dalai Lama seeking to destroy Germany from Tibet.[17] Yet such people manage to attract supporters and spin a web of supportive interlocking beliefs – though in Ludendorff's case even other Nazi ideologues eventually had enough of him. The *orectic fundamentalist* or *fanatic* may spin his web from within, but much more often invests shards of existing religious dogma with unconscious wish-fulfilling significance. Religion then expresses his character; fundamentally, relationships to internal objects and defences against them, and it may then become immensely precious to him. This is why religious beliefs and attitudes often hang together with beliefs and attitudes to politics, morality and sexual and gender issues: they are wish-fulfilling expressions of important elements of character structure. Character, as we saw, is shaped to a significant degree by religious doctrine, parental identifications and education. But it is also true that character selects religious doctrine. For example, only certain kinds of characters are likely to find the Biblical condemnation of homosexuality or the injunction to severely beat naughty children congenial or credible. Specific religious doctrines attract people with specific needs, the needs that those doctrines indirectly satisfy. The shoes fit and they like to wear them.

I want, then, to distinguish the fanatic from the fundamentalist who is merely devout, and from the ordinary casual or 'cultural' believer. Broadly, the fanatic is a fundamentalist in doctrine and in whom orectic processes dominate the personality. Because we are concerned here mostly with the role of narcissism in religion I will adopt a narrower stipulation and say that the fanatic is a fundamentalist with severe narcissistic character disorder and, generally, is a fundamentalist because of that disorder. (This leaves it open whether other pathological or near pathological conditions, for example hysterical disorders, can lead to behaviour much like that of fanatics as understood here.) The term 'fanatic' is unsatisfactory but I can think of no better.[18] It has the value of emphasizing that the circle of *orectic derangement* – of delusion or wish-driven divorce from reality – spreads further than the violent extremist centres while not including those fundamentalists whose beliefs are not wishfully motivated.[19] In the latter case we may wish to speak of *doxastic derangement* as a counterpart to orectic derangement. What I mean is this. The Yagwoia people of Papua New Guinea studied by

Jadran Mimica[20] believe (roughly) that bone strength is essential to the successful warrior, that semen is produced in the bones, and that therefore fellatio between young men and established successful older men is a way of passing on bone strength. The practice is institutionalized. Given the premises and the aim of producing strong warriors the practical conclusion follows. We know that the premises are wildly wrong. We might wish to say that the Yagwoia, at least in this respect, are doxastically deranged: their beliefs are wildly off, but it is easy to see given historical isolation and Yagwoia cosmology why they are maintained (until recently). Doxastic derangement is not uncommon in religious groups and can be sustained artificially. In his book *The Tenacity of Unreasonable Beliefs*, Solomon Schimmel[21] shows how Orthodox and Haredi Jews manage to hold onto beliefs which by any measure are plainly irrational. Their critical belief is in TSM: Torah (the five books of Moses) was handed by God to Moses on Mt. Sinai and every word of Torah is true. This belief is the touchstone of orthodoxy and without it, they believe, the entire edifice of Jewish belief collapses. The Haredi live in closed enclaves ensuring that neither they nor their children are exposed to television, the internet, goyim or any information that might challenge their beliefs. So it seldom occurs to them to question their beliefs. Nonetheless, some are by necessity exposed to secular learning. How do they manage that? Well, they hold that TSM and related tenets are 'axiomatic' or 'firm, unshakeable convictions' against which all other knowledge has to be measured. If there is conflict, that shows that the incompatible beliefs have to be rejected. 'We have been commanded not to exercise freedom of thought to the point of holding views opposed to those expressed in the Torah; rather, we must limit our thought by setting up a boundary where it must stop, and that boundary is the commandments and the injunctions of the Torah.' Of course, the best reason for believing something is that it is true. And the best way to get at the truth is unfettered enquiry. Many bright Orthodox and Haredi Jews choose to ignore critical Biblical scholarship and secular learning

> because they have invested so much of their intellectual, emotional, social and financial energy and resources into their belief system and religious way of life that they are afraid or reluctant to examine its foundations. It is because they sense that the pillars of all they believe and have invested in might be exposed as pillars of sand.[22]

One is reminded of Nietzsche's definition of faith as not wanting to know. Orectic and doxastic derangement are two general features of fanaticism to which we will return in Chapter 8. But for now, we must enter into some specifics.

96 Polemic

Features of fanaticism

There is no one specific feature that defines the fanatical mindset and there are many differences between the groups we will mention. But there are striking clusters of similarities that are to be expected when understood as more or less terse expressions of religiously shaped narcissistic character (or personality) disorders. Mindset is of course a matter of degree: but we are likely to find the usual clusters of arrogance and grandiosity shielding vulnerability and dependency, intense envy and aggression, paranoid thinking, idealization and delusional thought. As always, it must be kept in mind that members of a group do not share a uniform character; narcissistic disposition is only one factor that makes up any character; pathologically narcissistic dispositions are not restricted to the religious; and some people untouched by religion, many in the political arena, many patent scoundrels, may put on religious masks opportunistically.

I will briefly list some of the main threads that pass through the worlds of the fanatics and then discuss them in more detail in subsequent chapters.

One. The members of the group are the Elect, the Chosen Ones, the Saved, the possessors of the Truth. To be chosen is to be marked for a superior fate; one is indeed marked by virtue of *being* superior. The idea of being a people chosen by God with a special mission is mostly identified with Jews and their monotheistic derivatives but is not restricted to them. A Sinhalese religious nationalist expresses it typically: 'the Sinhalese nation . . . had come into being with the blessing of Buddha as a "chosen race" with a divine mission to fulfil.'[23] The Puritan Peter Bulkeley's famous words in 1651 possess Biblical and contemporary resonance:

> We are as a city set upon a hill, in the open view of all the Earth, the eyes of the world are upon us because we profess ourselves to be a people in covenant with God. . . . Let us so to walk that this may be our excellency and dignity among the nations of the world among which we live; that they may be constrained to say of us, only this people is wise, a holy and blessed people. . . . We are the seed that the Lord hath blessed.

Many contemporary American evangelicals and others see their nation as the theatre of a grand Biblical – Cosmic drama in which they are star players. On St. Augustine's ferocious doctrine, revived by Calvin, only the Elect ascend to heaven, the remainder are consigned to everlasting torment. Some Protestants believe that following the imminent return of Christ they, together with 144,000 'righteous Jews,' will be 'raptured' into heaven while the unrighteous majority perish. 'And everyone else goes to hell?' Amanda Lohrey asks one of her young Hillsong fundamentalists. 'Yeah, much as it sucks, you have to understand that Jesus was the only saviour.'[24] In another tradition we find Dostoevsky, writing in 1873:

> Is not the divine image of Christ in all its purity preserved in Orthodoxy alone? And perhaps the paramount, preordained task of the Russian people in the destiny of all mankind consists simply in preserving within itself this divine image of Christ in all its purity and, when the time comes, revealing this image to a world that has lost its way![25]

His argument and vision are fantasy. First, the Slavic world is to be conquered, and then Constantinople which would become the third Rome. Then the depraved West would yield; by moral force in the first instance but if that is unavailing then by force of arms. So, the procession of the chosen from the Slavophiles and Dostoevsky to Aleksandr Dugin and Vladimir Putin and the Russian Orthodox church whose aims are once again congruent with that of the state.

Two. The fanatic is deeply concerned to demarcate between believers and non-believers: skullcaps, turbans, hijab, pendant crucifixes, skin markings, genital circumcisions, special initiations and rituals, dietary restrictions and so forth. Marking the group assists in the preservation of a distinctive identity, but it is also part of the narcissistic struggle to be considered unique and special. Superiority and distinction have to be marked publicly or they are worthless. Small differences between similar groups are accentuated because the superiority which is predicated on membership of a special group is threatened most by those who are similar but excluded. The heretic and apostate are more feared than the infidel.

Three. There is only one correct way of living and it must be defended against encroachment by other religions, but especially against the forces of secularism. The pluralism of the modern world and its rapid change are unsettling and disorientating. Fanatics and their congeners naturally seek to simplify these conditions and invoke a time when choice was not oppressive. Hence the appeals to the mythical past of the Golden Age and its unambiguous scriptures. The Quran does not say

> that Islam is the true way of life for the people of Arabia, or for the people of any particular country or for the people of any particular age. . . . No! Very explicitly, for the entire human race, there is only one way of life which is Right in the eyes of God and that is al-Islam.[26]

98 Polemic

Fanatics of other religions disagree. Religious pluralism and religious deviancy are problematic: given only one true faith and way of life everything that challenges them is corrosive. As with racial categories, religious categories are seen as exclusive: one cannot have more than one religion at a time. Christianity and Islam (and some Jewish denominations) are universalist in principle, willing to embrace all comers – but only on condition of their accepting a proclaimed Truth. So, in practice, their implicit exclusivity inevitably creates the differences on which narcissism thrives. To the fanatic difference is at the same time necessary – to provide objects for devaluation and comparison – and intolerable and, paradoxically, must therefore be annulled. Those with no religion, or those who overtly offend against the fanatic's religious identity, such as homosexuals or blasphemers, are particularly unsettling and the rage stirred up against them is projected. That is why fanatics feel persecuted even when objectively they are not, as they are not by secular states, for example. Mere difference is offensive to them. Often enough, of course, they are persecuting each other. And the actual differences may seem unremarkable. In Russia the Orthodox church has turned on Jehovah's Witnesses and other Christian minorities (as well of course as the sexual and gender offenders); the murderous struggle between Sunni and Shia continues.

Four. There is a Holy Book, dominant prophet or charismatic leader. They are inerrant, and strict and sometimes literal obedience to their word is mandatory. In general, the Holy Books are the word of God and the prophet or televangelist may be a receptacle of God's word or (Holy Spirit), rather as shamans are receptacles and then masters of spirits. The Books therefore are timelessly true and comprehensive: gods don't change their minds. Swami Dayananda founder of the Society of Aryas and progenitor of the Hindu BJP, stated that 'the Indian scriptures – the Vedas – were the highest revelations ever vouchsafed to humanity and contained all knowledge, scientific as well as spiritual.'[27] Members of other religions disagree. The Quran, besides specifying correct conduct for all, is said to contain references to recent scientific discoveries such as atoms and viruses; likewise some mystical texts of Judaism. The Bible, the Quran, the other holy texts contain the law prescribing right conduct. For the fanatic, obedience to its statutes dissolves uncertainty. Hence, the more bewildering and uncertain the world, the more fiercely they cling to the Holy Book.

Five. In the Abrahamic religions, law and authority descend from God: this is a crucial idea. God's law always trumps human law. Civic law is either already fully contained in the Holy Book or must be derived from it. The conception of law animating much of the contemporary Christian right is that 'God's law is higher than mere human law, so human law should emulate God's. God's law is revealed in the Bible, so

The new atheism and the new fanaticism **99**

the Bible is the charter for modern lawmakers.'[28] Since God alone is sovereign and God's commandments are law the nation must also be under God's law, for the observant religious life can be lived only in a society of co-religionists in a political organization fashioned along religious lines. Hence the aims of fanatical religion take on political colour and lead ultimately to theocracy. Secular law is the enemy and must be dismantled by capturing the instruments of government and legislative power; the fanatics have recently had considerable success (Chapter 6).

Six. Fanatics and fundamentalists are deeply concerned to control sexuality, especially female sexuality, and to draw irrefragable boundaries between male and female. Women are subordinated. The conditions of marriage, reproduction, dress and demeanour are (mostly) controlled by men invoking ancient precepts. Ordination, perceived Biblically as rule over men, and access to education are denied or restricted (amongst Orthodox Jews, women are 'exempted from the duty of studying.') The patriarchal family is the indispensable unit within which sexuality is controlled. Issues around abortion, sex and gender identity, education and 'family values' are the battleground. The control of female sexuality is sometimes tellingly linked to the fear of emasculation and homosexuality: 'where adultery becomes common, that country is destroyed and enters the domination of the infidels because their men become like women and women cannot defend themselves.'[29] The possibility of men becoming women causes deep anxiety. Fear and loathing of homosexuality and blurred gender roles is the consequence. This is a major concern of all fanatics and fundamentalists, and in recent decades exploited politically to great effect in the West.

Seven. Like zealots before them, contemporary fanatics are assertive, clamorous and often violent. (An obvious exception is the fundamentalist Amish whose asceticism is a kind of violence to the self.) The physical violence is most conspicuous in the activities of some Islamists, and the political zealotry in the activities of the American Christian right and the racist and nativist movements in Europe and the sub-continent. The ever-present louring violence springs to mind but there is also the aggression of menace and vilification, the cruelty and abuse of children and the abuse of self fostered amongst the fanatics and fundamentalists. These are topics for Chapter 7.

Eight. The spirits are back. The statistics tell a story of a global revival of religion in numbers, especially in parts of the United States, Eastern Europe, parts of Africa, South America and Asia. The attrition of faith in Western Europe, Canada and Australia, nations better educated and less populated, is not countervailing. The figures are however difficult to interpret. Religious allegiance is claimed as an identity even where doctrinal commitments are absent or fuzzy. Many people claim to be Christians or Jews, for example, though they do not believe in God, let

100 Polemic

alone the resurrection or the origins of the Torah, and many with vague spiritual hankerings identify themselves as religious. Be that as it may, the fanatical style of religion is pretty clearly on the ascendant. To take one example, starting from a very low base at the turn of the nineteenth century there are now more than 500 million Pentecostals and charismatics worldwide. Alister McGrath, the prolific scourge of atheism, declares a new interest in things spiritual sweeping through postmodern Western culture which is 'fed up with the rather boring platitudes of scientific progress and longs for something more interesting and exciting.'[30] McGrath was one of the first to notice that there was indeed a significant transformation of global Christianity underway.

> Although Pentecostalism can be thought of as traditionalist in its Christian theology, it differs radically from other Christian groupings in placing emphasis on speaking in tongues and its highly experiential forms of worship, which involve prophesying, healings and exorcisms. A direct, transforming, personal encounter with God is seen as a normal feature of the Christian life. . . . Pentecostalism stresses a direct, immediate experience of God and avoids the rather dry and cerebral forms of Christianity which many find unattractive and unintelligible.[31]

Since God or the Holy Spirit and, on the dark side, Satan and demons, are experienced immediately, pesky epistemological and exegetical objections to traditional discursive theologies do not arise. Ecstatic worship and its lack of intellectual sophistication combine to make Pentecostalism and its kin effective in communicating their message and in bridging cultural gaps, especially in Africa where, according to McGrath, people are closely in touch with spiritual reality and find the appeal of atheism unintelligible. Through the story of the resurrection, McGrath tells us, the gospel is understood as deliverance from spiritual oppression, release from sorcery and from the baleful influence of ancestors.[32]

Alas, Africa is not alone in citizens highly attuned to spiritual forces. The lure of the spirits and shamans, of magical thinking and ecstatic worship, pseudo-explanation, prediction (prophecy) and control (EPC: see Chapter 3) has revived ominously elsewhere. Ecstatic elements had already appeared in the evangelicalism of the revivals that swept across the English-speaking world and Northern Europe in the Eighteenth and Nineteenth centuries.

> By 1966 Pentecostal practices were being taken up by ministers and lay groups in all the mainline denominations. Episcopalians, Lutherans, Presbyterians, Methodists and Baptists began to experience all

the gifts of the Holy Spirit, among them prophesying, healing, and the discernment of evil spirits, mentioned in 1 Corinthians 12.[33]

Most of the growth in church membership in the 1970s and 1980s occurred in the southern evangelical denominations and churches, probably (and somewhat paradoxically) in reaction to civil rights legislation. Healing revivals and exorcism, ecstatic worship, glossolalia, weeping, laughing, reaching out to the spirit, possession by the spirit and 'being slain in the spirit' become characteristic features of worship. A prosperity gospel preached by televangelists blossomed and made many of these new shamans and prophets very prosperous indeed. Many are in touch with God, can heal dire human afflictions and on occasion raise the dead.[34] Thus there has been a regression to a more primitive Christianity and, indeed, to a more primitive state of affairs altogether reminiscent of our Palaeolithic ancestors reaching out with open palms to the spirits hidden in their rock enclosures.

This then is a generalized summary of the religious fanatic's worldview. It is striking how the various beliefs and attitudes cluster in patterns that are significant from the perspective of psychoanalytic psychology, and indeed are predictable on the premise that narcissistic character traits underly them. I do not wish to underestimate the role of social, political and economic conditions in motivating the religious fanatic. But on the other hand we should not lose sight of the reciprocal way in which the salience of these factors, the ways in which these factors enter into the experience of the fanatic and fundamentalist, is conditioned by psychological traits. Nor do I wish to underestimate the role of other character traits and other defensive modes. But here I have proposed our task to be the exploration of the narcissistic aspects of religiosity, especially in its fanatical register. These aspects, I believe, are driving much of the religious extremism and violence in the world today. The following chapters continue that exploration.

Notes

1 See for example Dawkins 2006, Chapter 4 'Why there almost certainly is no God.'
2 Bremmer 2007; Whitmarsh 2015.
3 Williams 2015, 199.
4 Tammy Kitzmiller, et al. v. Dover Area School District, et al. (400 F. Supp. 2d 707, Docket no. 4cv2688). Eleven parents of students in Dover, Pennsylvania, sued the Dover Area School District over a schoolboard requirement that a statement presenting intelligent design as 'an explanation of the origin of life that differs from Darwin's view' was to be read aloud in ninth-grade science classes when evolution was taught. The board had also required that a book

advocating intelligent design be used as a reference in the biology teaching curriculum. The plaintiffs successfully argued that intelligent design is a form of creationism and that the schoolboard policy violated the First Amendment of the US Constitution. The case was seen as a major defeat for creationists, but also provided a dire omen of what could happen if religious fundamentalism was permitted to encroach on rational enquiry. Today in the United States we are seeing what such a pernicious encroachment means.

5 Some of these regressive changes relating to sexual morality, education and the law are discussed from a high altitude in the following chapters. Others include endeavours to restrict environmental protection measures, subverting the oversight activities of Federal scientific and related authorities, and retarding measures to address global warming. Under the Trump administration (2016–2020), many of their aims were achieved.

6 Nagel 2010; Kitcher 2011; Plantinga 2011; Taylor 2007; Johnston 2009.

7 Dawkins 2006, 1.

8 Hitchens 2007, 56.

9 Dawkins 2006, 306.

10 Quoted in Fitzgerald 2018, 466.

11 See Posner 2021, 29ff. Refrains of Christian nationalists that Jesus is king and Trump is his president come to save America, restore Zion and herald the end-times are clearly whacky, if not deranged. The ignorance and detachment from reality underlying such views are insufficiently remarked. Here there is little that can be called thinking: it is instead the expression of wishful phantasies substituting for thinking, as discussed in Chapter 8.

12 It's important to get the flavour of this. 'There was a tsunami and there are terrible natural disasters, because there isn't enough Torah study. . . . Black people reside there [New Orleans]. Blacks will study the Torah? [God said], Let's bring a tsunami and drown them. . . . Hundreds of thousands remained homeless. Tens of thousands have been killed. All of this because they have no God. . . . It was God's retribution. . . . God does not short-change anyone.' www.ynetnews.com/articles/0,7340,L-3138779,00.html. Ovadia's descendants are back, holding a knife to the throat of Israel's democracy.

13 Dawkins, Hitchens and Harris frequently encouraged ridicule. Dawkins is quoted as writing in his blog: 'We need to go further: go beyond humorous ridicule, sharpen our barbs to a point where they really hurt' (Plantinga 2011, 46). This indicates insensitivity to what motivates the religious. Philip Kitcher (2011) underscores the point. Darwinian atheists, he says, neither offer the best arguments against belief in the supernatural nor seem aware of the important functions that religions serve. Their ridicule is counterproductive because assaulting a person's religion can be experienced as profoundly threatening. Kitcher's own approach is to explore the threats the religious feel and to articulate secularism as positive responses to those

threats. Many of those threats are economic and social, so secular societies, he argues, must respond to social and economic injustice; they must provide support and a sense of purpose and connection to replace the amenities and satisfactions religion once provided.

14 Ruthven 2005, 11.

15 Pataki 2004a, 2004b.

16 Young Bruehl 1996.

17 Steigmann-Gall 2004, 88.

18 In an earlier work (Pataki 2007) I used the term 'religiose character.' Strozier et al. (2010) refer to the 'fundamentalist mindset' by which they mean much the same as I mean by 'fanatic.' But I think it matters to distinguish the fanatic from the merely devout, a distinction that history told in terms of fundamentalism obscures.

19 It is clear that not all the groups generally labelled as fundamentalist, terrorist or fanatic, even the suicide bombers among them, are primarily driven by religious motives; they may not even search for sanction in religion. Jerold J. Post (2007) has researched this area extensively and found amongst a wide array of designated fundamentalists and terrorists not religious inspiration but grievance, dispossession and marginalization. Amongst Hamas terrorists, for example, the most common configuration was loss of family through Israeli violence, humiliation, joblessness and hopelessness (175–91). Religion may be invoked, victory and eternal life are ensured with God on side of course, religious texts or rulings may justify, but these reassuring beliefs are causally secondary. These terrorists adopted fanatical measures out of despair; religion then gives despair cosmic significance and justifies or palliates action.

20 Mimica 2020.

21 Schimmel 2008.

22 Schimmel 2008, 47, 207.

23 Quoted in Ruthven 2005, 184.

24 Quoted in Lohrey 2006, 8.

25 Quoted in Scanlan 2002, 220.

26 Sayyid Abu Ala Mawdudi, *The Religion of Truth* quoted in Ruthven 2004, 48.

27 Quoted in Ruthven 2005, 172.

28 Maddox 2005, 267.

29 Maulvi Jalilullah Maulvizada interviewed by Ahmed Rashid in June 2007, quoted in Ruthven 2005, 111.

30 McGrath 2004, 191.

31 McGrath 2004, 194–195.

32 For superb discussions of Christianity in Africa see Horton 1997.

33 Fitzgerald 2018, 221; also 329.

34 Posner 2021, 61–71. Reading the history astonishes with the extraordinary cavalcade of rogues, charlatans and confidence tricksters weaving their way through Conservative Christian politics.

Chapter 6

Sexual morality and law

Religion and morality

Since the advent of monotheism, the domains of religion and morality have become so entangled that most people around the world today believe that one is inconceivable without the other. To have no religion, they believe, is to lack a foundation for morality and to be, in all probability, immoral. It is important to observe, then, that religion is, quite simply, one thing and morality another. They have independent sources, developed for the most part independently, and make differing claims upon us. Although monotheistic religions arrogate morality as their own – as if before their arrival there was only unrestrained lasciviousness and turpitude – it is obvious that rules of right conduct, right feeling, altruism, justice, obedience, respect and so forth far antedated these religions, various as these rules and conceptions may have been. Conceptions of justice and right conduct are internal to any viable social group. Our Palaeolithic ancestors could scarcely have survived had they not been governed by recognizably moral norms, at least as they applied within the intimate horde or group. Before monotheism, most societies regarded morality and religion as distinct domains. Animistic societies usually have rigid moral prescriptions but the spirits of animism are typically amoral, capricious and have no moral heft.[1] In such societies the idea that spirits should lay down laws of any kind is unknown. In Mesopotamia and Egypt, conceptions of justice and right conduct were highly refined, and the gods, particularly sun gods (Shamash, Re) watched over the preservation of laws. But it was the kings who framed the laws and set the standards of justice: 'Re installed the king/on the earth of the living/for ever and ever/to give law to the people, to satisfy the gods,/ to realize Ma'at [justice], to destroy Isfet [unlawfulness].'[2] The Olympian and Chthonian gods made neither moral nor civic law though they did occasionally enforce morality, often in frivolous ways lamented by the tragedians. Morality stood on the ground of tradition and public good sense. The conviction that an all-powerful god made moral laws whose transgression attracted severe penalties appears to have

DOI: 10.4324/9781315519814-9

been a late Israelite innovation. Of gods, only Yahweh, the Christian God and Allah legislate morality.

If one tried to sum up the most direct principle of pre-monotheistic religion in a single phrase it would be in the words *do ut des*: I give in order that you shall give. The gods give good things if treated well, welcome sacrifices and attention, and are angered if neglected. It is expected that every sacrifice is to be reciprocated. A Hittite hymn to Ishtanu goes: 'Be gracious to this man, your servant, then he will go on sacrificing to you bread and beer.' Perhaps the earliest Greek votive inscription, dated to about 700 BCE reads: 'Mantiklos has dedicated me to the far-shooting god with silver bow, from the tenth of his profit; you, Phoibos, give pleasure in return.' A question put to Zeus in Aeschylus: 'Where will you get a sacrificer like this man to honour you?' And, of course, it is the same, except more slyly, in later religions. A Christian prayer is unusually candid: 'Lord, give us grace; for if thou givest us not grace, we will not give thee glory – and who will win by that, Lord?'[3] Early Christians gave alms, oblations and prayers to lay up treasure, a home or maybe even a mansion, in heaven.[4] Most devoutly religious people still have some rewarding expectation, be it peace from the arrows of conscience or propinquity to God in heaven. Every religion promises salvation at a price.

Despite evident continuities with earlier religious traditions monotheism dramatically altered the relations between morality and religion. Right conduct and feeling are now prescribed not by tradition nor by king but by an irresistible supernatural power. On the one hand, this is a step towards moral universalism and a sundering of the connections between morality and king or state. There is only one moral law for all humankind, whether humankind knows it or not, laid down by an omnipotent being.[5] There is a higher power, a personal being with whom individuals may covenant and realize an emotional attachment. On the other hand, the plunge into the transcendent supernatural is a retreat from reality and descent into delusion. To arrive at the conception of a transcendent being ordering the cosmos certainly requires a capacity for abstraction – a kind of advance in intellectuality, as Freud noted. But the conception undermines the firm ground on which reason can stand, disrupts the understanding of human relationship, and derogates love of the one real world we have. The metaphysical difficulties of supernaturalism must here be put aside, as well beyond the scope of this work. We turn instead to the bleak picture of monotheism's moral and intellectual vices.

Sexual morality

The monotheistic distortion of human reality is particularly profound and pernicious in the area of sexual morality. Discussing the development and psychological impact of monotheism in Chapter 3, I emphasized

106 Polemic

that the conception of a unique and all-powerful god opened the avenue to intimate communion of an intensity scarcely known earlier except in the case of eccentrics.[6] It also created new ways of regulating self-esteem and distress by entering into the god's protective orbit or by identifying with it. With Yahweh, the architect of the world and human history, humankind moves to the centre of cosmic concern. This god *cares* about humankind, rewards obedience, punishes disobedience and demands love and loyalty as well as cult. Those who follow enter into a binding relationship of filiality. The relationship with God opens new channels for the dialectic of inflated narcissism: religious megalomania, and the struggle against it in exaggerated humility, asceticism and abjection. Where personal attachment is profound, failure to live up to divine demands risks the catastrophe of abandonment. But complete dependence on a being who, after all, is for most people remote, ungiving and in reality disappointing, engenders hatred and despondency. And since hatred of God – and here we must bear in mind the imbrication of God and parental representations – must be repressed it is turned upon the self or projected. Then guilt towards God – religious despair – becomes a new instrument of self-torture, and religious persecution of the Other becomes as common as rain. Paganism or idolatry is then not only error, it is infidelity and immorality. There are those who possess the Truth, and those who do not must be converted, marginalized or slain.

Relations to the gods of Judaism, Christianity and Islam as they developed over the centuries from Late Antiquity and the Middle Ages to the present retained these features and perpetuated their worst consequences. By and large, the gods are conceived as male, dominating and demanding – a severe father in heaven. At least it is so in the contemporary world with much of the Right of the religious spectrum: the fanatics and fundamentalists.[7] It is important to explore the extent to which their attitudes towards women, homosexuals and hot-button issues such as gender change and abortion can be derived from disturbed filial bonds. I don't mean to simplify attitudes that have many variations and complex psychological, moral, social and theological dimensions; my intention is to reveal something of one dimension, the unconscious motives created in infancy that contribute to the formation of adult conscious attitudes. I hope that whatever scepticism the reader may have regarding unconscious motivation as described in earlier chapters will at least partly be allayed by the light that its consideration sheds, and the order it imposes, on an array of religiously fanatical and related attitudes.

No contemporary observer can fail to notice the agitated concern with which fanatics and fundamentalists, and those who opportunistically join them, view the permutations of sexual choice and gender, the control of female sexuality and abortion, and the melting of divisions between male and female roles. In recent years other so-called 'woke' issues, such as sex education and school curricula have been cast into the arena. In some places the fanatics have succeeded in introducing book censorship and suppression of free thought not seen in many an age.[8] The heat that sex generates for these people is extraordinary and is radiating on a global scale. Currently, on almost any day, the media report: schism over the ordination of gay and female religious leaders in the Anglican churches; fierce dissension over abortion rights in the United States and Eastern Europe; puritan book censorship returning; issues of sex and gender expression roiling the United States, Eastern Europe and parts of Africa; the Russian Federation, with the inspiration of its Orthodox church, defending itself from Western sexual degeneracy by invading Ukraine; Indonesia criminalizing adultery and sex outside of marriage – homosexuality was already on the books; Uganda legislating the death penalty for homosexuality. In every instance mentioned the drivers of reaction to the humane and liberalizing tendencies in these societies are fanatical and fundamentalist religious groups.[9]

Origins: the fear of women

Many religious conservatives believe that the traditional patriarchal model of the family has a Biblical foundation. It is probably closer to the truth that the prevailing structure evolved from the monogamous Roman system, but the punitive, subordinating attitudes directed at women and children in the conservative religious family do have Biblical and possibly even earlier sources. Scholars have noticed the extraordinary cruelty towards women during and after the middle Assyrian period. It seems that it was then that women were first required to be veiled in public, and harsh legal penalties were applied to control their public presence and relationships. 'Neither wives nor widows nor women who go out on the street may have their heads uncovered.' Slaves and harlots, however, must go uncovered. Breaches of the law incur flogging and bitumen poured over the head. A woman who procures an abortion shall be impaled on stakes and not be buried. The punishment for adultery is death or disfiguration. Anyone – this time including men – who fails to report a conversation between a harem woman and an unauthorized man will be burnt in an oven. And so forth.[10] As the Bible shows, the cultural and theological influence of Assyria on the early Israelites was profound.

During the middle Assyrian and neo-Assyrian periods, a fundamental shift in religious conceptions occurred: a shift 'from faith in gods of immanence, spiritual representations of the forces of nature, deities who inhabit the world and wear the natural phenomena they represent like a suit of clothes, to gods of transcendence, deities outside, beyond and above nature rather than a part of it.'[11] The development is visible in

108 Polemic

changes to iconic representations of the gods, moving from concrete representations as forces of nature to abstract and symbolic forms. Moreover, as their empire became a world-dominating one, the Assyrians came to merge all the gods into a single figure of Ashur, of whom all the others were considered to be refractions. 'The foundations of the monotheism that the Hebrew tribes were to make the world's patrimony were being laid here in Assyria in the last part of the second millennium BCE.'[12] The belief in a transcendent god, a god no longer embodied in nature, leads to the desacralization of nature and inevitably to the devastating idea of Genesis (1:26) that men were superior to and masters of nature. Men now have dominion over fish and fowl and cattle . . . and over women too, whose physiology binds them to nature's cycles. It is no accident, as Kriwaczek says, that the religions that most emphasize God's utter transcendence relegate women to the lower rung, grant religious participation only grudgingly, and have the strictest avoidances when women's connection with nature, as in childbirth or menstruation, are most evident.[13] Women came to be seen as inferior to men, as having to serve and obey them. They are chattels but also seductresses.

It would seem then that Assyrian proto-monotheism went hand in hand with the derogation of nature and women, though, of course, the latter may have had other social and economic roots indigenous to Semitic herders and traders. Differentiation in economic function and responsibilities between men and women must have pre-existed these developments, but it is unclear whether earlier there were the established hierarchies of dominance that became so salient in some Semitic cultures. In any case, the creeds and attitudes of gender domination appear to have been passed on to the early Israelite scribes. The seductress Eve became the origin of all men's woes. The attitudes then passed to Christianity, especially in the person of St. Paul who enlarged on the earlier misogynism. 'Let a woman learn in silence with full submission. I permit no woman to have authority over a man; she is to keep silent. For Adam was formed first, then Eve' (I Timothy 2:11–13). The logic is uncertain, but Eve deceitfully compromised Adam and as a result a man has prescriptive rights over women, including how they should dress and wear their hair. Short hair is not permitted for women nor long hair for men (I Corinthians 11). There must be no confusion of genders. Women must be modest and subordinate. Many of the most rebarbative traditions of the Hebrew Bible were inherited by the early church and of, course, still reverberate.[14]

Although the devaluation and subordination of women, children and homosexuals has been a feature of all the orthodoxies of the peoples of the book, religious sentiment in the 20th century has, by and large, shown greater acceptance and accommodation. At least that is so with the exception of the fanatics, fundamentalists and opportunists who

Sexual morality and law   109

exploit their heft. Why the recalcitrance? Of course, one obvious narcissistic gratification for the man who accepts the Biblical view of women is that with a single act of faith, and with no effort on his part, he is elevated to superiority over about half the globe's population. This appeal can only be a part of the explanation, however; for one thing, many women accept the view as well. Moreover, it is evident that the Bible cannot be the unique source. The fear of and need to control women is found in cultures untouched by the Bible. And the Biblical injunctions could scarcely account for the intense anxiety about women having authority over men, the fear and loathing many fanatics feel when confronted with homosexuality, or the punitive attitudes towards children that we shall discuss in Chapter 7. These are passions beyond the evocative power of words or doctrine. When strong regularities cross cultures it is always worthwhile examining potential psychological determinants, and we now turn to some of these.

In the child's mind, and retained in the adult's unconscious mind, are images or representations of the strict, law-making, but protective father who provides shape and colour for the images of God, along the lines that Freud described. But usually underlying these images are earlier ones of the mother. When the relationship with the mother has gone well, and it generally does – is 'good-enough' in D. W. Winnicott's famous phrase – the images are comforting and radiate love. However, a number of developments converge to also make the mother an unconsciously feared and despised being, an object of great ambivalence. The child's (and adolescent's) fear of engulfment, and regressive merging with the mother, may make it necessary to push her away and render her obnoxious. Because she is so intensely longed for, sexually exciting and envied, but ultimately unpossessable, she arouses jealous and vengeful feelings, and consequently guilt and fear. And, of course, mothers give birth to unwelcome baby competitors. The child eventually comes to fear his own contumacious and insatiable desires and defends himself by disowning and projecting them onto the mother introjects: 'I am not the one with angry sexual cravings, she is!' That creates the figure of a dangerous seductress who must be controlled, kept at bay and, for good measure, devalued. Moreover, where mothers are in fact devalued in the family and cultural ambience, that will confirm the child's incipient estimation. A flight to the strict father may assist, in the case of the boy, in weakening attachment to this 'bad' sexual mother and, by identification with the father, to control his own desires. In fact, attraction to the father in both sexes is partly the result of a flight from the feared and devalued mother and the guilt and anxiety associated with her. Later, other 'strong' figures may be sought out: a stern omnipotent god, or 'strong' leaders who 'stay the course and never give up' come what may.

110 Polemic

We can now glimpse how the fear of subordination to women, the need to control their seductive sexuality and reproduction, and the punitive, derogatory and vengeful attitudes towards women distinctive of religious fanatics and their congeners is formed on the template of the dangerous seductress-mother introjects. All women are unconsciously perceived through this prism. Why is this combination of attraction and derogation, which to various degrees is almost universal, so salient in fanatical and fundamentalist religious cultures? Certainly, the actual treatment of women in these cultures witnessed by the child will affect his estimation of women. Religious teaching normalizes these estimations. But I conjecture that another part of the answer lies in the actual repressive, subordinating and cruel treatment to which female children, who will soon be mothers, are subjected. The derogation and humiliations leave their mark, and the sins of the fathers, through the mothers, are visited upon generations of children. The mothers identify with the aggressor and become the instruments perpetuating oppression. Identification with the aggressor explains why so many women in different traditions accept, justify and perpetuate the physical and moral mutilations which are their lot. This may be why, to list just a few examples, so many conservative Christian women ignore former president Trump's undisguised derogation of them. Why so many Muslim women are proud to perpetuate the obvious restrictions placed on them or defend sexual mutilations. Why Haredi women meekly accept that they lack the facility and privilege of Talmud study.

Hatred of the homosexual

Some of the hatred of homosexual men, or men who change their gender or biological sex, or who like to cross-dress, has a related provenance. They are perceived to be women, and so attract the kind of devaluating attitudes described above. The Greek elites were, by and large, pederastic, and the Romans were tolerant of homosexuality, but not so much of the passive homosexual, especially if they were high status Roman citizens. The passive homosexual was supposed to lack the manly and martial virtues, an odd view at the time since the proclivities of such men as Alexander of Macedon, Epaminondas and the Sacred Band, and Julius Caesar were well known. But the Judeo-Christian world became different. The ambient Canaanite and, later, Persian worlds were tolerant of homosexuality and there is evidence to suggest that early Israelite religion was also accommodating.[15] That is probably why the Biblical injunctions against it were so ferocious. Drawing irrefragable ethno-religious boundaries was a principal part of progressive Israelite self-definition, whether it concerned the god worshipped, what was eaten, or who one had sex with. Leviticus 20:13 states that: 'If a man also lie with

Sexual morality and law   **111**

mankind, as he lieth with a woman, both of them have committed an abomination: they shall surely be put to death; their blood shall be upon them.' In the influential Jewish philosopher Philo of Alexandria in the first century CE, a hysterical savagery appears that was to be amplified in Christian letters and later persecutions. The intolerable offence in his eyes was 'the disease of effemination':

> These persons are rightly judged worthy of death by those who obey the law [of Moses], which ordains that the man-woman who debases the sterling coin of nature should perish unavenged, suffered not to live for a day or even an hour, as a disgrace to himself, to his house, his native land and the whole human race.[16]

Philo insists that the accused should be taken to no court but summarily executed by the mob. The Latin church fathers followed. According to Clement, a well-groomed man is either bisexual or an out-and-out *cinaedus* who will 'prove himself a woman at night.'[17] Augustine also makes the underlying issue clear. Recoiling from his youthful homosexual love, he declares that no man should be permitted to use his body as a woman's. The horrors that proceeded from the progressive implementation of increasingly savage laws against homosexuals by the Christian emperors, the ghoulishly ingenious punishments meted out during the period of Christian totalitarianism dating from the fourth century CE, have been graphically described elsewhere.[18] It must be underlined that the sadistic persecution and murder of homosexuals was absent in the non-monotheistic world, absent in China and India, and briefly absent even in the finest days of Islam. That fact points to the influence of the Hebrew Bible, and indeed to the psychological structures created by monotheism.

The church fathers drew an association between pagan cults and homosexuality. In some cults priests cross-dressed and in those devoted to some of the Great Mother religions priests were eunuchs or self-castrates.[19] Pagan festivals were often occasions for reveling in the human bisexual disposition, for enacting role reversals. But even beyond the final extirpation of paganism, the Christian church continued its persecution of sexual and gender subversion relentlessly, often associating them not just with feminine but with demonic forces. A supposed association between the demonic and gender subversion projected onto liberal or Leftish irreligion is currently stirring the fanatical imaginations of the American Christian Right to an extent that would be comical if not so vicious.[20]

A male's adoption of what has traditionally been seen as the female role, whether in dress, demeanour or sexual object choice, is suggestive of emasculation and provokes castration anxiety, especially in those with

112 Polemic

unresolved and impaired filial relationships: the frightening reminder of the infant boy's fear of his father and the realization that he too could be castrated.[21] That anxiety has to be dealt with, and eliminating the objects that provoke it is one way of doing so. Paul's anxiety about women having short, and men having long, hair reflects a need to keep a rigid distinction between the sexes, and that suggests both castration anxiety and a fear of lapsing into homosexuality born of a temptation to it. The temptation, often largely unconscious, is of course widespread and it's part of the monotheist brand to suppress it. In the male case, the temptation is implicit in the turn to the father, and it is notable that, historically, persecution of homosexuals rises to the highest degree of ferocity at times of social anxiety: earthquake, famine, war and social turmoil exacerbate the persecution. These are times when a resolute father's protection is needed. In our day, economic distress and bewilderment are once again producing authoritarian figures allied with the church and the mob. In every instance over the last hundred years when a fascist alliance between such figures, church and the mob has evolved persecution of homosexuals followed. Homosexual impulses and phantasies reinvigorated in turning to the father introject may arouse guilt and shame and need to be repudiated and projected. Every trace or suggestion of such impulses in others must be eliminated, so all homosexuals, all reminders of sexual or gender diffusion, are repudiated. Experimental work by social psychologists has confirmed a positive correspondence between the strength of homophobia in individuals and arousal by homosexual pornographic images. In the religious fanatic the link between father and God introjects creates a familiar outcome. Because father and God images are so closely imbricated fear leads not just to the regressive reactivation and submission to the father and the passive homosexual attitude. It also leads to submission to God, to the passive attitude and castration anxiety coloured by the symbols of religious devotion. One thinks here naturally of the iconography of St. Sebastian and the cavalcade of martyrology. Natural or social disaster is interpreted as God's punishment for wicked deeds or wicked hearts. That wickedness is commonly thought to be homosexual desire or the pull of gender subversion, the supposed sins of Sodom and Gomorrah. If homosexuals are not extirpated, God will do what He did to Sodom. So persecution follows with God's imprimatur. 'It is not I who demand this, but God' is the catchphrase of Inquisitors down the centuries.

Some religions, most notably Catholicism, offer milder lines of defence against homosexual desires. The negative consequences of regressively turning to father can be mitigated by turning to Jesus, who is represented as non-sexual and safe, though not by the greatest artists. Homo-erotic feeling can be displaced, disguised and dispersed in group worship, prayerful adoration before a comely near-naked Christ, episodes of controlled group hysteria (as among Pentecostalists) with penetration by the Holy Spirit, and so forth. I don't mean to suggest that that is *all* that goes on in these practices but their sexual connotations can scarcely be overlooked. Since some religious institutions can function to defend against guilt for homosexual impulses, it is unsurprising that many people burdened by such guilt should enter them. These structured institutions provide a safe haven, though occasionally with tragic outcomes.[22] Where there is an absence of supportive, latently homosexual institutions of the types perfected by the Catholic church, as in the fundamentalist Protestant denominations, homophobes may have to defend against self-hatred more noisily by publicly despising and suppressing homosexual impulses in others. Many sensational cases involving prominent US evangelical pastors have emerged in recent decades.[23] In general, people who have not adequately resolved their infantile attachments, who live under the shadow of the images of the strict father or the seductress-mother, will be drawn to religions that allay their anxieties and validate their fears and prejudices. It is scandalous that religious groups and the politicians who exploit them still boast of these prejudices while pretending to occupy high moral ground.

Family and envy

With local variations in emphasis, opposition to gay marriage and gender conversion, persecution of homosexuals, subordination of women, opposition to abortion and to the ordination of women have been represented by a wide variety of religious groups as conditions for the preservation of the traditional (patriarchal) family. It is, of course, easy to imagine alternative nurturing dispensations because there have been, and there are, many alternatives, as ethnographic investigations demonstrate; but this is not the view of the traditionalists. The defence of 'the family' against sexual deviance, gender diffusion, reproductive choice and women wearing pants is not, I think, the main reason firing religious fanatics and their relations. The institution of the family satisfies a number of more or less unconscious desires of immense importance to them. The family creates a unit but at the same time it atomizes or disaggregates society. The resulting rigid structuring of social relations is reassuring to people who fear fusion or a loss of emotional boundaries: it creates an identity and opportunity for the exercise of power within a small circle. The family, on this rigid model, restricts lust and temptation: one's own – which is a help to many people – but more importantly, that of others. Achieving social conformity by locking everyone into a family helps to obviate the pain of envying 'the dissolute pagan.' The monotheisms are puritanical in essence and impose huge instinctual restrictions on those who take them seriously: the seriously religious

114 Polemic

often feel that they have renounced the sexual freedom, especially the perverse elements of that freedom, that the pagans are imagined to possess; and that which has been renounced but still longed for provokes envy and hatred when discovered in others. It provokes, in Dodds' apt phrase, 'the malice of the chaste for the unchaste.' For envy is not merely pained at another's possession of what one covets, it often seeks to spoil or destroy that thing and its possessor. On the influential view of Melanie Klein, envy is an expression of innate destructive drives that search out objects.[24] Shakespeare may have had something like that in mind: 'But jealous souls will not be answer'd so;/They are not ever jealous for the cause,/But jealous for they are jealous;/'tis a monster/Begot upon itself, born on itself.' Whether or not envy is begotten upon itself we understand how privation, frustration and loss stimulate envy. The intrusion of unconscious envy into adult consciousness is particularly painful and there are many defences against it, including spoiling, devaluation or destruction of the envied objects. Klein said that creativity is the most envied thing of all because its psychogenetic roots can be traced back to the life-giving breast. Conditions that are envied in others include freedom from envy and greed, the capacity for spontaneous and effortless enjoyment, the serenity that comes from feeling loved unconditionally, the absence of sexual inhibition, and vitality. The sexual freedom and licentiousness of the pagan lives, of course, mostly in the imagination of the chaste but include homosexual acts, changing gender roles and promiscuous and perverse sexuality, elements of which are harboured in every person's mind more or less consciously but magnified in the minds of the religiously inhibited. And this consideration throws an interesting shaft of light on one aspect of the anti-abortion or pro-life movement. The fanatic, the fundamentalist and their congeners want of course to control and punish women. It will be understood that I am describing one impulse that coexists in the mind with other and contrary impulses. But most of all they want to punish women deemed dissolute and promiscuous, who are imagined to be having unrestrained sex and making babies, to be freely enjoying themselves in perverse ways and being generative and creative. Those women in particular must be punished. My guess is that in *many* people with anti-abortion sentiments, the concern for the unborn is a cloak for the mitigation of unbearable envy – often projected onto the political landscape – wrapped in a package of self-deceiving dogma.

We have now traced some of the influences of religion in forming the fanatical mindset and some of the consequences of deriving moral norms from holy scripture. Too many children are exposed to views about women and sexuality derived ultimately from aspects of Biblical teaching and live in societies or cocooned cult-like groups partly shaped by them. They will receive little else of intellectual nourishment other than their Holy Books and derivative works. Consequently, they will remain at the mercy of these shallow works, with tragically impoverished insight into themselves or others. The enthusiasm for banning books is likely to graduate to burning them – if only metaphorically – and further diminish the ability of the young to educate themselves and enter into contact with human reality.

Law

Fanatics and fundamentalists believe that God legislates moral law. Amongst them there are also those who believe that the business of the state, perhaps the only business of the state, is to enforce the Mosaic (in the case of Muslims, Koranic) precepts. In their eyes, the Holy Books read like statutes. So the theonomic conception of law – all law derives from God – leads naturally into theocracy. Their views are influential even amongst those who do not go all the way to this extreme but feel that – somehow – God should be, as it were, more impactful in politics and law than the democracies currently allow. God needs their help.

The contrast between the nomocratic conception of law that has come down to us from Greece and most especially Rome and the theonomic or theocratic conception could not be starker. By the nomocratic conception I mean simply the understanding that a state should be governed by laws that are human creations and subject to amendment by humans according to changing circumstances. As we saw above, the nomocratic conception of kingship has antique roots in the earliest civilizations. The laws may descend from immemorial custom and be sanctioned by the gods, but they do not derive from the gods. The democratic form of nomocracy was first articulated in Greece. 'The laws,' Pericles said, 'are all the rules approved and enacted by the majority in assembly, whereby they declare what ought and what ought not to be done.' As J. M. Kelly remarks, 'In general Greek thought knew nothing of the idea that there exists a range of values, which, if human laws should conflict with them, render those laws invalid.'[25] Laws are obeyed, not because they are created by the gods or because of fear of the gods. 'In public affairs deep respect for the laws prevents us from breaking them,' said Pericles.[26] Socrates chose to die rather than break the laws he loved.

This nomocratic conception was elaborated by the Roman jurists who made of it what is still the basic framework of Western law, one of the great achievements of Western civilization. Roman law was venerated but not sacrosanct. It could be modified to meet changing circumstances, for the law derived, as the later Roman jurists said, from the fact. It was based on both custom and practice. 'It was the voice of the people speaking as God – "*vox populi, vox dei*" as the saying went – not

116 Polemic

the voice of God speaking to the people.'[27] With the accession of Constantine, Christian morality, mostly concerning the regulation of sexuality and an expanded range of sin, was progressively legislated and policed. After the Western Empire fell the Germanic kings 'continued the imperial mandate of the Christian emperors to suppress paganism, ensure that the Jews kept a low profile, and to impose Christian notions of public morality.'[28] Under Christian influence, law acquired an increasingly top-down theocratic caste whereby emperors and kings were seen as representatives of God on Earth and derived their authority to rule and to legislate from God. Justinian's Digest, the massive compilation of Roman law issued in the East in 533CE 'ultimately became the basis of the whole civil law of continental Europe and, later, of the many distant lands to which it was exported by colonialism or by cultural penetration.'[29] In Western Europe, the infusion of Germanic legal norms and bottom-up conceptions of political authority also played a significant part in the evolution of common law and the relations between rulers and the ruled. Fortunately, the forms of Roman legal process, the very idea of the rule of man-made law, though occasionally perverted by theocratic tendencies, were not fundamentally subverted. The view still held by many contemporary monotheists that the Ten Commandments is the basis of Western law is ludicrous.

The first articulate assault on the nomocratic conception of politics and law came from the many-sided Jewish priest and historian Flavius Josephus. Josephus ascribed to Moses the creation of an original and perfect constitution for humankind different from every other: God should be in charge of *everything*: '[Moses] did not make piety a part of virtue, but recognized and established the others as part of it. . . . All practices and occupations, and all speech, have reference to our piety towards God.' Josephus the high priest drew a comfortable conclusion:

> What would be finer and more just than a structure that had made God governor of the universe, that commits to the priests in concert the management of the most important matters, and, in turn, has entrusted to the High Priest of all the governance of the other priests.[30]

Josephus explicitly rejected Greek nomocracy in favour of theocratic rule based upon the Mosaic code and covenant. There was to be strict piety, control of passions, adherence to precepts laid down in Torah, limitation of opposition, and

> complete severance from the "talking shop" of Greek philosophy. . . . Law was not, as in the Greco-Roman view, to be brokered by different kinds of citizens sharing ideas in the public life of the agora; it was a given.[31]

Sexual morality and law   117

This conception of law, essentially the view of contemporary religious fanatics and fundamentalists, is voiced in the rhetorical question of many American evangelicals, Jewish and Muslim theocrats: 'Who is sovereign – God or state?' It is against this backdrop that Osama bin Laden's 'Letter to America' of November 2002 becomes paradigmatic:

> You are the nation who, rather than by ruling by the Shari'a of Allah in its Constitution and Laws, chose to invent your own laws as you will and desire. You separate religion from your politics, contradicting the pure nature which affirms absolute authority to the Lord your Creator. . . . You are the worst civilization witnessed by the history of mankind.[32]

America's unforgivable crime is the separation of the sacred from the secular, church and state.

This view in inverted form is identical to 'Christian Reconstructionism' as elaborated in detail by R. J. Rushdoony in the 1960s and 1970s. Despite – or because of – its rebarbative consequences it has increased its following among the Christian Right. Frances Fitzgerald summarizes the view:

> The Bible was to be the governing text for all areas of life, from government to education and the arts. In the "kingdom society" there was no room for diversity or tolerance of another religion, not even Judaism, for the Jews failed to live up to the covenants. With God on their side, Christians had no need for majoritarian politics, or for compromise or accommodation to reach their goal. . . . "Christianity is completely and radically anti-democratic; it is committed to spiritual aristocracy," [Rushdoony] wrote, and only "the right have rights."[33]

God's law is revealed in the Bible. The aim, then, is to progressively legislate every aspect of Biblical law. The state is not involved with human well-being.

> The state's job is to ensure that those who do not choose a godly life are at least compelled to observe its externalities, making society completely unthreatening for those who do. The "chosen" get to live completely unfettered by government, whose role is limited to restraining sinners.[34]

But how are these anti-democratic aims to be achieved? According to the ideology of Dominionism, in one incarnation or another currently motivating large elements of the hard Christian Right in the United States and elsewhere, national salvation will be achieved when chosen Christians

118 Polemic

occupy all significant public offices. The US will then be converted into a true Christian nation and, presumably, the conversion of the world will follow.[35] Other ways of subverting democracy and making the world safe for fanatics and fundamentalists recently swam into view. Capture a president at the mercy of the evangelical vote and drive him to subvert state institutions; or, again, as in Israel today, use a freak opportunity of a Parliamentary majority to dismantle the regulative institutions of the state, and legislate Jewish supremacy and theocracy. Many years ago Rabbi Ben Nun of the settler movement stated that

> Jewish immigration to Israel and settlement are beyond the [civic] law. The settler's movement comes out of the Zionist constitution and no law can stop it. . . . For those to whom the Bible and the religious prescripts are beyond the [civic] law there is no need to say anything further. . . . For us, what really matters is not democracy, but the Kingdom of Israel. . . . Democracy is a sacred idea for the Greeks, not so for the Jews.[36]

The current Israeli government is running with the idea.

The differences between the nomocratic and theonomic conceptions of law are absolutely fundamental in both concept and consequence. Under the first, humans create law, moral and civic; law is mutable and rationally fitted to circumstance. Under the second, law is received as divine revelation; it is immutable: gods don't change their minds. Some thinkers see theonomy as a great conceptual achievement because political and legislative power are wrested from the hands of individuals and provided with a transcendent and universal source. God rules, not any particular king or state, and that premise opens the path to moral and political universalism. In my view, theocracy is one of the worst ideas ever to have entered the mind of man. In the first place, it is, of course, not rule by God or rule according to the word of God; it is rule by those who manage to get themselves appointed as interpreters of the word of God. Where religions have been able to exert mundane power political, intellectual and indeed religious freedoms have had precarious tenure. We have the examples of Iran, Afghanistan and some other Muslim nations; we see the pernicious influence of religion on law in Russia, Poland, Brazil, Uganda and many other places where religion has heft. We watch with trepidation what may happen in Israel and the United States. (This is written in April 2023.) We can hear that the loudest voices calling for theocratic autocracy are those of mountebanks and hustlers.

Second, the doctrinal teachings of the Abrahamic religions, in all but their most liberal incarnations, are fundamentally theocratic. But the teachings are, to put it mildly, founded on the evidence of sand. It must be asked therefore what makes such theocratic teachings attractive to

Sexual morality and law   119

people. If what I have said so far about the narcissistic pathology of the fanatic is correct then those gains are likely to provide some insight. Religious fanaticism, I have been arguing, is largely a narcissistic character disorder in religious garb. For all the confidence and bellicosity at the malignant extreme of such disorders, they are, at heart, frangible, defensive and fearful. The fanatic splits his self into good and bad, projects the bad onto others, and identifies with the good, including with his idealized conceptions of parents and deity even when these are idealized for their aggression. This creates both a frightening paranoid world and an impoverished frightened self. The religious person in whom these trends predominate is consequently driven by fear: fear of autonomy, and fear of other people. In this circumstance, a political dispensation where he is not governed by his fellows and subjected only to the rigid authority of God provides perfect solutions to his psychological dilemmas. In the first place, his grandiose self-conceptions are gratified: only God is great enough to rule over him! The idea of being ruled by divine law excludes the possibility of being ruled by other people. The fanatic fears others because he unconsciously fears the consequences of his own projections and the retribution he expects for his unconscious aggression, envy and devaluation of others. Finally, in a theocracy, he can affirm the special relationship or identification with God and reap its narcissistic benefits. Nietzsche astutely detected the narcissistic element in this concession: 'By allowing God to judge, they themselves judge; by glorifying God they glorify themselves.'[37] The fanatics' relationship to God becomes the model for the entire polity. The great aim of fanatical theocrats is to make their individual delusion normative for their society, and then for the world.

Notes

1 Lewis 2003, 27.
2 Assman 2010, 49. Ma'at is not just law and order imposed from above. The Egyptian conception of justice also 'designates a justice from below, a salvational justice that comes to the aid of the poor and the weak, the proverbial widows and orphans. . . . According to the Egyptian view of things, it is not an organ of the state. Quite the contrary: the state exists so that justice may be realized on earth. . . . [J]ustice has been in the world since time immemorial: indeed it is difficult to see how people could live together without it. But in Egypt . . . it was situated in the human rather than divine world. Whereas the gods crave sacrificial offerings, humans crave the law. In its origins justice is something profane or secular' (Assmann 2010, 149–150).
3 Burkert 1998, 144. The other quotations in this paragraph are from pages 129 and 136.

4 Brown 2015.

5 The extent to which moral universalism is embodied in the Old or the New Testaments is controversial. Occasional remarks about how to treat strangers are hardly decisive. Loving your neighbours (and enemies) is not quite the same as loving humankind, though the phrase is of course open to interpretation. In the historical context it is more suggestive of a recipe for Israelite social cohesion then for interethnic bonding, as Wright (2010, 260) and others have argued. Recall St. Paul's endearing statement about loving your enemies so that it may be for them as burning coals (Wright 2010, 285).

6 For example, the orator Aristides. See Dodds 1965, 40ff.

7 Recall the distinction in the previous chapter. The religious fanatic, we say, is a fundamentalist with severe narcissistic character disorder; and in many instances is a fundamentalist as a result of that disorder. Their behaviour may be indistinguishable but it matters that the underlying motivational structures may be quite different.

8 One example for hundreds: 'Florida's board of education has approved the expansion of the state's so-called "don't say gay" bill, which now prohibits discussions of sexual orientation and gender identity at school across all grade levels. Wednesday's approval came at the request of the Republican governor, Ron DeSantis, who in the past two years has waged what critics call a "culture war" across the state through his bans on gender-affirming care, Covid-19 precautionary measures and abortion rights, among other facets.' Maya Yang *The Guardian* 20 April 2023. Florida and Texas lead in banning books but many states have followed. Among the banned, classics such as Toni Morrison's *Beloved* and Margaret Atwood's *The Handmaid's Tale*.

9 In the United States especially, conservative religion and reactionary politics have long been intertwined, as meticulously documented in Fitzgerald 2018. The current anti-abortion, anti-gay, anti-desegregation (and now anti-gender-affirmation) agendas are political formulations by influential operatives, starting from the late 1970s, to regain and extend the power of the Christian Right, resulting eventually in the weird alliance with the Republican Party of Donald Trump. The 'culture wars' gave the Christian Right focus. Although now fixated on abortion and sexual politics, the initial instigation was principally racist backlash against the federal government's efforts to desegregate tax-exempt private schools. 'The Christian right movement was born out of grievance against civil rights gains for blacks, and a backlash against the government's efforts to ensure those gains could endure' (Posner 2021, 124). White Christians are now portrayed as victims of civil rights for LGBTQ people, of coloured immigration, and of crafty Jews seeking their replacement, just as they were portrayed as victims of desegregation. This shows amongst other things the fungibility of the objects of prejudice and the prejudicial nature of religion.

10 Citing legal tablets from the time, Kriwaczek 2012, 224ff.

Sexual morality and law 121

11 Kriwaczek 2012, 228.
12 Kriwaczek 2012, 231.
13 Kriwaczek 2012, 230.
14 These attitudes are playing out brutally in Iran and Afghanistan and unexpectedly reappearing in Israel. They are also part of the dynamic of the anti-abortion movements and the fury over gender conversion in the United States and, more moderately, elsewhere.
15 Crompton 2006, 39ff.
16 Crompton 2006, 44.
17 Crompton 2006, 117.
18 Crompton 2006, Chapters 5 and 6; especially pps 133,146,153ff, 228, 249, 536ff; Catherine Nixey 2017. In the Theodosian Code, as it appeared in 438, the fate of passives was sealed: 'All persons who have the shameful custom of condemning a man's body, acting the part of a woman's, to the sufferance of an alien sex (for they appear not to be different from women) shall expiate the crime of this kind in avenging flames in the sight of the people' (Crompton 2006, 136). Under the Justinian code of 534, the welding of imperial law and Christian theology was complete and the active partner was also condemned to death. The people were warned that homosexual acts would 'incur the just anger of God, and bring about the destruction of cities.' Christian Councils subsequently issued canons, mostly but nor exclusively dealing with sex. Thus canon 50 of the Council of Elvira forbade Christians to eat with Jews; and canon 67 declared that 'it was forbidden for a woman . . . to have anything to do with long-haired men or hairdressers' (Crompton 2006, 154).
19 The milder customs of celibacy and wearing female attire persist in the Catholic church.
20 The Christian fear of demonic forces in Antiquity is colourfully described in Nixey 2017. A contemporary gem I cannot resist is the gift of a Republican congressman: ' "The Lord rebuke you, Satan, and all of your demons and all of your imps who come parade before us," he told the speakers at the hearing. "That's right, I called you demons and imps who come and parade before us and pretend you are part of this world. We have people that live among us today on planet Earth that are happy to display themselves as if they were mutants from another planet. This is the planet Earth where God created men male and women female." ' Reported in *The Guardian* 12/4/23.
21 In what follows I trace only the boy's odyssey. The girl's is both more and less complicated.
22 See Chapter 7.
23 See Fitzgerald 2018 for this cavalcade of confidence tricksters.
24 Klein 1957.
25 Kelly 2003, 20.
26 For the Periclean quotations see Bowra 1973, 81, 84. The secular tenor of these thoughts generally did not conflict with the Greek sense that the laws had divine sanction.

27 Pagden 2009, 116.
28 Brown 2015,146. The Frankish kings 'declared it was their duty to suppress public sins that brought down the wrath of God on the community as a whole. If the preaching of the bishops did not work in provoking repentance and the abandonment of sinful ways, royal governors would finish the job.' Brown 2015, 144.
29 Kelly 2003, 82.
30 Josephus citations in Goodman 2019, xii and 79.
31 Hannaford 1996, 93.
32 Quoted in Pagden 2009, 533.
33 Fitzgerald 2018, 342.
34 Maddox 2005, 272
35 The process of infiltrating political parties by knowing Christians is currently unfolding in Australia through the process of 'branch-stacking.'
36 Cited in Ruthven 2005, 161.
37 Nietzsche 1990, 170.

Chapter 7

Aggression in religion

Forms of religious aggression today

In the wake of decades of wars of religion, Pierre Bayle observed that the revealed religions contained the inexterminable seeds of war, slaughter and injustice. In this chapter I will suggest why that may be so. Earlier we said that all religions are involved in one way or another with the regulation of self-esteem and establishing conditions of safety, that is to say, with the narcissistic economy. Our account underlines the fact that in circumstances where religion dominates a child's upbringing and education, it may affect the formation of character, specifically the formation of the pathologically narcissistic character who is a religious fanatic. Religious education may of course affect a person in many other ways unconnected with the structure of their internal worlds. And because repressed infantile narcissism and narcissistic pathology are frequently expressed in aggression and group assertion (in the ways foreshadowed in Chapter 4) aggression may be said to be intrinsic to religion. Aggression is intrinsic to religion – as a constant brimming potential – because narcissism is intrinsic to it. I do not mean that all religious people are suffering from narcissistic disorders or that all religious groups, all of the time, are in some way involved in bullying people or exterminating them, though they are involved often enough. It is when the narcissistic elements of religion reach the pitch of fanaticism, which the monotheisms in particular are disposed to do, that aggression becomes its *modus operandi*. We also stipulated (in Chapter 5) that the fanatic is a fundamentalist in doctrine, one in whom orectic or wishful processes dominate the personality, and that most often he is a fundamentalist with severe narcissistic character disorder and became a fundamentalist *because* of that disorder. It was noted, however, that the circle of orectic derangement in religion spreads widely, is not restricted to narcissistic pathology, and aggression in religion is not restricted to the fanatic. We need to flesh out at least some of these claims with examples.

DOI: 10.4324/9781315519814-10

124 Polemic

Historically, the conspicuous expressions of religious aggression were wars, massacres of infidel populations, pogroms and the like. Religiously inspired wars were unknown before the advent of the monotheistic religions.[1] There were of course wars of conquest, massacre and rapine in earlier times, and armies were thought to be escorted and sometimes led by the gods themselves. But because the gods were shared or easily inter-translated it was impossible for the ancients to despise their neighbours' gods, though not infrequently they subordinated them to their favourites. Through the long history of conflict between ancient Greece and Persia, for example, there is scarcely a reproach of each other's religions, radically different though they were. In polytheistic dispensations, state hostility to religion arose only where the latter took on political colouring and threatened loyalty to the state, as happened with the intransigent early Christian church.

It is all too easy to multiply contemporary examples of violence and oppression where religion is causally involved in one way or another. Islamist terrorism and the internecine conflicts within Islam obviously have a religious dimension. Jewish supremacists relying on baseless Biblical covenants justify violent dispossession. Hindu-Muslim violence on the sub-continent is fed by religious enmity. Christian nationalists are supporting intolerant, aggressive dispensations in Russia, Europe, Israel, the United States and elsewhere. The intimidation and murder of heretics, apostates and blasphemers, speciously legitimated by religious teaching, continues in many nations.[2] But religious aggression appears not only in those familiar catastrophic explosions of violence. The oppression of minority religious groups, women and sexual and gender non-conformists are mostly expressions of religious aggression. The educational restrictions on girls in some Muslim nations and amongst Haredi Jews should be recognized as religious aggression. Below, I will briefly single out two other forms of religious aggression, become conspicuous in relatively recent times: religiously inspired punitive pedagogical practices and institutional child sexual abuse. But before getting there it will be useful to pre-empt some of the common strategies used to deny, obscure or palliate religious aggression.

Errors of the apologists

First, the '*tu quoque*': but you too! While there may indeed be violence in 'the name of religion' the argument goes, conceding that religion in one way or another may cause aggression, secular ideologies and movements have been much worse. Karen Armstrong writes:

> Born of modern scientific racism, the Holocaust . . . showed that a secularist ideology could be just as lethal as any religious crusade. . . .

The Holocaust was also a reminder of the dangers that can accrue from the death of God in human consciousness. . . . The symbol of God had marked the limit of human potential and, in the conservative period, had imposed a constraint upon what men and women could do. . . . But the Holocaust and the Gulag show what can happen when people cast off all such restraint or make the nation or polity the supreme value.[3]

Distinguished philosophers have resorted to this canard. Christian philosopher Alvin Plantinga, after indignantly chastising the new atheists, asserts that

They conveniently ignore the fact that modern atheist ideologies – Nazism and Marxism, for example – were responsible, in the twentieth century alone, for far more suffering and death than religion in its entire history.[4]

Charles Taylor writes of 'the terrible violence powered by atheistic and/or anti-Christian ideologies, like Marxist-Leninism and Nazism.'[5]

The first thing to notice about this line of argument is that even if it were sound it would do nothing to reduce the charge against religion. The charge is not that religion is the *only* cause of social violence and aggression but that it is *a* cause. For this strategy to have any hope of vindicating religion it would have to demonstrate one of two things. First, that unlike atheism and contrary to the overwhelming implications of the evidence, religion is only, or mostly, incidental to the violence with which it has been associated. Alternatively, that religious violence pales in comparison to that wreaked by atheists or atheistic dispensations. We shall find that the claims made by Armstrong, Plantinga and the others hang from historical ignorance on stilts.

Was the Nazi movement, was Nazi Germany atheistic? The answer is: almost certainly not. Historians such as Steigmann-Gall (2004), Robert Erickson (2012) and others have carefully documented the roots of Nazi ideology and its acceptance by Germans in the course of the 20th century. They have persuasively established that both are intricated with Christianity and are scarcely atheistic. Nazism had deep roots in developments in 19th-century Protestant theology and pervasive theological perceptions of Germany's circumstances before and after the First World War. By the latter half of the nineteenth century streams of Protestant Christianity eventually feeding into Nazism began to conceive of Germany as God's favoured nation. During the First World War, most Christian clergy came to view the war as 'a type of crusade in which God had chosen Germany to punish his enemies.'[6] After defeat, the resonant conception of the 'stab in the back,' so successfully exploited by Hitler,

126 Polemic

was first preached by the Protestant Court chaplain. It is clear that Hitler and most other leading Nazis were inspired by Christian social teaching, consistently held up Jesus as the Ideal, and remained professing Christians till the end. Some Nazi ideologues, such as Himmler, dabbled in a Nordic paganism that drew heavily on Christian themes. But it was theistic.[7] Many leading Nazis and supporters were in high church office; the majority of German clerics, especially but not only in the Protestant confessions, welcomed and continued to support Nazism, seeing it as an extension of Christian belief. It is clear also that the majority of German citizens saw Nazism as an expression of Christianity, or at least as consistent with it, and supported it. The Nazi ideologues who were atheists were few, ineffective and derided by Hitler and his close circle.

According to Steigmann-Gall, Hitler consistently insisted that Christianity was the centre of Nazi social thought. His mentor Dietrich Eckart, one of the main early ideologues of Nazism, wrote: 'In Christ the embodiment of all manliness, we find all that we need.' Like the influential Buch and Goebbels, Hitler regarded the teachings of Christ as direct inspiration for the 'German socialism' advanced by the party. In *Mein Kampf* he repeatedly returns to the vision of himself as an Aryan Jesus come with the sword: 'Hence today I believe that I am acting in accordance with the will of the Almighty Creator: by defending myself against the Jew, I am fighting for the work of the Lord.' The Nazi movement's goal, he says, is to 'translate the ideals of Christ into deeds.' In both public and private utterances, even after his bitter disappointment in failing to unite the German confessions and his increasingly vitriolic hostility to the churches, Hitler remained adamant in this belief.[8]

> Leading Nazis appropriated Christ, not just as *a* socialist or antisemite, but as the *original* socialist and antisemite. In various ways, the Nazis . . . staked a discursive claim to represent the "true" political manifestation of Christianity. They all held that Christianity was a central aspect of their movement, shaped its direction, or in some cases even helped explain Nazism[9]

> Nor did the Nazis who proclaimed a positive attitude towards Christianity in public reveal themselves as anti-Christian in private. The documentary evidence that the Christian professions of the leading Nazis were not mere opportunism is incontestable. Goebbels and Goering continued to baptize their children and Himmler's daughter said grace before meals.

Of course, the combination of Christianity and antisemitism required the rejection of the Old Testament and the transformation of Christ into an Aryan. But this was a simple prestidigitation following the lead of antisemitic historians such as Houston Stewart Chamberlain and Hitler's Protestant theologian mentors.

> Even as they argued that race was the supreme law of life, they [the Nazis] did not argue that it overrode religion, since in their view race was God's law. Rather, they commingled racial and religious categories of the Jew and conversely used Aryan and Christian as interchangeable categories as well. In the process, they revealed that their antisemitism was far from a secular or scientific replacement for Christian forms of Jew hatred.[10]

Not only the Nazi lights and theoreticians. Senior churchmen saw in Nazism the fulfilment of a Christian social vision. To quote one representative reception of the Nazi seizure of power, one with contemporary resonance: 'Our Protestant churches have greeted the turning point of 1933 as a gift and miracle of God.'[11] In the main, the public and military agreed. Some indirect measure of the agreement can be gathered from military statistics. By 1937 the earlier good relations between the Protestant church and the Party had broken down and some Party elements (though not Goebbels, Goering or Hitler) exerted pressure on Nazi members to abandon the churches. In 1937 the make-up of the SS was 60.0% Protestant, 21.1% Catholic, and those who had already left a church, 18.7%. Despite the pressure to abandon the churches, a year later there was only an 8.6% drop among the Protestants, who joined the third category – not, it is important to note, because they abandoned God or Christ but because the church was no longer seen as embodying the message of Christ. As Steigmann-Gall says:

> We have come to realize with growing empirical certainty that many Christians of the day believed Nazism to be in some sense a Christian movement. Even in the later years of the Third Reich, as anticlerical hostility grew, churchmen of both confessions persisted in their belief that Nazism was essentially in conformity with Christian precepts.[12]

The evidence appears conclusive that the majority of Germans, including most clerics, received Nazism as an embodiment of Christianity. Indeed that fact partly explains Nazism's rapid success in winning over the nation and retaining its allegiance. It may be argued that the Germans had lost sight of True Christianity, had succumbed to a ghastly distortion of it. Whatever one makes of that, we can see that the apologetical conflation of Nazism and atheism is mistaken. The apologetical strategy ignores the religion of the people and its leaders and confuses the leadership's eventual hostility to the churches with atheism.

128 Polemic

Karen Armstrong's casual assertion that the Holocaust was 'born of modern scientific racism' is as misconceived as her association of Nazism with atheism. The assumption that scientific racism is secular ideology is in itself peculiar. Much of the physical anthropology of the 19th and early 20th centuries was very bad science, to be sure, but it was no more part of 'secular ideology' than phlogiston theory. Western racial and racist thought about innate human differences has many sources.[13] In addition to the Bible (recall the sons of Noah), the notion of polygeny; ideas about blood purity during the medieval Inquisitions; aristocratic conceptions of inborn superiority; Romantic conceptions of innate personality and genius; the racist writings of some 19th century German and French counter-Enlightenment thinkers; and many others. These fed into the racist conceptions of the 19th and early 20th-century physical anthropologists. But the most disastrous idea animating racism, that there are determinate correspondences between physical and intellectual and moral characteristics appears for the first time in the Kabbalah, and exerted from there an influence.[14] The racist conceptions that reached their apex in the 19th and early 20th centuries were welcomed by devout American legislators and European imperialists as well as the Nazis. In the Nazi mind, conceptions of race were useful, but hardly efficient causes of genocide. Hannah Arendt famously said that 'there is an abyss between the men of brilliant but facile conceptions and men of brutal deeds and active bestiality.'[15] Explanation of the Holocaust obviously requires more than the invocation of mistaken anthropology. The paranoia and existential misery induced by the grave socio-economic conditions in Germany after the First World War, internal developments within Protestant theology and Hitler's murderous megalomania and the political support of the Christian faithful are clearly important factors. But the most significant element of the deadly brew was the Jew hatred, widespread in Christian Europe, that long antedated 'scientific' racism's misconceived typologies. Festering hatred underlay the Holocaust – a hatred profoundly shaped by both Protestant and Catholic churches and, especially, Luther. Armstrong's claim that the Holocaust was born of modern scientific racism is nonsense, and scarcely an indictment of secular ideology, let alone atheism. The best that can be said of Armstrong's other assertion that in the past God had 'imposed a constraint upon what men and women could do' is that it reveals a Sunday school reading of history. Mussolini, Franco and Hitler were believing Catholics. Popes have exterminated entire peoples.

The assertion that Marxist-Leninist atheism i.e. specifically its atheism, was responsible for the gulags and mass exterminations is a more ambiguous case, but also unsupportable. It invites us to ignore the ferocious history of the Russian Empire, the politics of its multi-ethnic constituency, the fact of war and civil war, the absolute desire of the

Communists to extirpate all opposition from the former regime, not to mention the disastrous economic policies and personality of Stalin. All these things (and others) contributed to one of the great evils of the twentieth century, but none of them are predicated on the Communists' belief that their victims had made a metaphysical mistake about the existence of God.

Of course, hatred of religion is another thing, but it is not entailed by atheism. Perhaps what the apologists mean is that the Communist's *hatred of religion*, and not their atheism, explains, if not the mass deportations and exterminations (which after all were a commonplace of conquest and control in central Asian history[16]), the dispossession and persecution of the Russian Orthodox church. It is true that the revolutionaries and their successors did not hold a favourable view of the Russian Orthodox church. But the animosity was not a consequence of their atheism but, principally, the church's egregious historical role in Russia. The men who persecuted the church happened to be atheists, but they did not persecute the church *because* they were atheists: they hated the Russian Orthodox church and had good reason to. At the time of the revolutions, the church was imbricated with the state and Tsardom, as it had been for centuries, and more or less as it is now. It was immensely wealthy and had a tight grip on the peasantry and on the allegiance of many Russian intellectuals. The revolutionary leaders viewed it as an ally and instrument of the repressive, autocratic Tsarist regime, as a recalcitrant centre of political power, not to mention a bottomless well of property and gold plate. Their immediate objective was to weaken the church and education or propaganda in Marxist materialism were perceived to have an important role in that. Undoubtedly godlessness was viewed by successive Communist regimes as a desirable characteristic in the Soviet man. And many of the Party's leaders certainly were godless. But the Party's motives for the repression of clerics and religion can be better understood in light of the obstacles the church presented to a ruthless modernist state desperate to extirpate traces of the old regime and culture. That the effort to extirpate the church failed miserably is evidenced by the fact that after 80 years of Soviet communism, it sprung back vigorously, to be embraced by Vladimir Putin, and to once again become an integral part of a repressive, autocratic and brutal state.

It is a fine irony that the religious apologists' favourite examples of atheist turpitude turn around to bite them. I am certain that atheists have initiated frightful aggression. But I do not know of instances where they have done so directly in the cause of atheism or because of their atheism. It seems to me that the apologists, in one way or another, conflate opposition to one established church or another with atheism. I suspect this is the result of a degree of wishful thinking. In any case,

130 Polemic

the historical matters touched on here should admit of fairly precise determination and resolution.

A different kind of apologetical response is found in William James. Many others have followed him.

> The baiting of Jews, the hunting of the Albigenses and Waldenses, the stoning of the Quakers and ducking of Methodists, the murdering of Mormons and massacring of Armenians, express rather that aboriginal neophobia, the pugnacity of which we all share the vestiges, and the inborn hatred of the alien and of eccentric and non-conformist men as aliens, than they express the positive piety of the various perpetrators. Piety is the mask, the inner force is tribal instinct. . . . At most we may blame piety for not availing to check our natural passions, and sometimes for supplying them with hypocritical motives.[17]

James accepts that piety may be a permissive cause in failing to restrain natural but murderous passions – a failure, one might think, that goes to the heart of religion. But the true or efficacious motives, he says, are aboriginal hatred of the alien and tribal instinct: religion is merely the mask. It is not self-evident that neophobia or some other destructive tribal instincts are aboriginal or innate. There is reason to suppose the existence of congenital differences in assertiveness and aggression which are amplified (or diminished) in the course of childhood development, but these are not the same as hatred or neophobia. Let that pass. Now, there are many conflicts in which religious, political, ethnic and other enmities are compounded and they can be difficult to unravel. Clearly, there are instances where religion is *not* causative though at a superficial glance it may appear to be; religious difference may mask the true motive from the observer (greed for the other's wealth, for example) or provide, hypocritically or self-delusively, an excuse for the aggressor. And there are instances where religion is merely a permissive cause, in that had religion been causative in its restraining role, aggression would have been obviated. James seems to believe that these are the *only* ways that religion is associated with aggression. In that he is certainly mistaken. Unambiguous instances – James' own examples on reasonable interpretations – where religion is not just a permissive cause of aggression or functioning as a pretence abound. The atrocities James mentions were not done by men driven by tribal instinct, who happened to be religious, and whose religion failed to restrain them; they were done by these men because they *were* religious and their tribal instinct or neophobia was either created or magnified by religion. If they were not religious they would not have been in the business of exterminating heretics and infidels, the conceptions of which are artefacts of religion. It seems not to occur to James that religion itself can create, shape and intensify the neophobias and exclusionary tribal identities that he thinks are the causative factors.

Several other palliations for religious aggression have been offered in related terms. Other psychological mechanisms – scapegoating is a favourite – are proposed.[18] These mechanisms are supposed to be shared with non-religious expressions of aggression and therefore render aggression only a contingent feature of religion. It seems likely that as long as the connection between religion and aggression is supposed to be merely contingent apologetical ingenuity will continue to be exercised. But we have already seen reason to think that (most) religions are intrinsically aggressive, and to that possibility we turn.

An intrinsic connection

In his bestseller *God is Not Great* Christopher Hitchens sweeps through the history of religious iniquity and concludes that religion is 'violent, irrational, intolerant, allied to racism and tribalism and bigotry, invested in ignorance and hostile to free inquiry, contemptuous of women and coercive toward children.'[19] Hitchens points the finger at Islamists, Protestant fundamentalists, Sri Lankan Buddhists, Japanese Buddhists, male circumcizers, female mutilators and many others operating under the aegis of religion. However, embarrassing religion with its history and bad eggs yields limited results. The apologist will concede the tragic lapses but urge that sin is our human lot. Besides, the perpetrators (the apologist may continue) are not practising True Religion, have gone astray, misuse religion and so forth. Regarding Hitchens' inductive argument, the apologist has a point. Accumulating incriminating associations between religion and its vicious consequences does not show that there is anything specific to religion that might necessarily generate these consequences. But if there is an intrinsic connection then, sinners though we may all be, religion is not off the hook.

Hitchens' view, shared by many other militant atheists, is that religious attitudes and beliefs are products of religious education based on crude and violent foundational texts: fundamentalists subordinate women and abominate homosexuals because they have imbibed scriptures that state that women are inferior and homosexuals are abominable. But education or even indoctrination in religious texts scarcely explains why so many people are prepared to suspend their humane feelings and follow the texts to brutal extremes. To explain the origins of religion, Hitchens offers commonplaces: the need to worship, credulousness and fear: fear of the weather, the dark and so forth. Missing in his account is an awareness of the deeper motives that make sense of its tenacity, profundity and tendencies to brutality: the motives we noticed earlier: principally, the ineluctable need to maintain self-esteem through

132 Polemic

attachment to internal parental objects and their incarnations in deities and religious groups.

In Chapter 4 I outlined the elements of a developmental process focusing on distortions of narcissism, particularly certain pathological means of regulating self-esteem. I will reprise a few steps of the process in broad strokes and then illustrate the interdependencies between narcissistic need and religious expression. Many psychological and environmental factors are intertwined with the developmental line of narcissism, but these, together with important biological and sociological dimensions of aggression, must be left aside. This omission certainly leads to a degree of oversimplification but I hope it is not fatal. I will scarcely touch on the extreme paranoid-schizoid end of the aggression spectrum manifested in some contemporary terrorism and the apocalyptic mindsets peculiar to certain religious sects or confessions. These things are intricated with narcissism, often malignant narcissism, but in especially convoluted ways.[20] However, the less dramatic cases of religious fanaticism and fundamentalism also offer much of interest. The chapter concludes on the note of its beginning: aggression is intrinsic to most religion because narcissism is intrinsic to it.

The religious induction of children usually commences early in life when the real and the imaginary are merged and the first mental representations of parents are being constructed. As ideas about supernatural figures are introduced to the talking child they merge with representations of parental figures and experienced in the inner world as 'real'; as other fictions and creatures of make-believe often are at this stage. Stories about their omnipotence and omniscience fit perfectly the child's exalted perceptions of parents, their own wishful phantasies and experiences of quasi-omnipotence. The omnipotence and benevolence of divine figures are particularly appealing because children want to live in a benevolent world, to love and to feel loved, and have their own narcissistic sense of omnipotence confirmed. To feel oneself at one with, or to bask in the radiance of, a powerful supernatural figure heightens self-regard and self-esteem. Relationships with benevolent supernatural figures can be particularly important when actual conditions of care are adverse; they can comfort and may resonate throughout life. But when parental figures are especially punitive or remote the divine figures are also likely to be experienced as punitive and remote. Stern religious teaching often enjoins crushing a child's natural (infantile) narcissism. It may be surrendered, but usually on condition that it can be indirectly restored by identification with an idealized parental or divine figure. If the rod is used, if parents are cold, then representations of self, parents and divine figures are likely to be coloured by pain and rage. In this atmosphere, children may still cling to the supernatural substitutes they have idealized as containers of their narcissism, or identify with them, but it will be to divine figures idealized for their aggression and

Aggression in religion **133**

destructiveness. The child manages to idealize attachment figures usually by splitting their representations into all good and all bad. She will attempt relationships only with the good aspects of objects and eliminate the bad, either by projection or, conversely, by introjection (swallowing it.) But if good objects are not sufficiently available then she will have to deal with the bad, and the strategies for dealing with bad objects come at a cost. Where projection dominates, a satanic external world is constructed, increasing paranoid anxieties. Introjection leads to phantasies of harbouring bad objects within and, ultimately, identifying with them, generating conceptions of oneself as secretly omnipotent but also as sinful and destructive. The strategies sustain a sense of security and the illusion of power but they are precarious. Since these object relations are intricated with religious objects, censure or depreciation of religion may threaten the entire defensive edifice on which self-esteem rests. Criticism threatens to unpick the links and release the terrible images of bad parental objects, self and divinity. Even when religious ideas have been abandoned or introduced only later in life, hard experiences may regressively reactivate the longing for lost idealized objects and attach or reattach them to religious objects.

Some examples may illustrate the aspects of narcissistic development described above. The psychoanalyst Otto Kernberg describes the worst-case scenario when the malignant narcissist, in whom narcissism and paranoia combine with the idealization of aggression, attains positions of power.

> The leader characterized by malignant narcissism experiences and expresses an inordinate grandiosity, needs to be loved, admired, feared and submitted to at the same time, cannot accept submission from others except when it is accompanied by an intense idealizing loyalty and abandonment of all independent judgment, and experiences any manifestation contrary to his wishes as a sadistic, wilful, grave attack against himself. Such leadership cannot but bring about a regime of terror, and an entourage that combines totally subservient, idolizing subjects, with totally corrupt and ruthless antisocial characters whose pretence of loving and submitting to the leader permits their parasitic enjoyment of his power.[21]

Adolf Hitler is, of course, the prime example of malignant narcissism, a man who identifies with idealized, omnipotent bad objects, living in a fearful paranoid world. He is the omnipotent Aryan Christ come with sword to purge the world of Jews:

> My feeling as a Christian points me to my Lord and Saviour as a fighter. It points me to the man who once in loneliness, surrounded by a few followers, recognised these Jews for what they were and

134 Polemic

summoned men to fight against them and who, God's truth! was greatest not as a sufferer but as a fighter. In boundless love as a Christian and as a man I read through the passage which tells how the Lord at last rose in His might and seized the scourge to drive out of the Temple[22]

No American president quite belongs in this camp but a number of them are notable for heedless destruction palliated by their Christianity. In 2003, G.W. Bush told Mahmoud Abbas that God told him to invade Iraq.

I'm driven with a mission from God. God would tell me, "George, go and fight those terrorists in Afghanistan." And I did, and then God would tell me: "George go and end the tyranny in Iraq," and I did.

And "now again," Bush said, "I feel God's words coming to me: "Go get the Palestinians their state and get the Israelis their security, and get peace in the Middle East." And by God, I'm gonna do it.[23]

It is hard to know whether Bush believed what he was saying. The idiom of God hovering, conversing with televangelists and pastors, is common to Bush's evangelical constituency. But the conviction and remorselessness in prosecuting his wars suggests at least a transient identification with God. Whatever we make of that – and Bush has since displayed decency and sanity – it is notable that in those dark times Bush was able to publicly express thoughts that are clearly deranged. In ancient Greece, gods only spoke to men in their dreams. Nevertheless, Aristotle remarked, if the gods wanted to speak to men they would choose the recipients more carefully.

The former president Donald Trump is not quite so high on God's contact list, though he appears to have had a conversation with the Almighty at least once, according to his spiritual advisers. Trump is improbable as God's anointed though large numbers of his Christian followers appear to believe it.[24] Kernberg's description of malignant narcissism fits him like a glove. He has not (yet) had the opportunity for large-scale material destruction but his injection into American society of louring violence, debased discourse and hatred of truth may yet fragment it irreparably. That his undisguised immorality, grandiosity and shamelessness give shape and purpose to his Christian constituency appears paradoxical, but only on the face of it. The white Christian nationalism he opportunistically champions is unconnected to love of country; it is founded on the illusion that his supporters own it. They were once the chosen, the light on the hill, but have since been dispossessed. Now they must make America great again and resume their rightful place of superiority at its head. It is a narcissistic illusion. Also conspicuous in

Aggression in religion **135**

the Trumpian fold is the envy and resentment directed at the educated coastal elites and the ascending immigrant classes; this latter phenomenon is known as downward envy. The indignation felt by many of his followers over distributive injustice and the sense that they are objects of condescension is not entirely unjustified, although it may be that some of that indignation is, in substance, wounded narcissism. But underlying the flurry of these emotions, some rationally fitted to their cause, some not, is unconscious envious hatred of creativity and intelligence – traits supposedly possessed by the elites that are consuming objects of envy. Trump embodies these blinding hatreds and provides what his crowds revel in: absolution from the need to think, rendered unnecessary by grandiosity and omniscience, and, ultimately, hatred of thought itself.[25]

The most common forms of religious aggression and assertion are exerted not by the lonely sociopath but by the religious group. In the individual's endeavour to retrieve lost narcissism the religious group is idealized and the grandiosity conferred on it is re-claimed through identification. The religious group then unconsciously represents the idealized parental and divine figures of childhood and aspects of the ideal self. Belonging to the idealized group is gratifying. If the group you belong to is special, you must be special: you belong to an exclusive church or religion, you are one of the Elect, you possess the Truth, every triumph of your religion is your triumph; you are secure in the embrace of God and in possession of your ideal self. This is a pleasing state of affairs with a dark shadow. Becoming a member of the Elect is an exclusionary process: being special means being one of the Few, not of the Many. But at the same time the Many, who are different, threaten the narcissist who requires the world to mirror them. The intolerance of difference generates a compulsion to force others to think and act as they do. So, proselytizing or converting others to their religion is doubly rewarding. Consciously, there is the knowledge of bestowing grace upon another; unconsciously, there is the pleasure of stripping converts of their identity, aggressively incorporating them into the group and erasing troubling differences. The process confirms religious faith, nourishes grandiose self-conceptions by testifying to its power and eliminates challenges to it. At bottom, conversion means: everyone must worship at *their* Idol, everyone must worship *them*. If conversion fails there is the option of elimination to which fanatical groups are often disposed. In milder times and milder religions, the thought that non-believers are consigned to hell may provide sufficient gratification.

Religious aggression is often defensively reactive to the instability of identifications underlying religious faith and the insistent intrusion of reality. Religious people often fear, inwardly, that religion, or much of it, is a house of cards. Faith, as Mark Twain's schoolboy said, is believing what you know ain't so. Many episodes in the social history of religion

136 Polemic

comprise more or less violent attempts by the faithful to shore up their faith against other faiths, heretics and self-doubt. Religious communities are often support groups for self-deception. Those who do not share the faith threaten it and must be converted, segregated or eliminated. Even small differences become major threats to those who require the world to narcissistically mirror them. It is frequently observed that sects of Christians have been more persecuted by other sects of Christians than by non-Christians, and Muslims by other Muslims, and Jews by nearly everyone. But as we saw, deviations other than the heretical are also felt to be intolerable. In the Christian dispensation of 2000 years, it is only recently that atheism, blasphemy, homosexuality, even mental illness and eccentricity, have not been religiously proscribed and punished.[26] There are still many places under religious influence where nonconformists are executed, and it is evident that there are many religious folk who believe that they should be. The idea that people should be killed for holding errant religious beliefs deemed a threat to the faithful is, I believe, an entirely Abrahamic innovation. Of some of those who hold false doctrines, Moses Maimonides wrote, 'under certain circumstances it may be necessary to slay them, and to extirpate their doctrines, in order that others should not be misled.'[27]

The narcissistic motivations underlying the religious phenomena we are examining find non-religious expressions; and, as noted earlier, there are other important non-narcissistic motivations at play in religious phenomenology.[28] Certainly, other activities and non-religious group identities can serve as vehicles for the satisfaction of thwarted and distorted narcissistic needs: membership of a supposedly superior race or football club, for example. But it does not follow that all ideologies or groups are equally amenable as instruments of narcissistic aggression. Religions, as we noted, are particularly fitted because their key ideological conceptions – commerce with a supreme being, membership of an Elect, moral rectitude, incorrigible knowledge – imbricated with early parental representations create or augment, and then feed, pathologically narcissistic trends. Perhaps only racial ideologies can compare with religions in providing the exceptionally conducive frameworks for organizing individual and group aggression.

I want briefly to mention two other expressions of religious aggression. The sexual abuse of children is of course not restricted to religious orders but appears to be unusually common in some of them, the Catholic church most notoriously. Abuse by Catholic priests has been studied intensively from a psychoanalytic perspective so quite a good psychodynamic understanding of it has evolved. Mary Gail Frawley-O'Dea has shown how both Catholic church doctrine and organization, especially in the training institutions, are causally implicated in the character malformations that are likely to lead to child sexual abuse.[29] I lightly sketch

Aggression in religion **137**

some of the key elements of her account. The church is a hierarchical and authoritarian institution that organizes relationships along the lines of dominance and submission. The aspirant who wants to get ahead knows that he has to submit to his father-bishop and mother-church. That structure of dominance encourages sado-masochistic modes of relating and, of course, attracts people with such needs in the first place. It is likely to stimulate rage and cruelty in one direction, combined with submissive, inhibited attitudes in another. 'Kiss up, kick down' is the expression used to describe this animus in many organizations. In recreating structures of dependency the institutions are infantilizing and induce regression. As a result of these factors, in episodes of sexual abuse, the assailant's feeling of powerlessness in relation to the seemingly omnipotent and aggressive parental representatives (bishops and church) is violently reversed in an unconscious attempt to identify with the omnipotent aggressor, while projecting his own powerlessness onto the child-victim – who represents his own powerless child self. These factors are reinforced by church teaching valorizing suffering and are therefore likely to induce indifference to the victim's suffering. That is the basic and common dynamic. Of course, it is not all. The sexual restrictions imposed by the faith, inherently emasculating, humiliating and frustrating, impacting people who are already likely to be suffering some degree of personality disorder, is an important element in instigating this form of abuse. Sexual desire, frustrated in every direction, is a potent drive. But it is important to see that the motivation in at least many of these cases is primarily aggressive and despoiling, not sexual: the offenders are without restraint sadistically seeking to sustain their self-esteem or narcissistic integrity in religious institutions, in the context of oppressive religious ideology.

Turning to education. Some of the most influential pedagogues in evangelical circles recommend beatings to break a child's will. They cater to a receptive, and perhaps growing, constituency. The psychologist and evangelist James C. Dobson's books *Dare to Discipline* and *The New Strong-Willed Child* are still bestsellers. The motivating idea is to convince the disobedient child that they are being beaten out of love and from parental obedience to God's will. The aftermath of tears is supposed to provide an opportunity for parent and child to come together in recognition of the parent's love and service to God. Indeed, the Bible is not deficient in references to sword and rod. We have seen that these Biblically endorsed punishments are likely to create in the child's mind an image of a cruel and unsparing God and an apocalyptic mindset. Religious folk who have endured and advocate harsh physical punishment tend to be intensely apocalyptic.[30] For a child an impending beating looms as a catastrophe, the end of the world. And, of course, where punishment and the affectation of parental love coalesce, children are

138 Polemic

more likely to repeat offences. The cycle of sin and punishment is kept in motion. The Biblical justification merges with religiously induced parental sadism in a cycle that continues through generations.

Donald Capps, a professor of Pastoral Theology, argues that religion is 'inherently disposed toward the abuse of children' because it provides theological legitimation for their punishment and promotes ideas and beliefs that are 'inherently tormenting to children.'[31] The doctrine of hell and eternal punishment, the aversive attitudes towards natural sexual feeling, and the breaches between friends occasioned by religious segregation, cause pain and torment in a child. These assaults on children's emotional integrity make them think abjectly of themselves. Capps goes further to frame an important hypothesis. Punishment and emotional abuse operate traumatically, he argues, in much the same way as childhood sexual abuse. Consequent to such trauma there is (i) repression of the traumatic experience which leads to the dissociation of part of the self which is intricated in the experience; (ii) a withdrawal of feeling or affect; (iii) a loss of confidence in the victims own judgement; and (iv) in some victims, ideas linked to the trauma 'get split off from the rest of their thought processes and are not incorporated into them.'[32] So it is, Capps observes, that intelligent religious people who can think independently and well about politics, science, art and mundane matters become unexpectedly bland, uncritical and deferential about religion.

To speak of religion, as I have been doing, as if it were some kind of personal agent, is to speak abstractly but economically. I have tried in this chapter to sketch the ways in which people whose narcissistic development is to a degree distorted and regulated by religion are typically prone to aggression and group assertion. Religion is intrinsically aggressive because repressed infantile and pathological narcissism are intrinsically aggressive. In the fanatic who (in my usage of the term) suffers from a severe narcissistic character disorder aggression and envy are not merely reactive, they search for objects to destroy or despoil. However, as I said above, the circle of orectic derangement in religion spreads widely, and aggression obviously is not restricted to the religious fanatic.

From the perspective of many religious people, and especially the fanatics, the world looks different. They are not the oppressors, they are the oppressed. They affirm, and perhaps believe, that their only wish is to make their way of life safe for themselves and for their children to continue their religious traditions. It is frequently observed that religious conservatives across the spectrum see themselves as besieged by secular modernity; they feel that their very existence is under threat and therefore react aggressively to defend themselves. I do not believe that this is in fact a major motivation. It is evident, and may be evident even to the educated fanatic, that in pluralistic dispensations secular states ensuring freedom of worship for all offer the best prospects for the survival of all

Aggression in religion **139**

religious groups. The threat fanatics and fundamentalists feel is not from secularization, nor indeed from other religions. The threat they sense is not to their survival but to the primacy and dominance of *their* religion, on which their self-esteem precariously hangs. The Islamists who insist on a world dispensation dominated by Islam, the Christian nationalists who insist on rescuing a Christian nation, and the ultranationalist Jewish supremacists appropriating Palestinian land, are concerned not so much about the preservation of their religion as that of its primacy. Everyone must recognize the primacy of their religion – and hence of them – the upshot of thwarted grandiosity. In their view, there must be 'one people under God' because difference in the narcissist's mind is persecutory. If they are opposed and persecuted – fanatics always feel opposed and persecuted – that just shows all the more how special they are.

The idea that one can only be a devout Christian, Muslim, Jew, Hindu or Buddhist in a devout society of your co-religionists is now animating the political programmes of many national governments and factions within nations. Violence is increasingly seen by fanatics as a legitimate means of achieving the necessary purifications. Democratic conceptions of political power and law are being challenged, and a regressively puritanical influence is exerted on morality, on sexual morality in particular. Religion is once again corroding canons of rationality, progressively refined since the birth of philosophy, in order to accommodate faith and superstition. The worst may have occurred in the past, but there are reasons to fear that the worst may be returning. An assault on cultural and religious pluralism and the tolerance associated with secular values is underway.

Notes

1 Perhaps this view of the non-Abrahamic world is too sunny. There appear to have been inter-religious massacres by various central Asian groups, including by Buddhists and pagan Mongols, at least by the second millennium CE. Whether these were at heart ethnically or territorially based is unclear. See Beckwith 2009, Chapter 7. The contemporary violence of Buddhist nationalists in Sri Lanka and Myanmar throws a question mark over the pacific character of this religion.

2 In *The God Delusion* Dawkins reports an experiment conducted by Israeli psychologist George Tamarin (Dawkins 2006, Chapter 7). Tamarin presented to over a thousand Israeli schoolchildren, aged between eight and 14, the account of the battle of Jericho and subsequent massacre in the book of Joshua. They were asked: 'Do you think Joshua and the Israelites acted rightly or not.' Sixty-six percent gave total approval and 26% total disapproval. In every case of approval, the justification for genocidal massacre was religious. For

example: 'In my opinion Joshua was right when he did it, one reason being that God commanded him to exterminate the people so that the tribes of Israel will not be able to assimilate amongst them and learn their bad ways.' The children were naturally expressing views heard from their parents or learned at school. Dawkins is right in concluding that the experiment shows 'the immense power of religion, and especially the religious upbringing of children, to divide people and foster historic enmities and hereditary vendettas.'

3 Armstrong 2001, 201.

4 Plantinga 2011, x. Others taking this line: Johnston 2009, 160, and the tireless McGrath 2004, 232ff.

5 Taylor 2007, 687.

6 (Streigmann-Gall 2004, 15). This matter is of course controversial. In my opinion the Christian apologists consistently confuse hostility to the Christian churches with atheism.

7 An authority sympathetic to religion writes: 'Heinrich Himmler and other formulators of Nazi ideology relied on a mixture of quasi-religious images and ideas, including symbols associated with the Knights Templar; nature worship from the German Volk movement of the 1920's; the notions of Aryan superiority from, among others, the Theosophists; and a fascination with the occult from a particular strand of German Catholic mysticism' (Juergensmeyer 2008, 168).

8 The quotations in this paragraph are, from Steigmann-Gall 2004, in order, 18, 46, 36, 27.

9 Steigmann-Gall 2004, 49.

10 Steigmann-Gall 2004, 29.

11 Heinrich Rendtorrf, Landesbischof of Mecklenburg, quoted in Steigmann-Gall 2004, 49.

12 Steigmann-Gall 2004, 5.

13 For a brief discussion, Pataki 2004b.

14 Hannaford 1996, 36.

15 Arendt 1976, 183.

16 Beckwith 2011.

17 James 1971, 331.

18 Notably by Rene Girard and Charles Taylor in several works.

19 Hitchens 2007, 56.

20 Most psychoanalytic discussions stress the role of humiliation, powerlessness, rage, and the splitting of self and object world and consequent paranoia, as essential to the violent fundamentalist (fanatical) mindset (Kernberg 2003; Terman 2010). This seems to be correct. But it should be noted that the susceptibility to humiliation is to some extent a function of the narcissistic self-idealization and grandiosity that is already in place *before* the triggering humiliating episodes. In this book I have focused on the conditions that lead to pathological narcissistic states. Susceptibility to humiliation and offense appear to be more prevalent in religious groups than in any other assembly of humankind. There are now numerous studies of Islamic and Christian right terrorism. Post 2007 and Juergensmeyer

2008 are balanced conspectuses that have survived the test of time. Amongst important psychoanalytic work in this area: Kohut 1978; Jones 2002; Kernberg 2003, 2022; Strozier et al. 2010.

21 Kernberg 2003, 692. Fromm 1973 is an important and prescient discussion of Hitler's psychopathology.

22 Cited in Dawkins 2006, 275.

23 Rupert Cornwell 'Bush: God Told Me to Invade Iraq' *The Guardian* October 6, 2005.

24 In 2016 and 2020 over 80% of white evangelicals voted for Trump. He is the televangelist President, a prosperity preacher whose rallies are modeled on tent revivals. An unlikely instrument of God but, according to James Dobson, Paula White, his spiritual adviser, led Trump to Christ. She declared: 'I can tell you with confidence that I have heard Mr. Trump verbally acknowledge his faith in Jesus Christ for the forgiveness of his sins through prayer' (quoted in Posner 2021, 25). The fact that Trump vanquished Hilary Clinton, a demon, is proof to many followers that a supernatural force must be backing him. His rise, after all, was prophesied in the Bible (Posner 2021, Chapter 2).

25 Trump's principal object of envy appears to be his predecessor, President Obama, who is intelligent, educated, urbane, articulate, reserved – things Trump conspicuously is not. Trump's animus, like that of other mob leaders, is to devalue and render things ugly. On the hatred of thought see Chapter 8.

26 On the treatment of the mentally ill under Christian dispensation see Robinson 1996.

27 Cited in Hannaford 1996, 112.

28 I also leave aside the particular modes in which religious assertion and aggression are expressed. People attracted to religion for various characterological reasons are likely to express forms of aggression specific to their character type. For example, the obsessional will be most concerned with purifying and purging; the hysterical with segregating and humiliating; the narcissistic with eliminating or absorbing. Religions structure the ideology and institutions necessary to satisfy these characterological needs. See Young Bruehl 1996.

29 Frawley-O'Dea 2007.

30 Jones 2002, 2010; Strozier 2010.

31 Capps 1995, xi. Richard Dawkins agrees. He cites the telling case of Pastor Robert's hell-houses which contain terrifying representations of infernal punishments designed to deter 12-year-olds from sin. Dawkins 2006, 320. I agree with Capps and Dawkins that religious education can be tantamount to child abuse.

32 Capps 1995, 52–53.

Chapter 8

Reason and religion

Reprise

I have been tracing some of the relations between the character of the religious fanatic, the features of the religions in which that character finds expression, and certain unconscious wishes, dispositions and phantasies, mostly of a malign narcissistic order. The focus on the narcissistic components of religiosity, and the somewhat artificial construction of the 'religious fanatic,' were partly intended to narrow the discussion to manageable proportions. Religions, I have emphasized, are complex, many and diverse, as are the degrees of commitment or profession to any one of them. Narcissism, the libidinal relation to the self frequently expressed in the dramatic confrontation of grandiosity and humility, does not exhaust the psychology of religion. But narcissistic concerns in religion, from the earliest attempts to regulate safety and self-esteem by identifying with powerful spirits to more recent endeavours to live according to moral norms sanctified by an all-powerful God, to live within the orbit of such a being, certainly are central. I contend that the maintenance of the narcissistic economy is a fundamental motive to religious commitment. I have remarked too, in several places, on the current drift in religions to those early primitive relations to spirits where they are once again animating the most vigorous of them today; worshippers hunger for enthusiasm, to be possessed by the Holy Spirit (or some such), or seek mystical or spiritual communion; just as bad spirits or demons responsible for disease and misfortune are cast out by modern day shamans.

It may be that the threads of theory I have been using to stitch unconscious motivational states to religious beliefs and attitudes are in fact frangible compared to, for example, social or evidential considerations motivating religious belief. Or perhaps a vague but still genuine yearning for meaning, wholeness or for the infinite is the thing that motivates most religious people. I doubt it, and shall return to this. My insistence on the less exalted psychological connections derives largely from four

DOI: 10.4324/9781315519814-11

sources: first, a conviction of the unparalleled significance of early dependent interpersonal or object relationships, and the human tendency to reconstitute these relationships symbolically in every department of later life, particularly when those early relationships were poor; second, an evident homology between certain unconscious wishes and phantasies and religious beliefs and practices; third, the naturalistic implications of the anthropology of religion, cast over a wide arc; and fourth, the illumination and order that the psychological perspective brings to the strangeness of religion.[1]

The subordination of reason

Of course, even if my motivational story is true, it doesn't follow that religious beliefs about spirits and so forth are false. There may be sound arguments or compelling evidence for the truth of religious beliefs, as well as strong unconscious motives for it. On the other hand, even if there are such compelling arguments and evidence, it doesn't directly follow that they have an influence on the majority of the religious because rational grounds in fact play no, or little, part in the motivation to religion. And even if religious claims about deity and so forth are true, much of the present critique highlighting religion's baleful psychological and social consequences would still apply. Our interest here is in the reasons (the underlying motives), often very different from the avowed reasons, for which the vast majority of religious people *do* believe, and I contend that those reasons have little connection with rational argument or evidence. To those who deny this I would say: look around you, consider the statistics on the global distribution of religious profession: it is not in the wealthier, educated, advanced parts of the world that religion is on the rise. It may not be irrational for a person to believe religious propositions about the existence of gods, an afterlife, the morality they live by and so forth, even if they cannot prove them but believe that there are experts who can.[2] But it does seem to me irrational, on matters of such grave import, not to want to test the evidence or the experts, or to settle into an intelligent scepticism. In fact, very few religious people bother with all that.

Then again, there are people who care not a whit for evidence or reasons as these are ordinarily understood; they have subtle reasons of the heart or overwhelming experiences of the divine. Not much can be said to them because an argument consisting of mere words is hardly likely to overturn such convictions.[3] Perhaps the only advice one can give them is to submit the reasons of the heart to the reasons of the head, as they hopefully do in the conduct of their ordinary affairs. Blaise Pascal, to whom we owe the phrase 'the reasons of the heart,' also famously said that 'the last proceeding of reason is to recognise that there

144 Polemic

are an infinity of things beyond it.' That may well be true, but it doesn't follow that what reason can't deliver something else can. Yearning for contact with infinity or embracing mystery are not strategies for knowing anything, in any meaningful sense. Somewhat connected to these views is another, expounded at very great length by Charles Taylor, that compels sympathy.[4] The heart of Taylor's book is that transcendence, which involves some kind of relation to God, is required for 'purposes of ultimate explanation or spiritual transformation or final sense-making.' One of the alleged devils in secularism, as he sees it, is the affliction of aimlessness, the 'loss of meaning': 'everyone understands the complaint that our disenchanted world lacks meaning. . . . You couldn't even have explained the problem in Luther's age.' I think that you probably could have, though the despair and futility felt by many in our age may have to be translated into the callousness of his. Taylor is throughout astonishingly blind to psychological connections and transformations. He perfunctorily links the malaise of meaninglessness to the eclipse of transcendence or religious belief, though the undermining of children early in life and the recession of love and belonging induced by rapid socio-economic transformation, seem better explanations. Yet it is true, as Taylor says, that there is a desire in human beings 'to gather the scattered moments of meaning into some kind of whole'; a longing for 'goals which could engage us more fully and deeply than our ordinary ends'; a sense 'that somewhere there is a fullness or richness which transcends the ordinary.' Taylor condemns exclusive humanism because it 'closes the transcendent window, as though there were nothing beyond. More, as though it weren't an irrepressible need of the human heart to open the window, and first look, then go beyond.' It is difficult to disagree about the human need for meaning, but what next? To face the abyss, close one's eyes, and then pretend that one has leapt over it? We have many irrepressible needs and it would be a delicious world if merely wishing satisfied them.

There are those, like Calvin and Plantinga, who believe that God has implanted in us a *sensus divinitatis*, a natural tendency to form belief in God and, presumably, many propositions about God.[5] If such a tendency was implanted in humans then it was cruel to do it so late and haphazardly. I don't believe that anyone with a smattering of anthropology could begin to take such a proposition seriously. Celsus (and perhaps Dante) wondered why, if following Jesus was a condition of salvation, he should not have come earlier to save countless good pagans from perdition. And then there is *faith* as a source of knowledge, of the existence of the divine, in propositions emanating from the divine, or as a precondition of knowledge about the divine. It is pointless here to add to the oceans of ink.

Reason and religion **145**

I have had to brush over these non-cognitive sources of knowledge knowing that many people, including philosophers, have found some of them compelling. But here the focus is on examining some of the unconscious factors that may underlie at least some of the expectations of them. I think we shall come to suspect that they are neither alternatives nor supplementary to reason; they are assaults on it.

If I now make a few brief remarks on the history of religion that is once again because its history throws light on the present. Since the advent of monotheism, with its claims to exclusive revealed truth and intrinsic intolerance of difference, reason has been a problem for religion and religion for reason. It has been asked why philosophy originated in ancient Greece. Walter Burkert's answer is surely correct: it was because of the weakness of religious organization there: 'no kings, no powerful priests, and no houses of tablets, which meant more mobility, more freedom, and more risk for mind and letters.'[6] Subsequently, in the Christian world, the debility or confinement of religious influence becomes the precondition for intellectual progress in the making of Western civilization. The long period of Christian totalitarianism was a time of intellectual stagnation, a few bright lights amidst much darkness.[7] Christianity crushed most of ancient thought and the benign religious and intellectual tolerance of the Graeco-Roman world. By the third century, original pagan thought was already struggling, but it took the authority of the Christian emperors and the influence of the church to cripple it. Progress in mathematics, physics, biology, medicine, astronomy, historiography, geography, philosophy, literature, theatre and political thought came largely to a halt. It is true that Christianity preserved some philosophy of service to it and, eventually, after the passage of many centuries, some thinkers became avid for the treasures of the ancients and the achievements of the Arabic philosophers and scientists. But its prolonged attitude to such learning can be characterized by Origen's pacific letter in the early third century:

> I would wish that you draw from Greek philosophy too such things as are fit, as it were, to serve as general or preparatory studies for Christianity, and from geometry and astronomy such things as may be useful for the interpretation of Holy Scriptures.[8]

A handful of Christian philosophers did make use of available materials from the Greek philosophers and scientists, but developed them only so far as they weren't led to conflict with scripture. Proving the existence of God and reconciling the divine properties with the natural world stimulate metaphysical ingenuity. The achievements of Duns Scotus, Thomas Aquinas and later Schoolmen in metaphysics and logic

146 Polemic

especially are considerable. But these achievements must be placed in context. Compared to what there was before and what came after, Late Antiquity and the Middle Ages provided little of intellectual substance or emotional depth. Some contemporary scholars point to achievements in administration and the arts, especially in the Eastern Empire; some argue that the growing interest in nature after the 13th century were developments internal to Christianity and not forced upon it; and there are those who place high value on the theological refinements of the period.[9] Here I can only submit my own attitudes to such claims. I cannot see the theology as anything but phantasies, for reasons that are touched on in this book. The idea that later interest in natural philosophy was a development internal to Christian curiosity seems to me a gross misreading of the history of ideas. Several recent revisionary works, mostly sponsored by a wealthy foundation, have argued for the essential amity between science and religion and the positive role of Christianity in stimulating scientific thought. I think this is nonsense on stilts. There is a simple rejoinder: very well, tell us of all the magnificent mathematical and scientific achievements in the Christian world from the 4th century to, say, the 15th. Such a story would not long detain us. The apologists who point to the sincere religious belief of several of the great scientists of the 17th and 18th centuries – by which time of course the stranglehold of the churches had been loosened by the Reformation and wars of religion – don't understand what problems in mathematics and physics are: they have an internal logic and development which grip the sighted and the blind alike. In relation to the arts, it is undeniable that these periods produced objects of great beauty and architectural grandeur. But for my part I am repelled by the arts' stultifying lack of interest in nature and the human form; those admired mosaic and iconic expressions of grave piety and spirituality have for me the tincture of self-delusion and hypocrisy. Nietzsche was right to say that Christianity robbed us of the fruits of the ancient world.

Why did that happen? The causes have been discussed from many angles and here I can consider only those directly relevant to this inquiry. These have to do with issues intrinsic to monotheist ideology and the narcissism intrinsic to it. They subtend from the monotheistic conception of revealed religion as the sole owner of all Truth that matters; its intolerance of divergence; and its anxious doctrine that our mundane existence is but a brief stopover to another place. These beliefs and attitudes lead to a devastating loss of interest in loving and probing the natural world. They are among the seeds that made monotheistic religions grow hostile to reason, though they are not the only ones.

We have already discussed monotheistic intolerance. The fear of heresy, apostasy and infidelity haunted the world of Late Antiquity and for more than a thousand years afterwards. First ecclesiastical condemnation

Reason and religion   147

of heretical propositions, books and authors, and then the burning of books and authors became institutionalized. In 1415 the Council of Constance burnt Jan Hus and condemned precisely 260 propositions attributed to John Wycliff, the most distinguished philosopher of the previous age. Wycliff was long dead by the time of the Council so his body was exhumed and burnt.[10] Such examples are familiar and this one must serve for many. They should be recalled for their resonance with our times, when books affronting religious sensibilities are being banned, and blasphemers and heretics are executed, in places where fanatics and fundamentalists have political clout.

The indifference to the natural world is typified by Augustine whose authority and influence were enormous. Augustine keenly desires knowledge of himself and God but, fettered to scripture, recoiling from his youthful homosexuality, he cannot see himself as part of the natural world. He loses interest in it. The Christian, he says, can remain ignorant of the number of the elements, of the heavenly bodies and the nature of animals, shrubs and stones. It is enough for the Christian to believe that the cause of all created things is God.[11] Augustine was a great introspective philosopher. It escaped him altogether that to know the self – or God – one must know the world. To know the world one must probe it.

The famous passage from Tertullian captures the overall tendency of this period, if not always the mettle of its best thinkers.

> What then has Athens to do with Jerusalem, the Academy with the Church, the heretic with the Christian? Our instruction comes from the porch of Solomon who himself taught us that the Lord is to be sought in the simplicity of one's heart. . . . We have no need of curiosity after Jesus Christ, nor of research after the gospel. When we believe, we desire to believe nothing more. For we believe this first, that there is nothing else that we should believe.[12]

Tertullian did not altogether forsake reasoning and Greek philosophy but evinced hatred for them. Reason is proud, presumptuous and oversteps its limits; it seduces the unwary away from religion. More than a millennium later Luther says that reason is a whore, the greatest enemy that faith faces. 'Whoever wants to be a Christian should tear the eyes out of his reason.' The schools of religious fanatics and fundamentalists today are conducted along this principle if not quite with the implicit savagery. In Chapter 5 we saw the principle operating in New York Yeshivas: science must be given credence but 'when push finally comes to shove and *madda* [secular learning] threatens inalienable Torah beliefs . . . which resist any modification and reinterpretation' then Torah must be given priority.[13] It is the same in the religious schools of the Islamic

148 Polemic

world and very probably in the homeschooling of American evangelicals. Even in an economically advanced and supposedly educated nation such as the United States the influence of religion has created distrust and animosity towards science and expertise, to education itself. The statistics vary, but currently somewhere over half the population believe that God created humans in their present form, support the teaching of Creationism, and believe that college education is bad for the nation. The fierce depths of this ignorance were on show recently in anti-Covid vaccination protests. Placards carried by enraged people blared: 'I don't need your science, I have my God (or, alternatively, Jesus).'

Narcissistic wounds

There is a direct line from Tertullian to the anti-intellectualism and crude fideism of today. But the attitudes have not only persisted they have recently been invigorated. One reason for the invigoration is that religion across its full spectrum has suffered a number of narcissistic wounds. Recall that a major function of religion, one that was once at its very centre, is explanation, prediction and control (EPC). Until about the middle of the 19th century, Genesis was still, in the West, considered the definitive account of the origins of the universe and humanity, while much of the rest of the Bible was considered the fount of morality, and provided a basic psychology. Although the fanatics and some philosophers are holding out, the claims of religion to provide explanatory accounts of such matters have been largely shattered.[14] Religion, and the people who identify themselves with their religion, have been thus marginalized – an unhappy outcome for the self-esteem of the religious. It is not so much that science is seen as having won the competition with religion, though there certainly was and is such a competition.[15] It is that, at least among most of the educated, much of religious doctrine is seen to compete with commonsense; though to be sure, some among that class choose deliberately to abandon commonsense in this instance and embrace mystery as if it were knowledge. There is nothing wrong with embracing mystery and acknowledging ignorance; there is everything wrong with supposing that mystery is some kind of knowledge.[16]

It is true that theories in physics, cosmology, psychology, genetics and so forth are incomplete, uncertain, often contested and difficult. At the cutting edge of science, all is tentative, everything is open to correction. It doesn't follow, of course, as some philosophers have suggested, that we should therefore opt for religious explanations where science falls short.[17] What we don't know, we don't know, and may never know. That uncertainty, however, is only a problem for the person who has a religious conception of knowledge as inerrant, and a religious *need* to know that must leap eventually into unquestioning faith. The fanatic

Reason and religion 149

suffering orectic derangement can allow no uncertainty and so becomes obtuse and insistent. An admission that their core religious beliefs may be wrong would subvert the very purpose of their faith. They cannot live with uncertainty, and the idea that their sustaining religious beliefs are at the mercy of evidence is offensive and wounding to them.

We have seen in earlier chapters why this is so. The need for certainty, for a kind of omniscience, is animated by the necessity of maintaining secure contact with a powerful attachment figure, either by identifying with it or by living in its orbit. The drivers to security are fundamentally attachment and narcissistic needs. In certain circumstances the needs create the illusion of knowledge, not indeed of everything but of all the things that matter for security and self-esteem. Most people are curious about 'final' things, about gods, their place in creation, the purpose of life, an afterlife, whether they are watched over and loved by the creator. The fanatic forecloses that curiosity. For him, *not knowing* is intolerable; it would be like being abandoned by his most important love objects. Poor reason, however, in everyday affairs and in scientific or other systematic disciplines, is shackled to the slow business of accumulating knowledge that may eventually turn out to be corrigible. Revision and uncertainty are always in prospect. There is no quick and easy way to scientific understanding, achievement in the humane disciplines or self-understanding. Moreover, progress in these things now appears to be undermining the essentials of the fanatic's beliefs. At the deepest level, reason threatens to subvert the relationship to God, the parental images (introjects), and the omnipotence and omniscience of the self. The identification with God, or an ineluctable need to live in the orbit of God, means that the denial of God or criticism or disrespect of his religion is a threat to the fanatic's being. In the grip of offended narcissism, in precarious identification with God, the eye is plucked out and the messenger becomes hateful. Now the doctrines of revealed truth, faith, the reasons of the heart, and supernatural experience can be employed to provide what reason cannot. Thought, unguided by reason or self-understanding, captive to the internal world and quasi-omniscience, becomes more or less phantastic and delusional.

Herein lies the great resource of the Holy Book. For people bewildered and threatened by the contemporary maelstrom of ideas and possibilities (all of us), who perhaps don't know much but must know everything that deeply matters, the Book arrives as an immeasurable gift. If the Book is the inerrant and congenial word of God, then knowing it dispels confusion and ignorance, and there is nothing further, as Tertullian enjoins, that one need believe. If the book is the word of God, conversing with it feels like associating with God. Extracts from the holy texts can be kept nearby and consulted regularly, placed in amulets or worn during prayer to keep in touch with God. The Book may be carried

150 Polemic

to war, its verses sung or waved aloft in public demonstrations. No copy of it may be desecrated. Frequent repetitions of holy passages in prayer and assiduous study are unconsciously like incorporating the mind of God: to thoroughly internalize the word of God is to *be* God. One is omniscient after all!

The evasion of reality

The religion of the fanatic and the fundamentalist and their intersecting circles may shield against the pain of abandonment, provide a sense of identity and belonging, and doubtless many of those other things for which religion is, often rightly, praised. It can engender good and charitable works, though often selective in their recipients. It may even deliver good health or well-being as the medical profession generally understand it. But being healthy or well is not just freedom from disease, a matter of sensation, contentment or self-satisfaction. A human being who is well, or doing well, has self-awareness and insight, freedom of thought and choice, tolerance, a robust sense of reality, and a mind not held captive by phantasy. The point I wish to present here is difficult to demonstrate in a short space and without the context of an overarching theory of mental functioning.[18] I shall state the point frankly, recognizing that many caveats are required: often what passes for thought is really the barely adorned expression of phantasy. Here is one example of what I mean. A passage from John Haldane's *An Intelligent Person's Guide to Religion* tells us that in paradise with God the blessed will gaze upon the divine nature and see

> the perfection of every positive quality . . . [and find] what they have always craved – absolute, unconditional, and everlasting love – their minds are themselves made more loving, but now without prospect of relapse, for the wound from which their darkness and disturbance issued as a consequence of wilful disobedience has now been healed.[19]

Many thinkers have painted pictures of heaven and post-mortem existence. Origen thought it might be like a school of higher education, others like a bounteous oasis. There is not much to decide the truth between them but it is striking that they are exactly as their creators would wish them to be. And – to put it dogmatically – they are philosophically incoherent: apart from a complete absence of evidence, there are insuperable philosophical difficulties with conceptions of post-mortem existence. Haldane's is a touching picture. It corresponds closely with the phantasy of the young child reconciled with mother after painful discord and now in loving harmony with her. It repairs the most terrible separation of all, death, which is separation from mother (the maternal introject), one's self and other loved objects. Such phantasies of surrender

Reason and religion 151

(of 'wilful disobedience') and merger are universal. It may be objected that my interpretation of Haldane's vision as the expression of phantasy rather than as a complex cultural product, a crystallization of millennia of thought and spiritual longing of which Haldane is a part, is reductive (and dogmatic). This much in the objection is true: the kind of religious picture described by Haldane is not refuted by psychology. But when its implausibility and unreality are taken into account the picture fades in the light of psychological understanding. I need to place my claim on the point of a needle: how can any person with a robust sense of reality, a measure of education and an appreciation of the wishful or orectic character of mind credit such a picture? It is not, strictly, that people who believe such pictures of post-mortem existence or bizarre theodicies reason badly, go wrong in philosophical argument.[20] Often they are fundamentally not reasoning at all: their reason has been recruited into the service of expressing phantasy.[21] The explorations of previous chapters will, I hope, make this view plausible.

Moreover, the picture is not just a delusion, in its religious frame it is also an evasion. The religious understanding of the picture disguises the true significance of the *human* relationship, the vast edifice of human love constructed around buried parental introjects. Such religious pictures, so to speak, switch the signs. Instead of pointing to the reality of what goes deep – the love between mortals, loss, despair, mourning – they point to the heavens, to gods, to incoherent wishful illusions. By giving such illusions a context in religious ideology opportunities for insight are caught in webs of incoherence and wasted. Religious ideology does not illuminate the things of this world or any other; it obscures them. Religious educational strategies and institutions, rituals and group associations are directed at maintaining wishful illusions. The practical task of all religions, from the Palaeolithic to the present, has been to soften reality for our human lot, to insist that we cannot be harmed, that we may be immortal, because the gods are either with us or in us, and will look after us. But in so far as they succeed, they detach the believer from reality, from the way things are in the world and, specifically, the way things are between people. Some thinkers maintain that reality is fungible, one take on it is as good as another. Others maintain that a good share of phantasy in life is no bad thing. Indeed we need illusions, dreams and art. Otherwise, as Nietzsche said, we might die of the truth. But they must make no claim to replace reality. The religious evasion of reality is a dangerous dereliction of love of the world.

Unfinished conclusion

In earlier chapters I distinguished the fanatic from the fundamentalist who is merely devout, and from the ordinary casual or simple believer. The fanatic, we said, is a fundamentalist in doctrine and practice and in

152 Polemic

whom wishful or orectic processes of a pathological kind dominate the personality. Because the role of narcissism in religion is the focus of this essay a narrower stipulation was adopted: the fanatic is a fundamentalist with severe narcissistic character disorder and, generally, is a fundamentalist because of that disorder. That stipulation was intended to leave open the possibility, indeed the likelihood, that other pathological or near pathological conditions, for example hysterical disorders, lead to behaviour much like that of fanatics as understood here. It was emphasized that the circle of orectic derangement – of delusion or wish-driven divorce from reality – spreads further than the violent extremist centres but does not include fundamentalists whose beliefs are not wishfully motivated. Their beliefs may satisfy their religious wishes and be buttressed by them but they need not have, on my usage here, the tincture of fanaticism. They, and to mixed degrees the simple or 'cultural' believers, may be described as doxastically deranged: their religious beliefs are incongruent with reality – though that naturally is not their view.

I am of course aware that a view suggesting that religious belief – any religious belief – is pathological or akin to pathology is controversial.[22] That something so widespread should, even at its extremes, be considered akin to the pathological seems counter-intuitive. It's like saying grass is unnatural. Yet, I think that we must seriously consider the possibility that many people's religious convictions supervene not only on insouciance, ignorance, conceptual impoverishment or bad reasoning (though all these things may play a part), but on delusional formations. Their religious beliefs and attitudes are in various ways engendered or sustained by unconscious wishes related to internalized objects that are needed to provide an adequate level of safety and self-esteem. By living in their orbit, by obedience, by identification, through their practices and institutions, religious believers take themselves to be maintaining contact with the gods and spirits. But at heart, they are maintaining relationships with the internal phantasy world of idealized objects and self-representations that sustain them. If the investments in these objects are too powerful or adhesive then, as with all pathological developments, the internal world will distort or replace the real one. We have traced some of the ways in which these investments can go wrong.

It is ironic that so much in religion stems ultimately from the irrepressible need for love. Religion is a product of human needs and the strongest of these is to have loving relations with a protective, good object. The model of these relations is the bond between mother and child, and much of human life consists in the effort to reconstitute that bond symbolically: in the meaning imposed on other relationships, in work, in art and in religion. The practical task of most religions today is the creation of conditions in which the worshipper's compelling desire for an intimate relation with perfectly good or caring objects can be satisfied in the belief that there are such objects. In the teeth of the evidence and reason, it is affirmed that spirits, gods, God, or at least something supremely good, exists somewhere – if not in this world, then in another. Religion is a space where wishful phantasies and expectations receive the continuing endorsement of the adult world. That can be sweet. I have tried to show some of the ways in which those wishful phantasies, shaped by religion, can go awry and become seeds of destruction, as the world is now witnessing.

Notes

1 The strangeness of religion seems singularly opaque to many distinguished theist philosophers. For example, Michael Dummett (2010), Charles Taylor (2007) and John Cottingham (2011) are perplexed by the fierce hostility religion meets in some philosophical quarters. They condescend to think that the critics envy the rituals and serenity provided by their religion. They may be right about the envy. But they seem blind to how offensive their religious beliefs may be to common sense, let alone to science, to the love of reality. I imagine though that they grasp very well the strangeness of religions not their own, of the Nupe or Nuer, for example.
2 Kenny 1992, 51–52.
3 There is a shocking letter from Dostoyevsky to Mme. Fonvizina which reads in part: 'If someone proved to me that Christ is outside the truth, and that in reality the truth were outside Christ, then I should prefer to remain with Christ rather than with the truth.' Quoted in Frank 1988, 299. This is the end of reason and the essence of fanaticism.
4 Taylor 2007.
5 See the extraordinary discussion in Plantinga 2011, 55–63.
6 Burkert 2004, 69.
7 The same has to be said of the even longer domination of Rabbinic Judaism, and of Islam after the end of the 12th century when the 'gates of independent reasoning' had been closed.
8 *Epistle to Gregory ch 1*. Quoted in Lloyd 1973, 167.
9 Examples of admiration: Herrin 2008; Norwich 1998; Brown 2018. The gross misreading of the rebirth of science Taylor 2007. Kenny 2007 paints a more realistic picture.
10 Kenny 2007, 102.
11 Lloyd 1973, 168.
12 Quoted in Lloyd 1973, 168.
13 Schimmel 2008, 46. Schimmel's book is an astute study of many aspects of the fundamentalist mindset. It has recently been revealed that many of the tax-payer funded ultra-orthodox schools in New York (and in Israel) do not teach science or higher mathematics, and often no English or any of the humanities.

14 For example Plantinga 2011. An excellent recent debate, with a useful bibliography, about the existence of God and the capacity of theistic arguments to deliver explanations is Oppy and Pearce 2022.

15 The profound difficulty science poses for religion is not that it has knocked out a few pins of traditional belief, that archaeology refutes Exodus and Joshua, or that Darwin renders intelligent design dispensable, serious as these kinds of matters are for religion. Science is not just a set of hypotheses about nature; it is about method and norms: about what constitutes evidence, sound inference, testability, empirical significance, rationality. Religion offends these. Religion's problems with demonstrating the truth of its core propositions are secondary to showing them to be coherent and of decent epistemological provenance. Some philosophers, notably Taylor and Plantinga, suggest that the Christian transcendent framework is on the same epistemological footing with science. Just what evidence, tests, or reasoning would be accepted as impeaching fundamental religious propositions is left unaddressed.

16 Some philosophers of religion find shelter in the perspectivism associated with postmodernism. These views appear to clip the wings of reason and science and make space for religion. Roughly, postmodernism rejects the contention that there is an objective standpoint, a God's-eye vantage, from which the world can be viewed. There is no one way the world is, no single Truth about the world. There are only 'local truths' conditioned by local cultures, practices, interpretations, and perspectives. There is no indubitable foundation on which to erect knowledge. There are no grand meta-narratives as science and metaphysics are supposed to be. Even our most comprehensive science, physics, is just another perspective amongst others equally valid. These conceptions elate some of the religious: reason is demoted and science and religion are once again on equal footing. John D. Caputo (2001) sanguinely affirms that there is 'no view from nowhere or timeless ahistorical answer: there is no one right answer to most questions. There are many different and competing beliefs and practices and we should make every reasonable effort to accommodate them, to let many flowers bloom. Including the flower of religion.' He thinks that the postmodern critique has undone the modernist critique of religion (presumably because it seems to undo all critiques). Later he says: 'there is not a reason on earth (or in heaven) why many different religious narratives cannot all be true' (62–3). The consequences of these muddled contentions are not difficult to discern. Postmodernism eliminates the tribunal of reason – all tribunals. This is devastating for postmodernism (is it true universally, or is it just a 'local' truth?), but more so for religion understood in any reasonably orthodox or traditional sense. God who is the ground of all being, who views the world from the perspective of eternity and omniscience, who has set down His inerrant Word in Holy Books is an impossible being. All religions have claimed precisely the foundationalism that postmodernism explicitly denies.

17 Haldane 2005, for example, is largely devoted to showing that where science cannot explain phenomena theism often can. This is a very troubled doctrine. It is immediately undermined by the reflection that explaining a mystery by a still greater mystery (God) is no explanation at all.

18 Pataki 2014 is an extended treatise on wish-fulfilling phantasy and the loss of reality testing.

19 Haldane 2005, 203.

20 For another example of phantasy masquerading as philosophical argument see the theodicy in Plantinga 2011, 58ff.

21 Shortly before his death Anton Chekov wrote to Diaghilev: 'I can only regard with bewilderment an educated man who is also religious.' I share the bewilderment.

22 There is a robust defensive psychiatric literature: e.g. Rizzuto 1998; Symington 1998; Loewenthal 2009; Sims 2009.

Appendix: on wish-fulfilment

I have referred several times to a conception of wish-fulfilment or substitutive satisfaction. The conception (henceforth FW) is a Freudian
innovation clearly represented in his view of religion as an illusion in
response to the recognition of dependency and narcissistic injury. It can
be distinguished from the ordinary conception of wish-fulfilment fairly
formally. In the ordinary conception a person wishes for something;
they get it; they know or believe that they get it and, as a result, cease
wishing. For their wishing to cease it is necessary that they at least believe that they get it: our cycles of desire and action are governed by
information, not, or not typically, by exhaustion. And it is because they
get it that they believe that they get it. Finally, it doesn't matter on this
conception whether a wished-for object is attained by personal effort or
by gift. Simplifying a little: where 'p' denotes any state of affairs:

(A) In the *ordinary sense* of wish-fulfilment a wish that p is fulfilled
only if:

   (i)   the wish is terminated: the agent ceases to wish that p;
   (ii) the agent comes to believe that p;
   (iii) p is actualized;
   (iv) the wish is terminated *because* of the actualization of p.

Throughout his work Freud developed the view that dreams, neurotic symptoms, conscious and unconscious phantasies, some psychotic
symptoms – delusions, hallucinations – jokes and art, slips of the tongue,
bungled actions, magical thinking, religion, the institutions of morality
and social organization are wish-fulfilling; or, recognizing that action
can fall short of its object, attempts at wish-fulfilment. These phenomena, if indeed they are wish-fulfilling, are so in a manner patently different from the ordinary conception: in them, the real objects of the wish
are *not* attained, only a substitute or semblance is. FW, then, is a form
of *substitutive satisfaction*. The phenomena are distinctive in that while
conditions (i) and (ii) are necessary, conditions (iii) and (iv) are not.

Characteristically, either the wished-for state of affairs is not actualized or, if it is, it has no causal role in the termination of the wish. The terminative or pacifying role must therefore rest entirely with (ii) believing that p – or, perhaps, with experiential states functioning informationally and pacifyingly in the manner of belief. Moreover, in most cases the agent initiates the wish-fulfilment. FW is something an agent *does*, either intentionally, sub-intentionally or by some expressive means.[1] To accommodate this we can distinguish two conditions replacing conditions (iii) and (iv):

(B) For any wish that p, it is fulfilled in the manner of FW only if:

   (i) the wish is terminated: the agent ceases to wish that *p* because:
   (ii) the agent comes to believe (or, perhaps, experience) that *p*.

      (v(a)) the agent initiates the wish-fulfilling process, in a sense that does not entail but does not exclude intention; or
      (v(b)) in self-solicitous types, fulfilment of the wish can be truly described in some such way as "A intentionally fulfils A's wish that *p*" or "A intentionally gratifies (consoles, appeases) A."

So at the rudimentary end of the series we have dreams in which representations caused by wishes in the primitive mental conditions described by Freud as under the sway of the 'primary process' achieve FW. Further along are representations of wished-for states of affairs generated intentionally in conditions of reverie, as in recalling fond memories though not with the express purpose of wish-fulfilment, being ephemerally mistaken for reality. At the furthest end of the spectrum are cases where fictive representations or enactments are used intentionally for the purpose of fulfilling wishes.

Freud does not always distinguish FW from ordinary wish-fulfilment; and he often fails to distinguish between the *representation* of a wish being fulfilled, and the *fulfilment* of a wish (either as process or end state). But his fundamental thought is that FW involves the fulfilment of a wish in the sense that the wish is terminated temporarily or pacified. Thus: '*Dreams are . . . guardians of sleep which get rid of disturbances of sleep . . .* a dream does not simply give expression to a thought, but represents the wish fulfilled as a hallucinatory experience . . . the dream does not simply reproduce the stimulus [the wish], but removes it, gets rid of it, deals with it, by means of a kind of experience.'[2] Freud describes the simplest form of FW, the hallucinatory wish-fulfilment of the infant, in a famous passage:

A hungry baby screams or kicks helplessly . . . the excitation arising from the internal need is not due to a force producing a *momentary*

158 Appendix: on wish-fulfilment

impact but to one which is in continuous operation. A change can only come about if in some way or other (in the case of the baby, through outside help) an "experience of satisfaction" can be achieved which puts an end to the internal stimulus. An essential component of this experience of satisfaction is a particular perception (that of nourishment, in our example) the mnemic image of which remains associated thence forward with the memory trace of the excitation produced by the need. As a result of the link that has thus been established, next time this need arises a psychical impulse will at once emerge which will seek to re-cathect the mnemic image of the perception and to re-evoke the perception itself, that is to say, to re-establish the situation of the original satisfaction. An impulse of this kind is what we call a wish; the re-appearance of the perception is the fulfilment of the wish; and the shortest path to the fulfilment of the wish is a path leading direct from the excitation produced by the need to a complete cathexis of the perception. Nothing prevents us from assuming that there was a primitive state of the psychical apparatus in which this path was actually traversed, that is, in which wishing ended in hallucinating. Thus, the aim of the first psychical activity was to produce a "perceptual identity" – a repetition of the perception which was linked with the satisfaction of the need.[3]

After a 'topographical regression' a memory of a previously satisfying experience achieves 'perceptual identity' and is mistaken for a perception of the original experience. It is for the infant *as if* its wish has been satisfied: the wish is temporarily pacified. The hallucinatory or fictive experience of satisfaction (henceforth: EOS) that pacifies the wish does not terminate, but occludes, the endogenous stimuli that gives rise to the wish. Hunger gives rise to a wish to be fed; the infant hallucinates being fed and this pacifies the wish but not the hunger. Clearly pacification will be the more effective the more remote a wish is from the needs which give rise to it. We are to imagine a similar process occurring in the rest of the wish-fulfilling series: symptom, religious illusion, art and so on. In essence, this is an informational conception of FW: wishing is pacified when a belief or, perhaps, an information-laden experience, registers that the wished-for state of affairs has been actualized. In the primitive conditions of infant experience or dream life, dominated by what Freud calls 'primary process,' representations of wished-for states of affairs brook no contradiction and function as wish-fulfilling: psychical reality is mistaken for external reality. One might say that from the perspective of the dreamer the fictive EOS or hallucination functions as irrecusable evidence for wish-fulfilling beliefs.

FW has broad compass yet with the exception of 'symbolic wish-fulfilment,' understood in a wide sense, Freud provides little guidance on

Appendix: on wish-fulfilment **159**

how the basic model can be extended to accommodate these other putatively wish-fulfilling phenomena. It does appear to have been Freud's view, and I think it is the correct view, that some forms of FW are brought about intentionally, either as adventitious consequences of intentional acts or as directly intended i.e. where FW is itself intended in an act of self-care or solicitude. Here, however, there is space only to consider the 'symbolic' cases.[4] Apart from the transparent dreams of young children, few dreams, let alone symptoms and their kin, have conscious content that is manifestly wish-fulfilling. These other phenomena are mostly *disguised* wish-fulfilments, partly the effect of unconscious primary processes and partly because of defences protecting consciousness from disruptive stimuli. Freud distinguishes latent from manifest content in dream and symptom. In the case of dreams, the latent content or 'dream thoughts' consist of recent day residues interwoven with older, aroused emotion-laden memories and wishes. This content is transformed into the manifest, consciously experienced dream – the fictive experience of satisfaction or EOS (or cluster of EOS's) – by the processes of the 'dreamwork': condensation, displacement, conditions of representability, secondary revision and symbolism. So dreams require interpretation: 'Dreams frequently seem to have more than one meaning. Not only . . . may they include several wish-fulfilments one alongside the other; but a succession of meanings or wish-fufilments may be superimposed on one another, the bottom one being the fulfilment of a wish dating from earliest childhood.'[5] Of his 'specimen' dream of Irma's injection Freud writes:

> The dream fulfilled certain wishes which were started in me by the events of the previous evening (the news given me by Otto [that Freud's patient Irma was still unwell] and my writing of the case history). The conclusion of the dream, that is to say, was that I was not responsible for the persistence of Irma's pain, but that Otto was. Otto had in fact annoyed me by his remarks about Irma's incomplete cure, and the dream gave me my revenge by throwing the reproach back on to him. . . . *I* was not to blame for Irma's pains, since she herself was to blame for them by refusing to accept my solution. *I* was not concerned with Irma's pains, since they were of an organic nature. . . . Irma's pains had been caused by Otto giving her an incautious injection of an unsuitable drug – a thing I should never have done.[6]

Freud's detailed analysis is too ramified to present here but the wish-fulfilments contained in the dream may be roughly divided into relatively obvious ones such as Irma's pains being organically caused, where the dream text practically wears the EOS on its sleeve ('Dr. M . . . confirmed it. . . . "There is no doubt it is an infection"'); and those that are disguised by the dreamwork. The 'incautious injection' with which

160 Appendix: on wish-fulfilment

Otto is rebuked leads Freud to partially repressed painful memories. Years earlier he had injected his patient Mathilde with a substance then considered harmless, resulting in her death; and on his advice Freud's friend Ernst began using cocaine for the relief of intractable pain, and by misuse quickly succumbed to it. So Otto with his thoughtless and probably dirty syringe is blamed not only for Irma's condition but also for the deaths of Mathilda and Ernst. If Otto is to blame then Freud is not. If FW is to succeed then it must be for the dreaming Freud *as if* Otto was responsible for the earlier deaths even though there is no conscious EOS to that effect. How does the dream do it?

At first pass, FW is effected by elements of the manifest dream representing multiple elements in the latent dream thoughts, utilizing condensation, displacement and symbolism. Condensation leads chiefly to the formation of 'collective and composite images' of figures or actions. So we are told that Irma 'stood for' Freud's eldest daughter, his wife as well as Mathilda, and that she acquired a series of still 'other meanings' and 'allusions': 'Irma became the representative of all these figures which had been sacrificed to the work of condensation, since I passed over to *her*, point by point, everything that reminded me of *them*.'[7] But how precisely does such representation by means of condensation facilitate FW? Freud's unsatisfactory answer is that in condensation 'ideas are formed which are endowed with great intensity' and 'the intensities of the individual ideas become capable of discharge *en bloc* and pass over from one idea to another.'[8] This is not helpful because we have no idea how to relate *meaning* or representation to *psychical intensity*, or the facilitations effected by relations of meaning to discharge. Moreover, it turns on the awkward proposition that in condensation one element of a composite figure stands for other elements of it. Whatever we come to make of these problems we can see why Freud also considers displacement as a form of representation, for it too involves a transfer of 'psychical intensity' or 'value' (distinguished from 'sensory intensity'), in which an element of low value comes to stand for one with high value.

Condensation and displacement do not exhaust the relation of representation. Freud eventually recognized an exclusive type of representation – symbolism – attended with conditions distinguishing it from the other types.[9] Symbols in this sense are semantically opaque to the subject because their meaning or referent is either repressed or innately and unreflectively given, conditions not imposed on the other processes. This is the sense in which a snake can symbolize a penis without condensation, or even displacement. Symbolism in this strict sense need not depend on processes of the dreamwork. Putting aside Freud's unhelpful explanation in terms of energic discharge, can we explain how representation, either as symbolism (strictly) or in the awkward manner Freud attributes

Appendix: on wish-fulfilment **161**

to condensation and displacement, facilitates and extends FW? Agnes
Petocz argued that the wish-fulfilling efficacy of the symbol rests on an
unconscious belief in the identity of symbol and symbolized.[10] As a consequence 'the symbol is mistaken for the symbolized and treated as if it
were the symbolized' leading, 'for reasons not properly understood,' to
a kind of 'gratification which is not as complete as would be the gratification obtained from the satisfaction, via primary objects and activities,
of the unopposed instinctual impulse.' Such a belief in identity cannot
be excluded, but it does not seem to be an indispensable condition for
symbolic FW. It may be that an operation on the symbol is simply taken
to be, is apprehended as, an operation on its referent, without belief in
their identity. The sorcerer who sticks pins in an effigy need not believe
the effigy *is* his enemy. The supposed causal relations between effigy
and referent are supported by an immense raft of beliefs and practices.
There appear to be many different ways in which symbolic relations are
established over the course of a life, and that may be true of unconscious
symbolism also. It would then seem likely that present figures and situations will be mapped onto past unconscious ones. So, given Freud's fixed
association between Irma and Mathilda, in representing Otto as giving
a toxic injection to Irma Freud *at the same time* pacifies his wish not to
have been responsible for the death of his earlier patient. The pacification of the contemporary desire goes together with that of the deeper
more painful one.

It seems to me that for FW to succeed there must be *some* occurrence of unconscious understanding or apprehension underwriting
them. Whether, as on Petocz's account, an unconscious belief in the
identity of Irma and Mathilda entails that an operation on the one is
experienced as if it were an operation on the other; or whether representations of Irma and Mathilda become condensed and interchange-
able through association; the pacification of Freud's wish that it was
Otto (and not Freud) who had killed Mathilda would require that it be
for him *as if* Otto had killed Mathilda. That would seem to entail *the
acquisition of a belief that Otto killed Mathilda* – for there *is* no EOS
whose content is Otto killing Mathilda. The passage from the EOS –
the tableau which has Otto (almost) injecting Irma – to the content
of Otto killing Mathilda requires a process of thought arriving at an
unconscious understanding or belief that it is so. This view presup-
posing a notion of *unconscious understanding* thus underlies symbolic
wish-fulfilment and gives us precisely what we want in the understanding of religious phenomena in which gods and spirits are understood
unconsciously, given the conditions prevailing in unconscious mental
life, as if they were parental or other significant attachment figures or
parts of the self.

Notes

1 In the common-sense-psychological classification of motives and acts *intentional action* is caused and rationalized by the conjunction of desire and instrumental belief; it may also involve executive states such as intending, deciding, and choosing; but the having of reasons is both causally and logically necessary. Various non-intentional modes of causal explanation are available. *Subintentional actions* including mental acts, are caused by desire without facilitation by instrumental beliefs. There are also forms of *expression* that have archaeology but no teleology, as when one clenches one's fists in (out of) anguish, or laughs.
2 Freud 1916/1917, 129.
3 Freud 1900, 565–566.
4 Pataki 2014, 2019 discuss the other forms of FW.
5 Freud 1900, 219.
6 Freud 1900, 118–119.
7 Freud 1900, 293.
8 Freud 1900, 595.
9 On symbolism in Freud see Petocz 1999.
10 Petocz 1999, 233.

Bibliography

Anderson, A. (1997) *The Treatise of the Three Imposters and the Problem of the Enlightenment*. New York: Rowman and Littlefield Publishers.

Arendt, Hannah (1976) *The Origins of Totalitarianism*. San Diego: Harcourt Brace.

Armstrong, Karen (2001) *The Battle for God*. New York: Random House.

Assmann, Jan (2007) Monotheism and polytheism. In Johnston, Sarah Isles (ed.) *Ancient Religions*. Cambridge, MA: Harvard University Press.

Assmann, Jan (2010) *The Price of Monotheism*. Stanford: Stanford University Press.

Astuti, Rita (2007) Ancestors and the afterlife. In Whitehouse and Laidlaw (eds.) *Religion, Anthropology and Cognitive Science*. Durham, NC: Carolina Academic Press.

Barrett, Justin L. (2004) *Why Would Anyone Believe in God?* Lanham, MA: AltaMira Press.

Barrett, Justin L. (2007) Gods. In Whitehouse and Laidlaw (eds.) *Religion, Anthropology and Cognitive Science*. Durham, NC: Carolina Academic Press.

Beaulieu, Paul-Alain (2007) Mesopotamia. In Johnston, Sarah Isles (ed.) *Ancient Religions*. Cambridge, MA: Harvard University Press.

Beckwith, Christopher I. (2011) *Empires of the Silk Road*. Princeton and Oxford: Princeton University Press.

Bellah, Robert N. (2011) *Religion in Human Evolution*. Cambridge, MA: Harvard University Press.

Bering, Jesse (2011) *The God Instinct*. London: Nicholas Brearley Publishing.

Black, D. M. (ed.) (2006) *Psychoanalysis and Religion in the 21st Century*. London: Routledge.

Blackford, R. and Schuklenk, U. (eds.) (2009) *50 Voices of Disbelief*. Chichester: Wiley-Blackwell.

Bonett, W. (ed.) (2010) *The Australian Book of Atheism*. Melbourne: Scribe.

164 Bibliography

Bowlby, J. (1969) *Attachment, Vol. 1, Attachment and Loss*. London: Hogarth Press.

Bowlby, J. (1980/1998) *Loss: Sadness and Depression, Vol. 3, Attachment and Loss*. New York: Basic Books.

Bowra, C. M. (1973) *The Greek Experience*. London: Cardinal.

Boyer, P. (2001) *Religion Explained*. London: Vintage Books.

Bremmer, J. N. (2007) Atheism in antiquity. In Martin, M. (ed.) *The Cambridge Companion to Atheism*. Cambridge: Cambridge University Press.

Brown, Peter (2015) *The Ransom of the Soul*. Cambridge, MA: Harvard University Press.

Brown, Peter (2018) *The World of Late Antiquity*. London: Thames and Hudson.

Burkert, Walter (1985) *Greek Religion*. Oxford: Basil Blackwell.

Burkert, Walter (1998) *Creation of the Sacred: Tracks of Biology in Early Religion*. Cambridge, MA: Harvard University Press.

Burkert, Walter (2004) *Babylon Memphis Persepolis: Eastern Contexts of Greek Culture*. Cambridge, MA: Harvard University Press.

Capps, Donald (1995) *The Child's Song: The Religious Abuse of Children*. Louisville: John Knox Press.

Capps, Donald (1997) *Men, Religion and Melancholia*. Ann Arbor: Yale University Press.

Caputo, John D. (2001) *On Religion*. New York: Routledge.

Cassidy, J. and Shaver, P. R. (eds.) (1999) *Handbook of Attachment*. New York: Guildford Press.

Charlesworth, Max (2002) *Philosophy and Religion*. Oxford: Oneworld Publications.

Chomsky, Noam (2018) *What Kind of Creatures Are We?* New York: Columbia University Press.

Clottes, Jean (2016) *What is Paleolithic Art?* Chicago and London: University of Chicago Press.

Collins, John J. (2007) Israel. In Johnston, Sarah Isles (ed.) *Ancient Religions*. Cambridge, MA: Harvard University Press.

Condemi, S. and F. Savatier (2019) *A Pocket History of Human Evolution*. New York: The Experiment.

Cottingham, John (2011) *Why Believe?* London: Continuum.

Crompton, Louis (2006) *Homosexuality and Civilization*. Cambridge, MA: Harvard University Press.

Dalley, Stephanie (ed.) (2008) *Myths from Mesopotamia*. Oxford: Oxford University Press.

David, Bruno (2017) *Cave Art*. London: Thames and Hudson.

David, Rosalie (2002) *Religion and Magic in Ancient Egypt*. London: Penguin.

Davidson, D. (1974) Thought and talk. In Guttenplan, S. (ed.) *Mind and Language*. Oxford: Oxford University Press.

Davidson, D. (1982/2001) 'Rational animals' [reprinted]. In Davidson, D (ed.) *Subjective, Intersubjective, Objective*. Oxford: Clarendon Press.

Bibliography   165

Dawkins, R. (2006) *The God Delusion*. Chicago: Houghton Miflin Company.

Dennett, D. C. (1989) *The Intentional Stance*. Cambridge, MA: MIT Press.

Dennett, D. C. (2006) *Breaking the Spell*. Harmondsworth: Penguin.

Dever, William G. (2006) *Who Were The Early Israelites and Where Did They Come From*. Grand Rapids: Wm. B. Eerdmans Publishing Co.

Dever, William G. (2020) *Has Archaeology Buried the Bible?* Grand Rapids: Wm. B. Eerdmans Publishing Co.

Dodds, E. R. (1951) *The Greeks and the Irrational*. Berkeley and Los Angeles: University of California Press.

Dodds, E. R. (1965) *Pagan and Christian in an Age of Anxiety*. Cambridge: Cambridge University Press.

Dummett, Michael (2010) *The Nature and Future of Philosophy*. New York: Columbia University Press.

Dunbar, Robin (2022) *How Religion Evolved and Why it Endures*. Oxford: Oxford University Press.

Eagleton, Terry (2006) Lunging, flailing, mispunching. *London Review of Books* 28, 20.

Erickson, Robert (2012) *Complicity in the Holocaust: Churches and Universities in Nazi Germany*. Cambridge: Cambridge University Press.

Evans-Pritchard, E. E. (1956) *Nuer Religion*. Oxford: Clarendon Press.

Evans-Pritchard, E. E. (1965/2004) *Theories of Primitive Religion*. Oxford: Oxford University Press.

Everett, Daniel (2018) *How Language Began*. London: Profile Books.

Faber, M.D. (2004) *The Psychological Roots of Religious Belief*. New York: Prometheus Books.

Fairbairn, W. R. D. (1952) *Psychoanalytic Studies of the Personality*. London: Routledge Kegan Paul.

Ferenczi, S. (1909) Introjection and transference. In *Sex in Psychoanalysis*. New York: Dover 1956.

Ferenczi, S. (1913/1956) Stages in the development of a sense of reality. In *Sex in Psychoanalysis*. New York: Dover.

Fitzgerald, Francis (2018) *The Evangelicals: The Struggle to Shape America*. New York: Simon &Schuster.

Fonagy, Peter, Gergely, György, Jurist, Elliot L. and Target, Mary (eds.) (2004) *Affect Regulation, Mentalization, and the Development of the Self*. New York: Other Books.

Fortes, Meyer (1959) *Oedipus and Job in West African Religion*. Cambridge: Cambridge University Press.

Fotopoulou, A., Pfaff, D. and Conway, M. A. (2012) *From the Couch to the Lab: Trends in Psychodynamic Neuroscience*. Oxford: Oxford University Press.

Frank, Joseph (1988) *Dostoevsky: The Stir of Liberation 1860–1865*. Princeton: Princeton University Press.

Frank, Joseph (2003) *Dostoevsky: The Mantle of the Prophet*. Princeton: Princeton University Press.

166 Bibliography

Frawley-O'Dea, Mary G. (2007) *Perversion of Power: Sexual Abuse in the Catholic Church*. Nashville: Vanderbilt University Press.

Freud, Sigmund (1900) *The Interpretation of Dreams* (SE, IV, V). London: Hogarth

Freud, Sigmund (1909) *Notes Upon a Case of Obsessional Neurosis* (SE, X). London: Hogarth.

Freud, Sigmund (1910) *Leonardo DaVinci and a Memory of His Childhood* (SE, XI). London: Hogarth.

Freud, Sigmund (1913) *Totem and Taboo* (SE XIII). London: Hogarth.

Freud, Sigmund (1914) *On Narcissism; An Introduction* (SE, XIV). London: Hogarth.

Freud, Sigmund (1916/1917) *Introductory Lectures on Psychoanalysis* (SE, XV). London: Hogarth.

Freud, Sigmund (1921) *Group Psychology and the Analysis of the Ego* (SE, XVIII). London: Hogarth.

Freud, Sigmund (1927) *The Future of an Illusion* (SE XXI). London: Hogarth.

Freud, Sigmund (1930) *Civilization and its Discontents* (SE, XXI). London: Hogarth.

Freud, Sigmund (1933) *New Introductory Lectures* (SE, XXII). London: Hogarth.

Freud, Sigmund (1939) *Moses and Monotheism* (SE, XXIII). London: Hogarth.

Fromm, Erich (1963/2004) *The Dogma of Christ*. London: Routledge.

Fromm, Erich (1973) *The Anatomy of Human Destructiveness*. New York: Henry Holt and Company.

Gale, Richard M. (1991) *On the Nature and Existence of God*. Cambridge: Cambridge University Press.

Gardner, Sebastian (1993) *Irrationality and the Philosophy of Psychoanalysis*. Cambridge: Cambridge University Press.

Gibbon, Edward (1776–1788/1993) *The Decline and Fall of the Roman Empire*. New York: Alfred A. Knopf.

Goodman, Martin (2019) *A History of Judaism*: London: Penguin Books.

Granqvist, Pehr (2020) *Attachment in Religion and Spirituality*. New York: The Guildford Press.

Guthrie, Stewart E. (1993) *Faces in the Clouds: A New Theory of Religion*. New York: Oxford University Press.

Guthrie, Stewart E. (2007a) Anthropological theories of religion. In Martin, Michael (ed.) *The Cambridge Companion to Atheism*. Cambridge: Cambridge University Press.

Guthrie, Stewart E. (2007b) Anthropology and anthropomorphism in religion. In Whitehouse, Harvey and James, Laidlaw (eds.) *Religion, Anthropology and Cognitive Science*. Durham, NC: Carolina Academic Press.

Haldane, John (2005) *An Intelligent Person's Guide to Religion*. London: Duckworth.

Hannaford, Ivan (1996) *Race: The History of an Idea in the West*. Washington, DC: Woodrow Wilson Centre Press.

Harris, S. (2004) *The End of Faith: Religion, Terror, and the Future of Reason.* New York: W.W. Norton.

Herrin, Judith (2008) *Byzantium: The Surprising Life of a Medieval Empire.* London: Penguin Books.

Higham, Tom (2021) *The World Before Us.* London: Viking.

Hill, David (2010) Fundamentalist faith states: Regulation theory as a framework for the psychology of religious fundamentalism. In Strozier, Charles B., Terman, David M. and Jones, James W. (eds.) *The Fundamentalist Mindset.* Oxford: Oxford University Press.

Hitchens, C. (2007) *God Is Not Great: How Religion Poisons Everything.* New York: Allen and Unwin.

Hong, Hobson A., Chong-Hwa Hong, Charles and Friston, K. (2014) Virtual reality and consciousness inference in dreaming. *Frontiers in Psychology* 5, 1133. https://doi.org/10.3389/fpsyg.2014.01133

Hopkins, J. (1982) Introduction: Philosophy and psychoanalysis. In Wollheim, R. and Hopkins, J. (eds.) *Philosophical Essays on Freud.* Cambridge: Cambridge University Press.

Hopkins, J. (2003) Emotion, evolution and conflict. In Chung, M. C. and Feltham, C. (eds.) *Psychoanalytic Knowledge.* Basingstoke: Palgrave MacMillan.

Hopkins, J. (2012) Psychoanalysis, representation, and neuroscience: The Freudian unconscious and the Bayesian brain. In Fotopoulou, A., Pfaff, D. and Conway, M. A. (eds.) *From the Couch to the Lab: Trends in Psychodynamic Neuroscience.* Oxford: Oxford University Press.

Hopkins, J. (2015) The significance of consilience: Psychoanalysis, attachment, neuroscience, and evolution. In Boag, S., Brakel, L. and Talvitie, V. (eds.) *Psychoanalysis and the Philosophy of Mind: Unconscious Mentality in the 21st Century.* London: Karnac.

Horton, Robin (1997) *Patterns of thought in Africa and the West.* Cambridge: Cambridge University Press.

Huizinga, Johan (1949/1971) *Homo Ludens.* London: Paladin.

Hume, David (1757/1992) The natural history of religion. In Antony, Flew (ed.) *Writings on Religion.* London: Open Court.

Hume, David (1992) *Writings on Religion,* ed. Antony Flew. London: Open Court.

James, William (1901–1902/1971) *The Varieties of Religious Experience.* New York: Collins/Fontana.

Johnston, M. (2009) *Saving God.* Princeton: Princeton University Press.

Jones, Ernest (1913/1974) The god complex. In *Psycho-Myth, Psycho-History.* Santa Monica: Hillstone.

Jones, James W. (2002) *Terror and Transformation: The Ambiguity of Religion in Psychoanalytic Perspective.* New York: Brunner-Routledge.

Jones, James W. (2010) Eternal warfare. In Strozier, Charles B., Terman, David M. and Jones, James W. (eds.) *The Fundamentalist Mindset.* Oxford: Oxford University Press.

Juergensmeyer, Mark (2008) *Global Rebellion.* Berkeley and Los Angeles: University of California Press.

168 Bibliography

Kelly, J. M. A (1992/2003) *A Short History of Western Legal Theory.* Oxford: Oxford University Press.

Kenny, Anthony (1992) *What is Faith?* Oxford: Oxford University Press.

Kenny, Anthony (2007) *A New History of Western Philosophy, Vol. 2, Medieval Philosophy.* Oxford: Clarendon Press.

Kernberg, O. F. (1975) *Borderline Conditions and Pathological Narcissism.* New York: Jason Aronson.

Kernberg, O. F. (2003) Sanctioned social violence: A psychoanalytic view part I. *The International Journal of Psychoanalysis* 84, 683–698.

Kernberg, O. F. (2014) *Aggressivity, Narcissism and Self-destructiveness in the Psychotherapeutic Relationship.* Ithaca and London: Yale University Press.

Kernberg, O. F. (2022) *Hatred, Emptiness and Hope.* Washington, DC: American Psychiatric Publishing.

Kirkpatrick, Lee A. (1999) Attachment and religious representations of behaviour. In Cassidy, J. and Shaver, P. R. (eds.) *Handbook of Attachment.* New York: Guildford Press.

Kirkpatrick, Lee A. (2005) *Attachment, Evolution and the Psychology of Religion.* New York: Guildford Press.

Kitcher, P. (2011) Challenges for secularism. In Levine, G. (ed.) *The Joy of Secularism.* Princeton: Princeton University Press.

Klein, M. (1952) The emotional life of the infant. In Klein, M. (ed.) *Envy and Gratitude.* London: Hogarth.

Klein, M. (1957) Envy and gratitude. In Klein, M. (ed.) *Envy and Gratitude.* London: Hogarth.

Klein, M. (1975) *Envy and Gratitude.* London: Hogarth.

Kohut, Heinz (1968/1978) The psychoanalytic treatment of narcissistic personality disorders. In Ornstein, Paul H. (ed.) *The Search for the Self.* New York: International Universities Press.

Kohut, Heinz (1972/1978) Thoughts on narcissism and narcissistic rage. In Ornstein, Paul H. (ed.) *The Search for the Self.* New York: International Universities Press.

Kohut, Heinz (1976/1978) Creativeness, charisma, group psychology. In Ornstein, Paul H. (ed.) *The Search for the Self.* New York: International Universities Press.

Kriwaczek, P. (2012) *Babylon: Mesopotamia and the Birth of Civilization.* London: Atlantic Books.

Laidlaw, James (2007) A well-disposed social anthropologist's problems with the 'cognitive science of religion'. In Whitehouse, Harvey and James, Laidlaw (eds.) *Religion, Anthropology and Cognitive Science.* Durham, NC: Carolina Academic Press.

Levine, G. (ed.) (2011) *The Joy of Secularism.* Princeton: Princeton University Press.

Levine, M. (ed.) (2000) *The Analytic Freud.* London and New York: Routledge.

Levine, M. and Pataki, T. (2004) *Racism in Mind.* Ithaca and London: Cornell University Press.

Lewis, I. M. (2003) *Ecstatic Religion: A Study of Shamanism and Spirit Possession.* London: Routledge.

Lewis-Williams, David (2010) *Conceiving God: The Cognitive Origin and Evolution of Religion.* London: Thames and Hudson.

Lloyd, G. E. R. (1973) *Greek Science After Aristotle.* New York: W. W. Norton and Company.

Loewenthal, Kate (2009) *Religion, Culture and Mental Health.* Cambridge: Cambridge University Press.

Lohrey, Amanda (2006) *Voting for Jesus.* Melbourne: Black Inc.

Maddox, Marion (2005) *God Under Howard.* Melbourne: Allen and Unwin.

Martin, M. (2007) Atheism and religion. In Michael, Martin (ed.) *The Cambridge Companion to Atheism.* Cambridge: Cambridge University Press.

McGrath, Alister (2004) *The Twilight of Atheism: The Rise and Fall of Disbelief in the Modern World.* London: Rider.

Meissner, W. W. (1984) *Psychoanalysis and Religious Experience.* Ann Arbor: Yale University Press.

Mimica, J. (2020) *Of Humans, Pigs, and Souls.* Chicago: HAU Books.

Nagel, T. (2010) *Secular Philosophy and the Religious Temperament.* Oxford: Oxford University Press.

Naipaul, V. S. (2010) *The Masque of Africa.* London: Picador Press.

Nietzsche, Friedrich (1990) *Twilight of the Idols/The Anti-Christ.* London: Penguin.

Nixey, C. (2017) *The Darkening Age:* London: Macmillan.

Norwich, John Julius (1998) *A Short History of Byzantium.* London: Penguin.

Olupona, Jacob K. (2014) *African Religions.* Oxford: Oxford University Press.

Onfray, M. (2007) *The Atheist Manifesto.* Melbourne: Melbourne University Press.

Oppy, G. (2011) "New Atheism" versus "Christian Nationalism". In Bubbio, P. and Quadrio, P. (eds.) *The Relation of Philosophy to Religion Today.* Cambridge: Scholars Press.

Oppy, G. (2018) *Naturalism and Religion.* London and New York: Routledge.

Oppy, G. and Pearce, Kenneth L. (2022) *Is There a God?* New York: Routledge.

Ostow, Mortimer (2007) *Spirit, Mind and Brain.* New York: Columbia University Press.

Pagden, Anthony (2009) *Worlds at War.* New York: Random House.

Panksepp, Jaak and Biven, Lucy (2012) *The Archaeology of Mind: Neuroevolutionary Origins of Human Emotions.* New York: W.W. Norton.

Pataki, T. (2000) Freudian wishfulfilment and subintentional explanation. In Levine, M. (ed.) *The Analytic Freud.* London and New York: Routledge.

Pataki, T. (2003) Freud, object-relations, agency and the self. In Chung, M. C. and Feltham, C. (eds.) *Psychoanalytic Knowledge.* London: Palgrave MacMillan.

170 Bibliography

Pataki, T. (2004a) Racism, the psychology of racism and envy. In Levine, M. and Pataki, T. (eds.) *Racism in Mind*. Ithaca and London: Cornell University Press.

Pataki, T. (2004b) Introduction to *Racism in Mind*. In Levine, M. and Pataki, T. (eds.) *Racism in Mind*. Ithaca and London: Cornell University Press.

Pataki, T. (2007) *Against Religion*. Melbourne: Scribe.

Pataki, T. (2010) Religion and violence. In Bonnett, W. (ed.) *The Australian Book of Atheism*. Melbourne: Scribe.

Pataki, T. (2014) *Wish-fulfilment in Philosophy and Psychoanalysis: The Tyranny of Desire*. London: Routledge.

Pataki, T. (2015) Wish-fulfilment revisited. In Boag, S., Brakel, L. and Talvitie, V. (eds.) *Psychoanalysis and the Philosophy of Mind: Psychoanalysis in the 21st Century*. London: Karnac.

Pataki, T. (2019) Wish-fulfilment. In Gipps, R. and Lacewing, M. (eds.) *The Oxford Handbook of Philosophy and Psychoanalysis*. Oxford: Oxford University Press.

Peoples, Hervey C., Duda, P. and Marlowe, F. W. (2016) Hunter-Gatherers and the origins of religion. *Human Nature* 27, 261–282.

Petocz, A. (1999) *Freud, Psychoanalysis and Symbolism*. Cambridge: Cambridge University Press.

Plantinga, A. (2011) *Where the Conflict Really Lies*. Oxford: Oxford University Press.

Posner, Sarah (2021) *Unholy: How White Christian Nationalists Powered the Trump Presidency, and the Devastating Legacy They Left Behind*. New York: Random House.

Post, J. M. (2007) *The Mind of the Terrorist*. London: Palgrave Macmillan.

Reich, Annie (1960) Pathologic forms of self-esteem regulation. *The Psychoanalytic Study of the Child* 15, 215–232.

Rizzuto, Ana-Maria (1998) *Why Did Freud Reject God?* New Haven and London: Yale University Press.

Robinson, Daniel N. (1996) *Wild Beasts and Idle Humours*. Harvard, MA: Harvard University Press.

Ronningstam, Elsa F. (ed.) (2000) *Disorders of Narcissism*. New York: Jason Aronson.

Rosenfeld, Herbert (1987) *Impasse and Interpretation*. London: Tavistock Publications.

Russell, Bertrand (1957) *Why I am not a Christian and Other Essays on Religion and Related Subjects*. New York: Touchstone Books.

Ruthven, M. (2005) *Fundamentalism*. Oxford: Oxford University Press.

Sandler, J. (1976) Dreams, unconscious fantasies and "identity of perception". *International Review of Psychoanalysis* 3, 1.

Sandler, J. (1989) Unconscious wishes and human relationships. In Sandler, J. (ed.) *Dimensions of Psychoanalysis*. London: Karnac.

Sandler, J., Person, Ethel S. and Fonagy, P. (eds.) (2012) *Freud's 'On Narcissism: An Introduction'*. London: Karnac.

Sandler, J. and Sandler, A. M. (1998) *Internal Objects Revisited*. London: International Universities Press.

Scanlan, James P. (2002) *Dostoevsky the Thinker*. New York: Cornell University Press.

Schimmel, S. (2008) *The Tenacity of Unreasonable Beliefs: Fundamentalism and the Fear of Truth*. Oxford: Oxford University Press.

Sims, Andrew (2009) *Is Faith Delusion: Why Religion is Good for Your Health*. London: Continuum.

Steigmann-Gall (2004) *The Holy Reich: Nazi Conceptions of Christianity 1919–1945*. Cambridge: Cambridge University Press.

Steiner, J. (1993) *Psychic Retreats: Pathological Organizations in Psychotic, Neurotic and Borderline Organizations*. London: Routledge.

Strawson, Galen (2009) *Selves*. Oxford: Clarendon Press.

Strawson, Galen (2018) *Things That Bother Me*. New York: New York Review Books.

Stringer, Chris (2012) *Lone Survivors: How We Came to be the only Humans on Earth*. New York: St. Martins Griffin.

Strozier, Charles B. (2010) The apocalyptic other. In Strozier, Charles B., Terman, David M. and Jones, James W. (eds.) *The Fundamentalist Mindset*. Oxford: Oxford University Press.

Strozier, Charles B., Terman, David M. and Jones, James W. (eds.) (2010) *The Fundamentalist Mindset*. Oxford: Oxford University Press.

Suttie, Ian D. (1935/1960) *The Origins of Love and Hate*. London: Penguin.

Symington, Neville (1998) *Emotion and Spirit: Questioning the Claims of Psychoanalysis and Religion*. London: Karnac Books.

Tambiah, Stanley J. (1990) *Magic, Science, Religion and the Scope of Rationality*. Cambridge: Cambridge University Press.

Taylor, C. (2007) *A Secular Age*. Cambridge, MA: Harvard University Press.

Terman, Charles (2010) Fundamentalism and the paranoid gestalt. In Strozier, Charles B., Terman, David M. and Jones, James W. (eds.) *The Fundamentalist Mindset*. Oxford: Oxford University Press.

Thomson, J. A. Jnr. (2011) *Why We Believe in Gods*. Charlottesville: Pitchstone Publishing.

Trocme, Etienne (1997) *The Childhood of Christianity*. London: SCM Press.

Tylor, Edward B. (1873/2016) *Primitive Culture* (2 vols). New York: Dover Publications.

Whitehouse, Harvey (2007) Towards and integration of ethnography, history and the cognitive science of religion. In Whitehouse, Harvey and James, Laidlaw (eds.) *Religion, Anthropology and Cognitive Science*. Durham, NC: Carolina Academic Press.

Whitehouse, Harvey and James, Laidlaw (eds.) (2007) *Religion, Anthropology and Cognitive Science*. Durham, NC: Carolina Academic Press.

Whitmarsh, Timothy (2015) *Battling the Gods: Atheism in the Ancient World*. New York: Alfred A. Knopf.

172 Bibliography

Williams, Bernard (2015) *Essays and Reviews: 1959–2002*. Princeton: Princeton University Press.

Wilson, Bryan R. (ed.) (1974) *Rationality*. Oxford: Basil Blackwell.

Wilson, David Sloan (2002) *Darwin's Cathedral: Evolution, Religion, and the Nature of Society*. Chicago: University of Chicago Press.

Winch, Peter (1979) Understanding a primitive society. In Wilson, Bryan R. (ed.) *Rationality*. Oxford: Basil Blackwell.

Winnicott, D. W. (1965) *The Maturational Processes and the Facilitating Environment*. London: Hogarth Press.

Winnicott, D. W. (1974) *Playing and Reality*. Harmondsworth: Pelican.

Wollheim, R. (1971/1991) *Freud*. London: Fontana.

Wollheim, R. (1979) Wish-fulfilment. In Harrison, R. (ed.) *Rational Action: Studies in Philosophy and Social Science*. Cambridge: Cambridge University Press.

Wollheim, R. (1984) *The Thread of Life*. Cambridge: Cambridge University Press.

Wollheim, R. (1993) *The Mind and its Depths*. Harvard, MA: Harvard University Press.

Wright, David P. (2007) Syria and Canaan. In Johnston, Sarah Isles (ed.) *Ancient Religions*. Harvard, MA: Harvard University Press.

Wright, Robert (2010) *The Evolution of God*. New York: Littlemore.

Young Bruehl, Elisabeth (1996) *The Anatomy of Prejudices*. Cambridge, MA: Harvard University Press.

Index

Note: References following "n" refer notes.

aboriginal neophobia 130
abortion 106–107
adaptive illusion, God as 37
afterlife, belief in 12–13, 34–36
Against Religion (Pataki) 90
agency detection device (ADD) 32
aggression: narcissism 77; religious 123–125, 130–133, 135, 138; *see also* intrinsic religious aggression
animals 19; art 21, 22; Palaeolithic 22, 27n50; spirits 20, 23; worship 27n50
animism 9, 27n53, 32, 40, 48, 56; anthropomorphism of 52; spirits of 9, 104
anthropocentrism 55, 56
anthropomorphism 50–53; of animism 52
anti-abortion 114
antisemitism 126–127
Arendt, Hannah 128
Aristotle 56, 134
Armstrong, Karen 124, 125, 128
art 16–18; animals 21, 22; and language 19; Palaeolithic 22; parietal 19, 20, 22, 30
Assmann, Jan 57, 119n2
atheism 57, 58, 100, 125, 127–129; new 87–92
Atrahasis 51, 55
atrocities 130

attachment theory 32, 59–64, 66n40
Augustine 52, 147

Barrett, Justin 32, 45n30
Bayle, Pierre 123
Beaulieu, Paul-Alain 51, 56
beliefs: in afterlife 12–13, 34–36; in children 34; ethnocentric 93; fundamentalists 152; Jewish 94, 95; in magic 80–81; orectic 94; of Protestantism 92; religious 2, 12, 15, 18, 22, 31, 39, 42, 48, 61, 63, 93, 94, 136, 142–144, 146, 149, 152; in spirits 7, 9–10, 28–29, 31; supernatural objects 18; unconscious 161; Yagwoia people 95
Bellah, Robert N. 24n4, 70
Ben Nun, Rabbi 118
Bering, Jesse 34–38; origins of religion 36
Bible 98–99, 117
bin Laden, Osama 117
Bowlby, John 43, 61; attachment system 32
Boyer, P. 38, 44n8
Brown, Peter 122n28
Bulkeley, Peter 96
burial practices 12–13
Burkert, Walter 27n48, 51, 145
Bush, G. W. 88, 90, 134

174 Index

Calvin 96, 144
Capps, Donald 138, 141n31
Caputo, John D. 154
castration anxiety 111–112
Catholicism, defence against
   homosexuality 112–113
caves 19–23
Celsus 58, 144
Chamberlain, Houston
   Stewart 127
Chekov, Anton 155n21
children: belief in 34; education
   81; emotional abuse 139;
   linguistic skills 35; magic,
   belief in 80–81; motivation
   to 137; narcissism 73–77, 79,
   80, 132, 138; punishment to
   137–138; religious induction
   of 132–133; sexual abuse of
   136–138; wish-fulfilling 80–81
Chomsky, Noam 18, 26n39
Christianity 58, 98, 100, 116,
   117, 126, 127, 145
Christian Right, United States
   117, 120n9
circumcision 79
Clottes, Jean 13, 20, 22, 23,
   27n48, 27n51
cognitivism 28–29, 91; afterlife,
   belief in 34–36; belief in
   children 34–35; haunted-house
   effect 33, 34; hypersensitive
   agency detection device
   (HADD) 32–33, 35, 37,
   45n30; ignoring of features
   of religiosity 37–39; illusion
   of God 37; immaterial
   minds 34; intuitions 34–35;
   psychoanalysis 38–39; and
   religion 31–32; spirits 33–34;
   superstition 37; theory of mind
   (ToM) 32–38, 45n30, 62;
   wishful/comfort theories 33,
   36, 38–39
communion 49, 50, 53, 54, 56,
   58, 106; and attachment
   59–64; monotheism and
   53–59; with spirits 69
condensation ideas 160–161

conversion 118, 135
Cottingham, John 153n1
Crompton, Louis 121n18

Darwin, Charles 89, 101n4
David, Bruno 13, 16, 26n34,
   27n42
Davidson, D. 45
Dawkins, Richard 38, 44–45n8,
   64, 88, 89, 102n13, 139–140n2,
   141n31
deity 52–53
delusions 59–60
Dennett, Daniel 38, 49n9, 88
discrimination, religious 77
Dobson, James C. 137
Dodds, E. R. 13, 114
Dominionism 117
Dostoevsky, Fyodor 97, 153n3
doxastic derangement 94–95
dreams 157, 159
Dummett, Michael 153n1
Dunbar, Robin 12, 29–30, 26n40

Eagleton, Terry 64–65n16
eccentrics 106
Eckart, Dietrich 126
ecstatic states 29
education: for children 81;
   religious 123, 131
ego-ideal 74
emotion/emotional: attachment
   63; conflict 42; and religion
   37–39, 42
Enlene cave 20
envy, family and 113–115
Erickson, Robert 125
ethnocentric beliefs 93
Evans-Pritchard, E. E. 24n7
Everett, Daniel 16–17
evil spirits 42–43, 48
experience of satisfaction (EOS)
   158–161
explanation, prediction and
   control (EPC) 49, 52, 56,
   63, 148

Faber, Martin 66–67n40
Fairbairn, W. R. D. 75

Falwell, Jerry 90
family, envy and 113–115
fanaticism 123; features 96–101;
    fundamentalism and 92–95;
    religious 119
fanatics 93–94, 96–98, 123,
    138–139, 152; difference
    96, 98; and fundamentalists
    99, 105–106; mindset 114;
    religious 98–101
female sexuality 99, 110, 114
Fitzgerald, Frances 117
Fortes, Meyer 82n3
Frawley-O'Dea, Mary Gail 136
Freud, Sigmund 42–43, 54,
    59–61, 63, 66n33, 66n40,
    72, 74, 84n23, 105, 109;
    condensation ideas 160–161;
    delusions 59–60; ego-ideal
    74; evil spirits 42–43, 48;
    illusion 59; on magic 78–82;
    on narcissism 73, 78–82,
    82n1; pure pleasure-ego 73;
    wish-fulfilment theory 43,
    59–60, 67n40, 80–81, 83n13,
    156–161
Fromm, Erich 71
fundamentalism 92–95, 99, 123,
    131, 139, 152; beliefs 152;
    fanatics and 99, 105–106;
    mindset 93, 103n18; Islamic
    88, 89

gender: domination 108;
    subversion 111; *see also*
    women
genocide 128
gods 8–9; hatred of 56, 106;
    human-to-god relationships
    49–50, 55, 58–59, 76; illusion
    of 37; internal working models
    (IWMs) 62, 63; intimacy with
    54; law of 98–99, 115, 117,
    119; love of 56; moral laws
    104–105; of polytheism 56;
    proximity to 61–62; of religion
    46; spirits and 8–9, 32–33,
    49–53
God Delusion, The (Dawkins) 89

Granqvist, Per 61–63
Guthrie, S. E. 33, 38

Haldane, John 150–151, 155n17
hallucinatory states 15, 30–31
hallucinatory wish-fulfilment
    157–158
Haredi Jews 95, 124
Harris, Sam 88, 102n13
hatred 57; aboriginal 130; of
    God 56, 106; of homosexual
    110–113; of religion 129
haunted-house effect 33, 34
Higham, Tom 15, 25n27, 25n33
Himmler, Heinrich 126, 140n7
Hitchens, Christopher 88, 89,
    102n13, 131
Hitler, Adolf 125–126, 128, 133
Holocaust 124–125, 128
Homo erectus 11, 16–17
homophobia 112–113
homosexual/homosexuality
    94, 99, 107, 114, 131;
    Catholicism's defence against
    112–113; hatred of 110–113;
    laws against 111; Leonardo's
    72; religious institutions 113
Horton, Robin 24, 24n7, 42,
    46n40, 48–49, 63
Huizinga, Johann 15, 25n28
human agency 9, 33, 34, 41
Hume, David 41, 52, 65n24, 88
Hus, Jan 147
hypersensitive agency detection
    device (HADD) 32–33, 35, 37,
    45n30

ideal self 74–75, 77, 135
identification, narcissism and
    70–73
idolatry 57–58
illusions 59; of God 37;
    wishful 151
immaterial minds 34
inculcation of religion 75–78
indoctrination, power of 44
infantile modes of thinking 81
infantile narcissism 73–77, 79,
    80, 132, 138

176 Index

infant's attachment 61–63
innate behavioural system 61
Instruction for Merikare 54–55
intellectualism 29, 31, 39–42, 48
intentional action 162n1
intentional stance 32, 36, 45n9
internal working models (IWMs) 62, 63
intrinsic religious aggression 131–132; child sexual abuse 136–138; narcissism 132–138; punishment of children 137–138
intuitions 34–35
Islam 97–98; fundamentalism 88, 89
Israelite religion 53–54

James, Henry 14
James, William 130
Jesus Christ 70–71, 97, 126
Jews/Jewish: belief 94, 95; Haredi 95, 124; immigration 118; Orthodox 95
Johnston, Mark 3n2, 89
Josephus, Flavius 116
justice 104, 119n2
Justinian law 116, 121n18

Kalapalo people 70
Kant, Immanuel 25n32, 88
Kardiner, Abram 48
Kelly, J. M. 115
Kernberg, Otto 133, 134
Kirkpatrick, Lee A. 61, 67
Kitcher, Philip 89, 102n13
Klein, Melanie 114
Klein, Richard 16–18
Kriwaczek, P. 108

Laidlaw, James 45
language 26n39; art and 19; complexity 18; human tribe 19; and spirits 16–18
Lascaux cave 21
law: conception of 117; of God 98–99, 115, 117, 119; nomocratic conception 115, 116, 118; Roman 115–116;

theonomic conception of 115, 118
Laws, Curtis Lee 92
Les Trois reres cave 20
Lewis, I. M. 46, 68–69
Lewis-Williams, David 14, 20, 30–31, 43n43
Lohrey, Amanda 97
Ludendorff, Erich 94

magic: belief in 80–81; in Christian prayer 83–84n21; Freud on 78–82
Maimonides, Moses 136
malignant narcissism 75, 132–134
manipulative mode of religion 49
McGrath, Alister 100
Mimica, Jadran 94
mind-body split 34, 35
monotheism 1, 64, 65n19, 78, 104–105, 108, 145, 146; and communion 53–59; *see also* polytheism
morality 75, 77, 120n5; Christian 116; religion and 104–105; sexual 105–107
Mosaic distinction 57; religion 79, 83n21
Moses and Monotheism (Freud) 78–79, 83n21
motivation 142–143; to children 137
mystical/mysticism 29–31

Nagel, Thomas 89
narcissism 54, 56, 123, 132, 135, 146, 149; aggression 77; children 73–77, 79, 80, 132, 138; Freud on 73, 78–82, 82n1; and identification 70–73; intrinsic religious aggression 132–138; malignant 75, 132–134; motivations 136; pathological 79, 96, 123, 136, 138; relations 73–75; religion and 77–78, 142, 152; shamanism and 68–71; wounds 148–150

Nazism 125–128
Neanderthals 11–13, 15–18
neophobia 131; aboriginal 130
new atheism 87–92
Nietzsche, Friedrich 57, 71, 95,
 119, 146, 151
Nixey, Catherine 121n18,
 121n20
nomocracy 115, 116, 118

omnipotent modes of thinking
 79–81
Oppy, Graham 24n1, 24n9
orectic derangement 94, 123,
 138, 149, 152
Origen 52, 145, 150
Ostow, Mortimer 66n40
Otto, Rudolf 49

paganism 57, 58, 106, 111
Palaeolithic: animals 22, 27n50;
 art 22; Middle Palaeolithic 11,
 15, 18; religion 10–16, 18;
 Upper Palaeolithic 19, 21, 22
Panksepp, Jaak 15, 25n29
Pan, Peter 79
parental attachment 62
parental superegos 93
parietal art 19–20, 22, 30
Pascal, Blaise 143
Pataki, Tamas 90, 103n18,
 155n18
pathological narcissism 79, 96,
 123, 136, 138
patriarchal family 99, 107
Pentecostalism 100
perceptual identity 158
pervasive guilt 57
petitionary prayer 83–84n21
Petocz, Agnes 65n24, 80, 161
physical violence 99
Plantinga, Alvin 89, 125, 144,
 154n14, 154n15, 155n20
pluralism, religion 97–98
polygeny 128
polytheism 51–53, 56–59;
 see also monotheism
Posner, Sarah 103n34
Post, Jerold J. 103n19

postmodernism 154n16
post-mortem existence 12,
 150–151
powerful beings 70
primitive child 80–81
primitive man 23–24n1, 43,
 79–81
Protestant Christianity 92, 96,
 125–127
psychoanalysis 38–39, 49, 60–62,
 72–73
psychotic states 30
punishment: of children 137–138;
 of women 114
pure pleasure-ego 73

Quran 97–98

racial identity 93
racism, scientific 124–125, 128
rationality 90
reality, religious evasion of
 150–151
reason 148–149, 151; religion
 for 145; subordination of
 143–148
religious beings, three categories
 of amongst Kalabari 8
resurrection 92, 100
revolutionary monotheism 57
right conduct 104, 105
ritual behaviour 11, 12, 15
Robertson, Pat 91
Roberts, Oral 83n15
Roheim, Geza 48
Roman law 115–116
Rushdoony, R. J. 117
Ruthven, Malise 92

scapegoating 131
Schimmel, Solomon 95, 153n13
science, and religion 146,
 154n15, 154n16, 248
scientific racism 124–125, 128
self 73–75
self-esteem 71, 73–75, 77
self-loathing 57
sensus divinitatis 144
sexual abuse, of children 136–138

178 Index

sexuality, women 99, 110, 114
sexual morality 105–107
shamanism 15, 20, 27n49,
    27n53, 30, 31, 41; and
    narcissism 68–71; religion 15,
    20, 27n49, 27n53, 30, 31, 41;
    spirits and 21–23
souls 39–42; spirits and 8, 50–51
spirits 41–42, 49; animal 20,
    23; of animism 9, 104;
    belief in 7, 9–10, 28–29,
    31; and cognitivism 33–34;
    communion with 69; concept
    of 8, 28–29, 33–34; entering
    into 18–21; evil 42–43, 48;
    God and 8–9, 32–33, 49–53;
    identification of 19; Jesus
    Christ 70–71; language and
    16–18; mystical path to
    29–31; ontology of 34, 37;
    possession 69, 72; powerful
    70; and religion 7–10, 15,
    18; and shamanism 21–23;
    supernatural 1, 3n2, 7, 10,
    23n1; *see also* gods
Steigmann-Gall, Richard
    125–127, 140n6
Strawson, Galen 46n38
Stringer, Chris 12, 17
Strozier, Charles B. 103n18
subintentional actions 162n1
subordination of women 99,
    107–110
substitutive satisfaction 156
superiority 97
supernatural agency 33
supernatural beings 1, 3n2, 7, 10,
    23n1, 33; belief 18
supernatural realms 29–30
superstition 37
Suttie, Ian 82n10
symbolic burial 12
symbol/symbolism 14, 16,
    160–161
Symington, Neville 79

Tamarin, George 139
Tattersall, Ian 18

Taylor, Charles 89, 125, 144,
    153n1, 154n15
Tertullian 147–149
theocracy 115–119
theonomy 115, 118
theory of mind (ToM) 32–38,
    45n30, 62
therianthrope 20, 23
Thomson, J. A. Jnr. 32
Torah 95, 100, 147
totalitarianism, Christian
    111, 145
Totem and Taboo (Freud) 29,
    42–43
trance states 29, 30
transcendence 20, 29, 46, 105,
    107, 108, 144
True Religion 2, 3n2, 64
Trump, Donald 89, 90, 98, 110,
    120n9, 134–135, 141n24,
    141n25
Twain, Mark 135
Tylor, Edward B. 24n6, 24n8, 42,
    43, 46n36, 46n40; conception
    of animism 40, 48; definition
    of religion 9–10, 39–40;
    Intellectualism 29, 31, 39–42,
    48; intellectualist 48; souls
    39–42

uncertainty 98, 148, 149
unconscious: belief 161;
    infantile wishes 60–61;
    understanding 161
United States: Christian Right
    117, 120n9; conversion to
    Christian nation 118

Vedas (Indian scriptures) 98
violence: physical 99; religious
    124–125, 131, 139

Williams, Bernard 88
Winch, Peter 24n7
Winnicott, D. W. 109
wish-fulfilment theory 43,
    59–60, 67n40, 80–81, 83n13,
    156–161

wishful illusions 151
wishful theory of religion 33, 36, 38–39
Wittgenstein, Ludwig 24n7
women: Biblical view of 107–109; defence of the family against 113; derogation 108, 110; devaluation 108; in patriarchal family 99, 107, 113; punishment to 114; sexuality 99, 110, 114; subordination of 99, 107–110; victims 69

Wright, Robert 65n19, 120n5
Wycliff, John 147

Xenophanes 52

Yagwoia cosmology 95
Yosef, Ovadia 90–91
Young-Bruehl, Elisabeth 93

Taylor & Francis eBooks

www.taylorfrancis.com

A single destination for eBooks from Taylor & Francis with increased functionality and an improved user experience to meet the needs of our customers.

90,000+ eBooks of award-winning academic content in Humanities, Social Science, Science, Technology, Engineering, and Medical written by a global network of editors and authors.

TAYLOR & FRANCIS EBOOKS OFFERS:

A streamlined experience for our library customers

A single point of discovery for all of our eBook content

Improved search and discovery of content at both book and chapter level

REQUEST A FREE TRIAL
support@taylorfrancis.com

Printed and bound by CPI Group (UK) Ltd, Croydon, CR0 4YY
10/10/2024
01043238-0005